Oepression

The aim of the **Overcoming** series is to enable people with psychologically based disorders to take control of their own recovery program. Each title, with its specially tailored program, is devised by a practising clinician using the latest techniques of cognitive behavioral therapy – techniques which have been shown to be highly effective in changing the way patients think about themselves and their problems. The series was initiated in 1993 by Peter Cooper, Professor of Psychology at Reading University and Research Fellow at the University of Cambridge, whose original volume on overcoming bulimia nervosa and binge-eating continues to help many people in the USA, the UK, and Europe.

All titles in the series are available by mail order from
Robinson Publishing Ltd. Please ring 0171 938 3830 for details.

OVERCOMING DEPRESSION

A *self-help guide using cognitive behavioral techniques*

Paul Gilbert

Robinson
LONDON

To my family

Robinson Publishing Ltd
7 Kensington Church Court
London W8 4SP

First published by Robinson Publishing Ltd 1997
Reprinted 1997, 1998

A copy of the British Library Cataloguing in Publication Data for
this title is available from the British Library.

ISBN 1-85487-434-9

Important Note
This book is not intended to be a substitute for medical advice or treatment.
Any person with a condition requiring medical attention should consult a
qualified medical practitioner or suitable therapist.

Printed and bound in the EC

Contents

Acknowledgments

Many people have contributed enormously to the writing of this book. At times depressed people read some chapters and gave very important feedback and views of their own. Sadly, in order to protect confidentiality, I cannot name them but my heart-felt thanks goes out to them. They have saved me from some insensitivities and obscurities and have helped clarify certain points. I am also indebted to the many depressed people who have shared their stories with me and shown me the many faces of depression.

Many colleagues have, over the years, shared discussions on treating depression. Steven Allan, my research colleague, needs special mention for his preparedness to read the whole book and spend many evenings discussing ideas, and for sharing his therapeutic experience. Special thanks also go to Professor M. Pervez for his encouragement and many helpful comments on the text. Other colleagues who have read sections include Ken Goss, Liza Monaghan, Phil Brewin and Mia Gregory. To all these I owe my thanks.

I also owe my thanks to those who tried to educate me. Professor Ivy Blackburn started me off in cognitive therapy many years ago. Dr William Hughes introduced me to psychoanalytic approaches, Dr E. MacAdam to family therapy and Dr H. Ghadiali to group therapy from a Jungian perspective. Special thanks go to Dr John Price who has had a deep impact on my thinking about depression, especially in regard to some of the theories outlined here. He has also shared many therapeutic ideas with me. His theories on depression, put forward in the 1960s and 1970s, are now gaining research evidence. He deserves credit for being one of the first to see depression as a state of defeat.

I am forever amazed at the patience of my own family. Jean,

Hannah and James all allowed me the time to write but also rescued me from over-involvement. I have no doubt at all that much of my current contentment with life resides in their loving support – not to mention the tea and sympathy.

I would also like to thank Professor Peter Cooper for asking me to write this book and as editor giving me the freedom to write it as I saw best. Gratitude also to Mark Crean of Robinson Publishing for his encouragement and hard work on the manuscript. Special thanks must go to the copy-editor, Nancy Duin, who toiled with my English. Of course, any confusions, bad spellings and other annoying things are obviously my responsibility. For these I apologize in advance.

Foreword

Many, perhaps the majority, of those who go to see their family doctor have some type of psychological problem which makes them anxious or unhappy. There may be a fairly obvious reason for this – the loneliness of widowhood or the stresses of bringing up a family – or it may be that their mental state is part of their personality, something they were born with or a reaction to traumatic experiences in their lives. Despite being so common, I soon discovered after starting in general practice over ten years ago that this type of mental disturbance (usually described as a *neurosis* to distinguish it from the *psychosis* of those with a serious mental illness like schizophrenia) is particularly difficult to deal with. What are the options? Well, there are always drugs – minor tranquillizers, antidepressants and sleeping pills. It is certainly easy enough to write a prescription and more often than not the patient feels a lot better as a result, but there is no getting away from the fact that drugs are a chemical fix. Sometimes this is all that is necessary to tide someone over a difficult period, but more usually the same old problems recur when the drugs are discontinued.

The alternatives to drugs are the 'talking therapies' ranging from psychoanalysis to counselling that seek to sort out the underlying cause of anxiety or unhappiness. Psychoanalysis is out of the question for many, being too prolonged – often lasting for years – and too expensive. Counselling certainly can be helpful for no other reason than that unburdening one's soul to a sympathetic listener is invariably therapeutic. But once the counselling sessions were over, I got the impression it was only a matter of time before the psychological distress reappeared.

Here, then, is one of the great paradoxes of modern medicine.

Doctors can now transplant hearts, replace arthritic hips and cure meningitis but, confronted by the commonest reason why people seek their advice, they have remarkably little to offer. And then a couple of years ago I started to hear about a new type of psychological treatment – cognitive therapy – which, it was claimed, was not only straightforward but demonstrably effective. I was initially sceptical as I found it difficult to imagine what sort of breakthrough insight into human psychology should lie behind such remarkable claims. The human brain is, after all, the most complex entity in existence, so it would seem unlikely that someone had suddenly now at the end of the twentieth century found the key that unlocked the mysteries of neuroses – a key that had eluded human understanding for hundreds of years.

The central insight of cognitive therapy is not, it emerges, a new discovery, but rather is based on the profound observation originally formulated by the French philosopher Descartes that the essential feature of human consciousness was 'cogito ergo sum' – 'I think therefore I am.' We *are* our thoughts and the contents of our thoughts have a major influence on our emotions. Cognitive therapy is based on the principle that certain types of thought that we have about ourselves – whether, at its simplest, we are loved or wanted or despised or boring – have a major effect on the way we perceive the world. If we feel unloved, the world will appear unloving, and then every moment of every day our sense of being unloved is confirmed. That, after all, is what depression is all about. These types of thoughts are called 'automatic thoughts' because they operate on the margins of our consciousness as a continual sort of internal monologue. If these thoughts are identified and brought out into the open then the state of mind that they sustain, whether anxiety or depression or any of the other neuroses, can begin to be resolved.

So this type of therapy is called 'cognitive' because it is primarily about changing our thoughts about ourselves, the world and the future. The proof of the pudding, as they say, is in the eating and the very fact that this type of therapy has been shown to work so well, in countless well-controlled studies, is powerful confirmation that the underlying insight that our thoughts lie behind, and sustain, neurotic illnesses is in essence correct.

Nonetheless, some may be forgiven for having misgivings. The concept of cognitive therapy takes some getting used to and it is certainly hard to credit that complex psychological problems can be explained by such an apparently simple concept. There is perhaps an understandable impression that it all sounds a bit oversimplified or trite, that it fails to get to the root cause of the source of anxiety or depression.

So it is necessary to dig a bit deeper to examine the origins of cognitive therapy and perhaps the easiest way of doing this is to compare it with what for many is the archetype of all forms of psychotherapy – psychoanalysis. Psychoanalysis claims to identify the source of neuroses in the long-forgotten and repressed traumas of early childhood, so it is less concerned with thoughts themselves than with the hidden meaning which (it claims) underlies them. The important question, though, is whether psychoanalysis does make people better, or at least less unhappy. Many people certainly believe they have been helped, but when Professor Gavin Andrews of the University of New South Wales reviewed all the studies in which the outcome of psychoanalysis had been objectively measured in the *British Journal of Psychiatry* in 1994, he was unable to show that it worked any better than 'just talking'.

In cognitive therapy, the importance of human thoughts lies precisely in their content and how that influences the way a person feels about themselves, a point well illustrated by one of its early pioneers, Aaron Beck. Back in the sixties, while practising as a psychoanalyst in Philadelphia, Beck was treating a young woman with an anxiety state which he initially interpreted in true psychoanalytic fashion as being due to a failure to resolve sexual conflict arising from problems in childhood. During one session he noticed that his patient seemed particularly uneasy and, on enquiring why, it emerged she felt embarrassed because she thought she was expressing herself badly and that she sounded trite and foolish. 'These self-evaluative thoughts were very striking,' Beck recalled, 'because she was actually very articulate.' Probing further he found that this false pattern of thinking – that she was dull and uninteresting – permeated all her relationships. He concluded that her chronic anxiety had little to do with her sex life but rather arose from a constant state of dread that her lover might desert her because he found her as uninteresting as she thought herself to be.

Over the next few years, Beck found that he was able to identify similar and quite predictable patterns of thinking in nearly all his patients. For the first time he realized that he was getting inside his patients' minds and beginning to see the world as they experienced it, something he had been unable to do in all his years as a psychoanalyst. From that perspective he went on to develop the principles of cognitive therapy.

Compared to psychoanalysis, cognitive therapy certainly does appear much simpler, but we should not take this to mean that it is less profound. The central failure of the founders of psychoanalysis was that they did not recognize the true significance of thoughts in human neurosis. Once that significance was grasped by those like Aaron Beck then human psychological disorders became more readily understandable and therefore simpler, but it is the simplicity of an elegant scientific hypothesis that more fully explains the facts. It can't be emphasized too strongly the enormous difference that cognitive therapy has made. Now it is possible to explain quite straightforwardly what is wrong in such a way that people are reassured, while allowing them to be optimistic that their problems can be resolved. Here, at last, is a talking therapy that works.

Professor Gavin Andrews in his review in the *British Journal of Psychiatry* identified cognitive therapy as 'the treatment of choice' in generalized anxiety, obsessive compulsive disorders and depression. It has in addition been shown to be effective in the treatment of eating disorders, panic attacks and even in the management of marital and sexual difficulties, in chronic pain syndromes and many emotional disorders of childhood. Its contribution to the alleviation of human suffering is remarkable.

James Le Fanu, GP

Introduction

Why cognitive behavior therapy?

Over the past two or three decades, there has been something of a revolution in the field of psychological treatment. Freud and his followers had a major impact on the way in which psychological therapy was conceptualized, and psychoanalysis and psychodynamic psychotherapy dominated the field for the first half of this century. So, long-term treatments were offered which were designed to uncover the childhood roots of personal problems – offered, that is, to those who could afford it. There was some attempt by a few health service practitioners with a public conscience to modify this form of treatment (by, for example, offering short-term treatment or group therapy), but the demand for help was so great that this had little impact. Also, whilst numerous case histories can be found of people who are convinced that psychotherapy did help them, practitioners of this form of therapy showed remarkably little interest in demonstrating that what they were offering their patients was, in fact, helpful.

As a reaction to the exclusivity of psychodynamic therapies and the slender evidence for its usefulness, in the 1950s and 1960s a set of techniques was developed, broadly collectively termed 'behavior therapy'. These techniques shared two basic features. First, they aimed to remove symptoms (such as anxiety) by dealing with those symptoms themselves, rather than their deep-seated underlying historical causes. Second, they were techniques, loosely related to what laboratory psychologists were finding out about the mechanisms of learning, which were formulated in testable terms. Indeed, practitioners of behavior therapy were committed to using techniques of proven value or, at worst, of a form which could potentially be put to test. The area where these techniques proved of most value was in the treatment of anxiety disorders, especially specific phobias (such as fear of animals or heights) and agoraphobia, both notoriously difficult to treat using conventional psychotherapies.

After an initial flush of enthusiasm, discontent with behavior therapy grew. There were a number of reasons for this, an important one of which was the fact that behavior therapy did not deal with the internal thoughts which were so obviously central to the distress that patients were experiencing. In this context, the fact that behavior therapy proved so inadequate when it came to the treatment of depression highlighted the need for major revision. In the late 1960s and early 1970s a treatment was developed specifically for depression called 'cognitive therapy'. The pioneer in this enterprise was an American psychiatrist, Professor Aaron T. Beck, who developed a theory of depression which emphasized the importance of people's depressed styles of thinking. He also specified a new form of therapy. It would not be an exaggeration to say that Beck's work has changed the nature of psychotherapy, not just for depression but for a range of psychological problems.

In recent years the cognitive techniques introduced by Beck have been merged with the techniques developed earlier by the behavior therapists to produce a body of theory and practice which has come to be known as 'cognitive behavior therapy'. There are two main reasons why this form of treatment has come to be so important within the field of psychotherapy. First, cognitive therapy for depression, as originally described by Beck and developed by his successors, has been subjected to the strictest scientific testing; and it has been found to be a highly successful treatment for a significant proportion of cases of depression. Not only has it proved to be as effective as the best alternative treatments (except in the most severe cases, where medication is required), but some studies suggest that people treated successfully with cognitive behavior therapy are less likely to experience a later recurrence of their depression than people treated successfully with other forms of therapy (such as antidepressant medication). Second, it has become clear that specific patterns of thinking are associated with a range of psychological problems and that treatments which deal with these styles of thinking are highly effective. So, specific cognitive behavioral treatments have been developed for anxiety disorders, like panic disorder, generalized anxiety disorder, specific phobias and social phobia, obsessive compulsive disorders, and hypochondriasis (health anxiety), as well as for other conditions such as compulsive gambling, alcohol and drug addiction, and eating disorders like bulimia nervosa and binge-eating disorder. Indeed, cognitive behavioral techniques have a wide application beyond the narrow categories of psychological disorders: they have been applied effectively, for example, to helping people with low self-esteem and those with marital difficulties.

At any one time almost 10 per cent of the general population is suffering from depression, and more than 10 per cent has one or other of the anxiety disorders. Many others have a range of psychological problems and personal difficulties. It is of the greatest importance that treatments of proven effectiveness are developed. However, even when the armoury of therapies is, as it were, full, there remains a very great problem – namely that the delivery of treatment is expensive and the resources are not going to be available evermore. Whilst this shortfall could be met by lots of people helping themselves, commonly the natural inclination to make oneself feel better in the present is to do precisely those things which perpetuate or even exacerbate one's problems. For example, the person with agoraphobia will stay at home to prevent the possibility of an anxiety attack; and the person with bulimia nervosa will avoid eating all potentially fattening foods. Whilst such strategies might resolve some immediate crisis, they leave the underlying problem intact and provide no real help in dealing with future difficulties.

So, there is a twin problem here: although effective treatments have been developed, they are not widely available; and when people try to help themselves they often make matters worse. In recent years the community of cognitive behavior therapists have responded to this situation. What they have done is to take the principles and techniques of specific cognitive behavior therapies for particular problems and represent them in self-help manuals. These manuals specify a systematic program of treatment which the individual sufferer is advised to work through to overcome their difficulties. In this way, the cognitive behavioral therapeutic techniques of proven value are being made available on the widest possible basis.

Self-help manuals are never going to replace therapists. Many people will need individual treatment from a qualified therapist. It is also the case that, despite the widespread success of cognitive behavioral therapy, some people will not respond to it will need one of the other treatments available. Nevertheless, although research on the use of cognitive behavioral self-help manuals is at an early stage, the work done to date indicates that for a very great many people such a manual will prove sufficient for them to overcome their problems without professional help.

Many people suffer silently and secretly for years. Sometimes appropriate help is not forthcoming despite their efforts to find it. Sometimes they feel too ashamed or guilty to reveal their problems to anyone. For many of these people the cognitive behavioral self-help manual will provide a lifeline to recovery and a better future.

Professor Peter Cooper
The University of Reading, 1997

Preface

Depression is a horrible state to be in. Having worked with depressed people for many years and having heard many different stories, the thing that stands out is the sheer misery of it. Another way I encountered depression was personally, nearly twenty years ago. In the context of some major set-backs in my life, I suddenly found myself caught up in one. Even though I had studied depression, I was not as prepared as I thought I would have been to deal with it. My depression was of the milder kind but even so it was associated with panic attacks, many sleepless nights, a terrible sense of having failed in important areas of my life and a deep dread. Researchers rarely talk about dread, but I think it is a good word to sum up what people feel when they are depressed. I can't say I felt particularly sad, as you might if you lose a loved one, more frightened, irritable and joyless. Hence, I would choose the word dread or 'living in dread' to describe it. I also discovered that one does strange things when one is depressed. Occasionally, I would sit in lukewarm baths at four in the morning to try to reduce the agitation. I would take taxis to work because I couldn't face the bus, and if I had to give a talk or lecture you'd have to drag me out the loo! However, I was not so knocked out by it that I couldn't function, as some people can be. And on the whole I chose to see it as a 'brain state change' brought on by stress. Indeed, my first book on depression was called *Depression: From Psychology to Brain State*. Not the most inspiring of titles, perhaps, and it is now out of print, but my own experience had convinced me that something had 'happened in my brain' and I wanted to explore how social and psychological factors could produce biological changes.

Sadly, some people seem at risk of certain types of depression, and we now know that genes appear to play a role. However, while I do not want to underplay the biological dimension of depression, some forms are surprisingly common and genes probably play a major role only in a minority of cases. Life events and early childhood experiences seem by far the more common sources. I suspect this was true for me. My early years were spent in West Africa. It was a place of tremendous freedoms and I would roam happily in the outback. For nearly a year we lived in the 'bush' with no running water or electricity – and no school! My memories are still vivid of that time and when the skies are dull and cold I remember with great fondness the excitements, the blue skies and expansiveness of Africa. When I came home to England to go to boarding school I found the confinement and harshness of it difficult. I also found that I was behind in my education and had serious problems with the English language. To this day I do not like confinements and can easily feel trapped in places. The life events that triggered my depression were all related to feeling trapped and failing.

I see depression as a state of mind that we have a potential for, just as we have the potential to feel grief, fear, sexual arousal and so forth. And like any state of mind, depression is associated with very real changes in the brain. In my own work I have explored the reasons for this by thinking about the typical things that tend to trigger depression. This led to a consideration of whether the capacity for depression might be something that evolved along with us as we plodded the conflict-ridden trail from reptiles to monkey to humans. I won't go into the details of that except to say that depression probably affects animals. As with humans, depression seems to strike mostly when an animal loses status (is defeated), loses control and/or is trapped in adverse environments. When these things happen the brain seems to switch into depressed-like states. In humans, signals of being valued as a person have evolved as important mediators of mood states.

The other thing to consider, if we stay with an evolutionary view for a moment, is that although the brain is a highly complex organ it is also something of a 'contraption'. Deep in our brains are structures that evolved with the reptiles. Neuropsychologists even called this part of the brain 'the reptilian brain'. Evolution does not create totally new designs. Rather, old designs are adapted, added to or altered as a species evolves. It is rather like developing a car, but each new design must include the old – you can't go back to the drawing board and start afresh. So the brain has various structures within it that stretch way back many millions of years. This is why we can see the brain as a cobbling together of different bits that do different things. We have the potential for great violence, terror, lust, love and compassion. We are a mosaic of possibilities arising out of this jerry-built brain of ours.

Provided these various parts of the brain work together then it functions reasonably well, but if they get out of balance then it functions less well. Due perhaps to childhood trauma or difficulties and later stressful life events, we sometimes find it difficult to keep this mixed array of possibilities under control. They start pulling in different directions. The brain may tell us that there is far more danger than there is, and we panic; it may tell us that we are inferior, worthless and to give in, and we feel depressed; it may tell us that we need to get our own back, and so we seethe with the desire for revenge. Each of these parts has its own job to do, but they must work in harmony. In depression we lose this harmony and have thoughts and ideas that lead us to feel more defeated, inferior and worthless, and thus more depressed.

What we find in depression is that people experience all kinds of thoughts and feelings coming from different systems within the brain, and these can be difficult to control or make sense of. Another way to think of this is that we have different parts to ourselves and can play different roles, e.g. child, hero, lover, parent, friend, enemy, helper and so on. Evolution has provided many brain systems that enable us to enact different roles. Each part tends to see the world in its own way. For example, the hero part strides out and risks all. The coward part says, 'You must be joking. I'm not going out there.' Now if the two work together then they will make a sensible compromise and evaluation of risk. But if the hero does not listen to the coward then the hero puts the self in danger. On the other hand, if the coward does not listen to the hero, the coward just hides in the corner. In reality, of course, there are no actual 'parts' as such; what we experience is the activation, to a greater or lesser degree, of different brain systems. When we pay attention to our thoughts and feelings we can actually recognize which brain systems are turned on. Our thoughts and feelings are windows on these different systems in us.

So what to do if you feel depressed? The first thing to say is that the thoughts we have when we are depressed tell us that the depression system is switched on. That may not seem very helpful, until we realize that there may be ways to turn it off again and bring ourselves back into balance. For example, when we are depressed we may think in ways that seem right 'to the depression', but which may seem very wrong to other parts of ourselves. The rational and compassionate parts of ourselves may have a very different view of things. The more we can say, 'OK, my depression is a part of me; one of my many brain systems, but it can't be relied on to be accurate or helpful', the more we can step in to try to take control of it.

Secondly, as we get depressed the depression system tends to throw other systems out of balance. For example, we may become more irritable or anxious. And as a result we may judge ourselves and/or others more harshly, which feeds the depression. Typical of depression is to devalue things, usually ourselves and accomplishments, but we may also devalue others. We may start to believe that things are darker than they are.

Thirdly, depression is about how the brain is operating at any particular time. So depression is very much felt 'in the body' and is about feelings. Depression was designed (evolved) to slow us down, to weaken self-confidence and make us more sensitive to possible social losses and threats. It does this by changing the way our bodies work. However, if we can get other systems to challenge the depression, by learning how to think differently about ourselves and events, then we have an opportunity to get things back into balance. This book will discuss how to recognize important depressing thoughts to work with and how to challenge them.

This book is for people who would like to know more about depression – what it is and how to help oneself. It is not a cure-all, nor a substitute for therapies like drugs or psychotherapy, nor can a book like this change the painful realities of living. It is simply one approach. Each person's depression is, in part, similar to other people's and in part unique to that person. What understanding can do is to offer a way to move out of depression rather than plunge further into it. There are many ways to challenge some of the negative thinking of depression. I will try to point out some pitfalls to watch out for and suggest some methods that will enable you to develop a more rational and compassionate approach to yourself.

The book is divided into three parts. The first is the most technical. I have included this because many of the depressed people I see say that they would like to know more about depression itself. If it seems too technical, you can skip those bits you find difficult to follow; in fact, you can skip the whole of Part I if you like. Part II outlines some basic approaches to self-help. Here we will explore the role of thoughts and feelings, and how to challenge some of the thoughts and feelings that lead to a downward slide. There is a chapter devoted to how depressed people treat themselves (which is often very badly) and how to treat yourself more kindly. The more you learn to value yourself (or at least to stop devaluing yourself), the greater the chances of turning the depression system off. Each chapter in Part II is followed by a series of exercises you can try. In Part III the basic approaches covered in Part II are applied to special problems. These include the need for approval, anger, shame, lack of assertiveness, disappointment and perfectionism.

You will read of many other people's depression. All names have, of course, been changed. Also, to avoid any chance of identification, the details of all the stories have been altered. Sometimes two or three cases have been rolled into one, again to avoid identification. The focus of each problem is on the specific themes that reveal the dilemmas and complexities of depression.

Our journey together may be a long one, but I hope it will equip you with some ideas of how to move out of depression. Recovering from depression usually requires time, effort and patience, but if you know what you are trying to achieve, and have a way forward, you are likely to be more successful in your efforts. So let's begin.

PART I

Understanding Depression

What is Depression?

If you suffer from depression, you are, sadly, far from being alone. In fact, it has been estimated that there may be over 100 million people in the world today who suffer from it. Depression has afflicted humans for as long as records have been kept. Indeed, it was first named as a condition about 2400 years ago by the famous ancient Greek doctor Hippocrates, who called it 'melancholia'. It is also worth noting that although we cannot ask animals how they feel, it is likely that animals also have the capacity to feel depressed. Animals can certainly behave as if they are depressed. So, to a greater or lesser degree, we all have the potential to become depressed, just as we all have the potential to become anxious, to grieve or fall in love.

Depression is no respecter of status or fortune. Indeed, many famous people throughout history have suffered from it. King Solomon, Abraham Lincoln, Winston Churchill and the Finnish composer Jean Sibelius are well-known examples from history. What is important to remember is that depression is not about human weakness.

What Do We Mean by 'Depression'?

This is a difficult question to answer precisely because a lot depends on who you ask. The word itself can be used to describe a type of weather, a fall in the stock market, a hollow in the ground and, of course, our moods. It comes from the Latin *deprimere*, meaning to 'press down'. The term was first applied to a mood state in the seventeenth century.

If you suffer from depression, one thing you will be aware of is that it is far more than just feeling down. In fact, depression affects not only how we feel, but how we think about things, our energy levels, our concentration, our sleep, even our interest in sex. So depression has an effect on many aspects of our lives. Let's look at some of these.

Motivation   Depression affects our motivation to do things. We can feel apathetic and experience a loss of energy and interest – nothing seems worth doing, everything is so pointless that it's hopeless even to try. If we have children, we can lose interest in them and then feel guilty. A work project that we might have been very keen about becomes boring. We have to drag ourselves around. Each day can be a torment of having to force ourselves to perform even the most minor of activities.

Emotions   People often think that depression is only about low mood or feeling fed-up – and this is certainly part of it. Indeed the central symptom of depression is called 'anhedonia' – derived from the ancient Greek meaning 'without pleasure' – and means the *loss of the capacity to experience any pleasure*. Life seems empty; we are joyless. But – and this is an important *but* – although we lose the ability to have positive feelings and emotions, we can experience an increase in negative emotions, especially anger. We may be churning inside with anger and resentment that we can't express. We might become extremely irritable, snap at our children and relatives and, at times, lash out at them. We may then feel guilty about this, and this makes us more depressed. Other very common symptoms are anxiety and fear. When we are depressed, we can feel extremely vulnerable. Things that we may have done easily before seem frightening, and at times it is difficult to know why. So the two 'A's' – anger and anxiety – are very much part of depression. Other negative feelings that can increase in depression are sadness, guilt, shame, envy and jealousy.

Thinking   Depression interferes with the way we think in two ways. First, it affects concentration and memory. We find that we can't get our minds to settle on anything. Reading a book or watching television becomes impossible. We also don't remember things too well, and we are prone to forget things. However, it is easier to remember negative things than positive things.

The second way that depression affects our thoughts is in the way we think about ourselves, our future and the world. Very few people who are depressed feel good about themselves. Generally, they tend to see themselves as inferior, flawed, bad or worthless. If you ask a depressed person about their future, they are likely to respond with: 'What future?' The future seems dark, a blank or a neverending cycle of defeat and losses. Like many strong emotions, depression pushes us to more extreme forms of thinking. Our thoughts become 'all or nothing' – we are either a complete success or an abject failure.

Images When we are depressed, the imagery we use to describe it tends to be similar. We may talk about being under a dark cloud, in a deep hole or pit, or a dark room. Winston Churchill called his depression his 'black dog'. The imagery of depression is always about darkness, on being stuck somewhere and not able to get out. If you were to paint a picture of your depression, it would probably involve dark or harsh colours rather than light, soft ones. So darkness and entrapment are key internal images.

Behaviors Our behavior changes when we become depressed. We engage in much less positive activity and may withdraw socially and want to hide away. Many of the things we might have enjoyed doing before becoming depressed now seem like an ordeal. Because everything seems to take so much effort, we do much less than we used to. Our behavior towards other people can change, too. We tend to do fewer positive things with others and are more likely to find ourselves in conflict with them. If we become very anxious, we might also start to avoid meeting people or lose our social confidence.

Depressed people sometimes become agitated and find it extremely difficult to relax. They feel like trapped animals and pace about, wanting to do something but not knowing what. Sometimes, the desire to escape and run away can be very strong. But where to go and what to do is unclear. On the other hand, some depressed people become very slowed down. They walk slowly, with a stoop, their thoughts seem stuck, and everything feels 'heavy'.

Physiology When people become anxious about something,

their bodies can produce a surge of adrenaline. And depression can result in other biological changes, affecting our bodies and our brains. Now there is nothing sinister about this. To say that our brains work differently when we are depressed is really to state the obvious. Indeed, any mental state, be it happy, sexual, excited, anxious or depressed, will be associated with physical changes in our brains. Recent research has shown that some of these are related to stress hormones such as cortisol, which indicates that depression involves the body's stress system. Certain brain chemicals, called *neurotransmitters*, are also affected, the most well studied being the monoamines. Generally, these chemicals are reduced in the brain when we are depressed, and this is why some people find benefit from drugs that allow the monoamines to build up.

Probably as a result of the physical changes that occur in depression, we can experience a host of other unwanted symptoms. Not only are energy levels affected, so is sleep. If you are depressed, you may wake up early, sometimes in the middle of the night or early morning, or you may find it difficult to get to sleep. There are some depressed states, however, in which sleep is increased. In addition, loss of appetite is quite common and food may start to taste like cardboard; as a result, sometimes there is weight loss. Other depressed people may eat more and put on weight.

Social relationships   Even though we might try to hide our depression, it almost always affects other people. We are less fun to be with. We can be irritable and find ourselves continually saying 'No'. Now the key thing here is that this is quite common and has been since humans first felt depressed. So we need to acknowledge these feelings and not feel ashamed about them, for if we do, it will just make us more depressed. There are various reasons why our relationships might suffer. There can be conflicts that we feel unable to sort out. There might be unvoiced resentments. We might feel out of control. Our friends and partners might not understand what has happened to us. Remember the old saying: 'Laugh and the world laughs with you. Cry and you cry alone.' Depression is difficult for others to comprehend at times.

Are All Depressions the Same?

The short answer to this is no. There are a number of different types. One that researchers and professionals commonly refer to is called 'major depression'. According to the American Psychiatric Association, one can be said to suffer from major depression if one has at least five of the following possible symptoms, which have to be present for at least two weeks.

- Low mood
- Marked loss of pleasure

} You have to have one of these symptoms

- Significant change in appetite and a loss of at least 5 percent of normal body weight
- Sleep disturbance
- Agitation or feelings of being slowed down
- Loss of energy or feeling fatigued virtually every day
- Feelings of worthlessness, low self-esteem, tendency to feel guilty
- Loss of the ability to concentrate
- Thoughts of death and suicide

} You must have at least four of these symptoms

Such a list of symptoms is important to professionals, but it does not really capture the variety and complexity of the experience of depression. For example, I would include feelings of being trapped as a common depressed symptom, and many psychologists feel that hopelessness is also one. I have included this list here to give you an idea of how some professionals tend to think about depression.

Researchers distinguish between those mental conditions that involve only depression and those that also involve swings into mania. In the manic state, a person can feel enormously energetic, full of their own self-importance and confident, and may have great interest in sex, and if the mania is not too severe, they can accomplish a lot. People who have swings into both depression and (hypo) mania are often diagnosed as suffering from *bipolar illness* (meaning that they can swing to both poles of mood – high and low). The old term was manic-depression. Those who only suffer depression are diagnosed as having *unipolar depression*.

Another distinction that some researchers and professionals make is between *psychotic* and *neurotic* depression. In psychotic depression, the person has various false beliefs called 'delusions'. For example, a person without any physical illness might come to believe that he or she has a serious cancer and will shortly die. Some years ago, one of my patients was brought into hospital because she had been contacting lawyers and undertakers to arrange her will and her funeral as she was sure that she would die before Christmas. She believed that the hospital staff were keeping this important information from her to avoid upsetting her, and she tried to advise her young children on how they should cope without her (causing great distress to the family, of course). Sometimes people with a psychotic illness can develop extreme feelings of guilt. For example, they may be certain in their minds they have caused the Bosnian war, or done something terrible. Now psychotic depression is obviously a very serious disorder, but compared to the non-psychotic depressions it is, on the whole, rare.

Another distinction that is sometimes made is between those depressions that seem to come out of the blue and those that are related to life-events, e.g. when people become depressed after losing a job, the death of a loved one or the ending of an important relationship. Today, however, although we recognize that people clearly differ in the exact nature of their depressions and the patterns of their symptoms, this distinction is less creditable. In psychotherapy, one often finds that, as one gets to know a person in depth, what looked like a depression that came out of the blue actually had its seeds in childhood. Sadly, this does not mean that some of us are not more biologically vulnerable to depression than others, only that distinguishing between depressions in terms of cause is fraught with problems.

Clearly some depressions are more serious, deep and debilitating than others. In many cases, depressed people manage to keep going until the depression eventually passes. In very serious depression, this is extremely difficult, and getting professional help is important. Depressions can vary in terms of onset, severity, duration and frequency.

Onset	Depression can have an acute onset (i.e. within days or weeks) or come on gradually (over months or years). It can begin at any time but late adolescence, early adulthood and later life are particularly vulnerable times.
Severity	Individuals can vary as to whether their symptoms are mild, moderate or severe.
Duration	Some will come out of their depression within weeks or months, whereas for others it may last in a fluctuating, chronic form for many years. 'Chronic depression' is said to last longer than two years, and 10–20 percent of depressed people suffer from it.
Frequency	Some individuals may only have one episode of depression, whereas others may have many. About 50 percent of those who have been depressed will have a recurrence.

The fact that depression can recur may seem alarming, but this should really come as no surprise. Suppose, for example, that since a young age you have always felt inferior and worthless. One day this sense of inferiority seems to get the better of you and you feel a complete failure in every aspect of your life. Now it may be that a drug will help you to recover from that episode, but even if you become better, you may still retain, underneath, those feelings of failure and inferiority. Drugs do not retrain us or enable us to mature and throw off these underlying beliefs.

How Common is Depression?

As I have already indicated, depression is, sadly, very common. If we look at what is called major depression, the figures look like this.

	Women	Men
Suffering depression at any one time	4–10%	2–3.5%
Lifetime risk	10–26%	5–12%

Those being treated in hospital: 1 per 1000
Those being treated as psychiatric outpatients: 2–3 per 1000

What this suggests is that about one in four or five of us could have some kind of depressive episode at some point in our lives. It also implies that depression is about three times more common in women than in men. Depression is also found more often in certain deprived sections of society – e.g. in areas of high unemployment. New research also indicates that rates of and risks for depression have been steadily increasing throughout this century, but the reasons for this are unclear. Socio-economic changes, the fragmentation of families and communities, the loss of hope in the younger generation – especially the unemployed – and increasing levels of expectations may all be implicated.

Key Points
- Depression, in its various forms, is very common and has been for thousands of years.
- Depression involves many different symptoms. Emotions such as anger and anxiety are common and at times more troubling than the depression itself. We can also have a strong desire to escape – for which we may feel guilty.
- There are different types of depression.
- Some depressions are quite severe, while others are less so but still deeply disturbing and life-crippling.

My key message to you, if you suffer from depression, is that if you feel a failure, if you have a lot of anger and hatred inside, if you are terrified out of your wits, if you think life is not worth living, if you feel trapped and desperate to escape, whatever your feelings, you are not the only one. Millions of depressed people throughout the world feel like you do. Of course, knowing this does not make your depression any less painful, but it does mean that there is nothing *bad* about you because you are in this state of mind. These feelings are sadly often part of being depressed. True, some people who have not been depressed may not understand it or may tell you to pull yourself together, but this does not mean that there is anything bad about *you*. It just means that *they* find it difficult to understand.

2

What Causes Depression?

This chapter looks at a number of different ideas about what causes depression. Understandably, when we feel depressed we often want to know what has caused it. Sometimes causes are easy to find, such as the break up of a relationship. At other times, they are less easy to discover.

Theories about the causes of depression fall into three main types: those that focus on biology; those that focus on psychology (and the way we think); and those that focus on our social lives and life-events. Some of the ideas may seem rather complex and can be difficult to grasp. Don't worry if you find this is the case. It is not at all essential that you understand the various theories to be able to use this book. I include them here because people are often interested in them. In fact, if you prefer you can skip the rest of this section and go straight to Part II. But if you wish to look at the different theories about depression, you may find that there is something in each of them that may be useful for you. However, no single theory can claim to have all the answers.

Concern with what might cause depression has been of interest for millennia. Over 2000 years ago, the Greeks thought that depression was caused by too much 'black bile' in the body. Indeed, the word 'melancholia' means 'black bile'. But, as they were well aware, this raises another question. What causes the black bile to increase? The Greeks had a rather sophisticated view about this. They thought that there were people who by nature had more black bile – melancholic types. But they also believed that stress, diet and seasonal changes could affect the amounts of black bile in the body. The Greeks recognized that we could be upset by things that happen to us and that these upsets could affect our bodily processes – that is, affect the black bile.

Today, of course, we no longer think in terms of 'black bile' but in terms of chemical changes in the brain or, to use the technical term, 'neurochemistry'. Unfortunately, though, those who study depression are not always as sophisticated as the Greeks were. Some argue that changes in brain chemistry cause depression and that's that. But while it is certainly true that we know a lot more about what happens in the brain when someone *has become depressed*, we still can't say that the chemical changes that take place in the brain actually *cause* depression. For example, we know that the secretion of adrenaline is associated with anxiety, but this does not mean that adrenaline is the sole cause of anxiety or that the elimination of this hormone is the cure for anxiety. We might experience surges of adrenaline and then anxiety because a mugger is demanding our money, but to rid ourselves of such anxiety, it would be better to get away from the mugger rather than (say) take a drug.

What is often missing from our theories of depression is a notion of the *interactions* between the world we live in, the way we think and give meaning to things, and our bodies. If you go to a doctor, he or she may accurately diagnose depression and then offer you drugs, and these drugs may well lift your spirits, help you to sleep better, tone down the anxiety and so forth. But they won't necessarily help you think through what might have contributed to the chemical imbalance in the first place, nor how you might exert more control over it.

On the other hand, some psychologists place all the blame for depression on the way that we think about things or the kinds of relationships we have. They may not give enough weight to the fact that, when we are depressed, our brains work in a different way compared to when we are not depressed. But mind and body are one. For example, if we are anxious, angry, overjoyed or feel sexy, changes take place in our brains. In other words, in different states of mind we also have different 'brain states'. The fact that our brains are working differently when we are depressed means that getting out of depression can be difficult. And certainly at times anti-depressant drugs can be very helpful (provided the side-effects are not too severe), and in some cases, they are essential. But we need to think about *interactions* between different aspects of our lives. We need to think about how the brain, our thoughts and our social environments are all interconnected.

Biological Aspects

As I have mentioned above, when we are depressed, changes occur in the way our brains work. The sleep system is affected, the areas of the brain controlling positive rewards and positive emotions are toned down, and the areas controlling negative emotions are enhanced. Of special importance are the changes in the way messages are relayed in the brain. Modern research is not at all clear what all these changes are, but it is believed that some of the most important ones take place in pathways in the brain known as the *monoamine pathways*. The exact neurochemistry is rather complex, but what we can say is that antidepressant drugs work by boosting the parts of the monoamine system that control positive emotions and tone down those areas that control negative emotions. Different antidepressants do this in slightly different ways (see pages 291–4). The key question is: why have these changes occurred in the brain?

There are at least three ways that our brains can be affected to make us vulnerable to depression.

Genes
The first possibility is that there is a biological sensitivity. We switch into depressed states because something goes wrong with the way that neurochemicals are produced and used in the brain. This malfunction may be due to our genes, the segments of DNA that control a vast number of chemical processes. For this view to be accepted, depression must be found to run in families – i.e. there must be a tendency for depression to be inherited.

The strongest evidence would be if identical twins, separated at birth, were in adulthood found to have a similar risk of depression. In fact, this has been found: if one identical twin becomes depressed, the chances of the other twin developing depression are much higher than for any individual selected at random from the general population. The more severe the depression – e.g.

psychotic or bipolar – the greater the risk. For non-identical twins, the risk is higher than for the rest of the population, but not as high as for identical twins. So on the basis of this evidence, it does seem that some forms of depression involve the genes. Genes may also affect the threshold or ease by which depressed brain states are activated by life-events.

We must be careful not to draw from these findings conclusions that are too simplistic, such as 'All depressions are inherited diseases.' In the first place, much depends on the definition of depression. Not all types of depression involve the genes, although the evidence is increasing that there is a *genetic component* for at least some. In addition, some people appear to have an increased risk of certain types of depression if some of their close (genetic) relatives suffer from certain disorders, including anxiety and alcoholism. However, common sense tells us that everyone except identical twins varies genetically – we are not exact copies of each other. And research with infants has shown that differences in temperament can show up in the first days of life – for example, some infants are inhibited and cautious while others are more explorative.

Development

Genes are essential for life. They control the colour of our eyes and hair, trigger developments so that, as we grow, our sexual organs develop, and so forth. And genes play a role in personality and susceptibility to anxiety and depression. But the brain is not a closed system following a preset pattern irrespective of what is happening in the outside world. Indeed, the quality and forms of our early relationships actually help to shape the various types of connections that nerve cells make in the brain. We now know that the brain is very 'plastic' in this regard. The way the brain matures during infancy and early childhood depends on social input. The brain of a child who is loved and wanted might mature differently to that of a child who is abused and constantly threatened.

What this means is that various types of experience shape the brain, and this phenomenon links what happens outside of us with what happens inside our heads and bodies. To give one example: If we are stressed, hormones such as cortisol and various stress chemicals affect the brain and, over time, these change the way that transmission takes place in the brain. They affect what are called 'receptors' and the types of connection that one nerve cell, or neurone, makes with another. So the brain and the outside world are linked right from birth, and a vulnerability to depression may be laid down early in life. For instance, there is increasing evidence that those susceptible to chronic forms of depression have histories of abuse, and that the stress systems of some of these people have an increased sensitivity.

This suggests that a biological sensitivity to depression might result from early experiences that affect the way the brain grows and matures. Again we should not be too pessimistic about these findings because psychological interventions can still be very helpful. As individuals come to recognize their own personal sensitivities, psychological understanding and training can do much not only to help them cope better but may also change their sensitivities.

Uncontrollable Stress

Another way that our brains can be switched to a depressed state involves *current stresses*. Some years ago, the researcher Professor Martin Seligman found that, if animals were given stresses that they could not control, they would become very passive and behave like depressed people. These extremely important findings were later taken up by other researchers who wanted to see what changes took place in the brains of animals subjected to uncontrollable stress. It was found that some of the changes were similar to those associated with depression – for example, activity in areas of the brain that control positive emotions and behavior was reduced. Moreover, if other animals were subjected to the same stress but had the means to control that stress, different changes took place – the areas of the brain that control positive emotions and active (rather than passive) behavior were toned up. The same stress, but with different levels of control, can produce quite different biological effects. If you are stressed and can do something about it, your brain will react in one way, but if you can't do something about it, it will react in a different way. The way you cope with stress is the key issue.

These findings are very important, for although we cannot test them directly, they strongly imply that the more control we can take over the stresses in our lives, the less likely it is that our neurochemicals will take a dive.

Evolutionary Aspects

Evolutionary theory suggests that we suffer various painful states of mind because we have *innate potentials to switch into them*. For example, if someone we love dies, we can find ourselves in a deep state of grief. We might have learned to share these feelings or to keep a stiff upper lip, but there is, in all of us, a potential *grief state of mind*. Similarly, we all have the potential for aggressive fantasies and attitudes. For example, if someone harms your child, your inner desire for revenge could be intense. And we all have the potential for feeling sexual or anxious.

Let's think about anxiety. We now know that both humans and animals have an innate – that is, inborn – system in their bodies that can be triggered when they feel threatened. This is called the *fight/ flight system*. The automatic secretion of adrenaline by the adrenal glands serves the function of alerting us to danger and enables us to take immediate action. Depending on what type of danger it is, we tend to behave in certain ways. For example, when threatened by a mugger our heart rate might go up and we want to fight or run away. However, a blood phobic might faint at the sight of blood. Moreover, the things that become the focus of phobias are usually not things that can harm us. For example, guns, electric light sockets and cars kill far more people than spiders. Yet an extreme fear of spiders (even without any previous traumatic experience with them) is common, but an extreme fear of guns is rare. People may even know rationally that very few spiders can hurt them but may have an intense fear of them none the less. It is as if there is a biological program in the brain for 'fear of spiders'.

The basic idea is that certain brain states can be switched on because our brains are set up (designed) to switch on those states if circumstances require it. This approach suggests that some of the biological changes that take place in depression are caused by the activation of a 'potential, depressed brain state,' one that is no different in principle to a potential anxious state, a potential anger state, a potential sexy state, a potential grief state and so on.

However, this does not mean that all depressions are the same or only reactions to life events. As noted before there are different types of depression and a combination of genes, early life sensitivity, life events and other factors can combine to influence vulnerability and the type of depression a person may suffer from. This is why some depressions are more severe and long lasting than others.

But, you may well ask, what is the point of depression? The adaptive value of anxiety is easy to see and so is anger's – they both help us to defend ourselves – but depression seems so unhelpful. The first thing to say is that humans have the capacity to amplify any mental state. We can see and anticipate dangers that animals cannot. We can worry about things far in the future – how a party will go or how a job interview will turn out. The underlying physical system that allows us to feel anxiety – that is, the fight/flight system – is millions of years old in an evolutionary sense, but in humans, it can now be triggered in numerous ways. Still, you might ask, even if we allow for the fact that humans can amplify a potential state such as anxiety, what is the value of depression? In fact, there are a number of possibilities.

Stopping Us Chasing Rainbows
One view of the adaptive function of milder depression is that it helps us to give up our aspirations if they are unlikely to succeed. Because a depressed mood reduces the pleasure for certain things, we are more likely to give them up. Unless there was something (such as a low mood) that could persuade us to give up pursuing the unobtainable, we could easily continue to pursue it and so waste a lot of time and energy.

Helping Us to Cope With Loss
This theory suggests that many forms of depression are like grief. We all have the potential for grief when we lose contact with someone close to us. When we are in a state of grief, we can become anxious, pine for the lost person, feel that life has become empty (at least for a while) and become sad and depressed. The pining and sadness is designed to help us try to reconnect. Clearly, if we did not have the capacity for grief, this would suggest that we did not care whether we were close to others or not. But from an evolutionary

viewpoint, closeness to others is vital for our survival and we are usually highly motivated to make good supportive relationships. We can become very distressed without them. Therefore, 'attachment losses' are painful because we are biologically set up for them to be so. The reason we need closeness and feel good when we feel connected with others (and bad when we feel disconnected) is biological; it is an evolved need, especially in children.

Sometimes people become depressed even though they have not recently experienced any actual major loss, but later it turns out that they have never felt loved or wanted by their parents. Although they may want to be close to others, in their early family life, closeness was associated with punishments and threats. Thus, we can have a deep yearning for closeness with others but also a basic belief that we are unlovable and/or that other people are unreliable and will severely disappoint us. The depression is not just an illness but has to do with our being in a state of wanting closeness but being unable to get it.

In everyday life, we can develop different styles of relating to others. Some people experience what is called 'anxious attachment'. They are frightened of being rejected or abandoned, become anxious if left on their own and angry at separations. In contrast, other people may decide that attachments and closeness to others are just too painful and difficult and so they avoid closeness. Yet others move between anxious and avoiding styles. Sometimes they seem to want a lot of closeness and reassurance of being loved (and lovable), but at other times they are aloof and distant. Now all of us can have these styles to varying degrees and stress can increase their severity. For example, when we are under stress, we often want more reassurance from our loved ones. Depression can arise when we feel that we cannot get this and feel cut off from others and alone.

Helping Us to Avoid Fighting Against Overwhelming Odds

Another evolutionary theory suggests that some depressed states are associated with being subordinated and defeated in some way. Depression makes us give up attempting all sorts of challenges and reduces our aspirations; it knocks out our optimism and 'go for it' attitude; it leaves us with feelings of inferiority and shame.

According to this theory, there are biological differences between animals who have high rank and those who have low rank. In addition, it is now known that animals that have been subordinated or have suffered a lot of attacks from others show similar behavior and biological changes to those humans who suffer from depression. So the theory suggests that some depressions are related to potential states of mind that can be triggered by certain no-win situations and/or where there is enforced subordination (feeling one has to do things one does not want to, often because of fear). This is why depressed people often feel inferior, worthless, and at the bottom of the pile (low social rank) and find it difficult to be assertive. There seems to be no point in trying anything – it seems to involve far too much effort. This puts a powerful brake on aspirations and reduces hope.

Thus depressed people may come to label or judge themselves and/or are judged by others in ways that are not only negative but also suggest they have been allocated a low rank or status. In extreme cases, they might actually be ostracized and pushed out. Thus, judgments such as 'unlovable', 'worthless', 'bad', 'inadequate', 'useless' and so on are, in effect, assignments of status that locate the individual in a low rank in the pecking order. Mood, then, is in part an energy control system that signals a person's self and to others the readiness (confidence) of that individual to challenge and seek out those things that are important: e.g. friends, sexual partners, good employment, etc.

There are lots of ways that feelings of defeat can be turned on in us. Sometimes we feel defeated by how we think others treat us. We try our best but it just does not seem to work out right. Sometimes others are or have been very critical of us, and we come to believe their harsh judgments. We feel inhibited or thwarted by them and sometimes even frightened of them. And, of course, we can defeat *ourselves* by being very critical and dismissive of ourselves. We tend to make disparaging comparisons and think that others are in some way better or more intelligent than we are. Depressed states of mind often focus on feeling worthless, inferior, not up to it, and inadequate compared to others. The messages that others, or we ourselves, are making are not messages of love, acceptance and value but of criticism and put-down.

This depressed brain state is particularly likely to be activated in situations of enforced subordination and entrapment. If we are in unhappy marriages or terrible jobs or live in a place that we hate but can't get away from, we can come to feel that we are stuck, with no way out. Here are two examples. When David, a highly paid executive, had to put in increasing long hours, he came to hate his job and the situation was made worse when a new, overly critical boss took over. However, David had a big mortgage, had got used to a certain lifestyle, and could see no way of getting another job. He felt trapped in a position where he was being constantly pressured and criticized. Cathy lived in a poor area with high unemployment, and she had an abusive husband. Having little money of her own, and feeling totally responsible for her two children, she felt trapped, put-down and unsupported.

Another way we can have feelings of defeat is when we aim too high, try to be perfect or to never make mistakes. Since this is impossible to achieve, we will feel constantly defeated due to the high standards we set ourselves. When we don't reach them or succeed in our goals, we may have a sense of failure and defeat. But this very depression may prevent us from following the impossible route of continuing to challenge overwhelming odds.

Yet another way we can feel defeated is when there are chronic conflicts in our relationships that we never seem able to win. Often these involve much (usually unexpressed) anger, accentuated by a feeling that we always lose these battles. For Fran, the conflict was with her mother. Whatever she did, her mother would always find fault and tell how she should have done it. Fran never felt able to tell her mother what she felt about her, and developed a deep sense of being no good, and that whatever she tried to do it would never be good enough. If they did have arguments, it always felt to Fran that her mother was by far the stronger person who exerted a hold over her.

So it is clear that certain states of mind can be turned on in us by certain situations. There are two other reasons for exploring these ideas with you. First, it will help you to make sense of some of your experiences of depression. Second, and perhaps most important, if you grasp the essentials of this approach you will see that what happens to people when they are depressed has to do with the *activation of an inner potential state.* If you think of depression as being a part of you that has been triggered, you will be able to exert more control over it. Your depression is one of many potential states of mind; it is no more the 'real' you than any other state of mind you might be in.

Human nature is like a piano keyboard. We can play some lovely tunes but also make some dreadful noises. One of the tricks of life may be to know which tuneful notes we are capable of and learning how to play them when we want to. If we consistently judge ourselves to be unlovable or inferior and worthless, we may also be consistently activating depression brain systems. Thus, it follows that one way of turning off these distressing systems is to change the way we think about ourselves so that we don't keep activating them.

Psychological Aspects

Our understanding of the psychology of depression has been growing in recent years. In fact, there are now many ideas and theories about how the way we think and our attitudes and conduct can make us vulnerable to depression. Back in 1917, Freud argued that depression arises when anger at a loss is directed against the self. This has become popularly known as 'anger turned inwards'. As we shall see later, it is true that, when we are depressed, we also often feel very angry – sometimes with others but often with ourselves.

Recently, some psychologists have looked into how we behave and act when we become depressed. They have found that we are unable to behave in ways that bring us positive rewards or much pleasure. Many people become locked into depression because there does not seem to be much in their lives that gives them satisfaction or pleasure or boosts their self-esteem. They may not have a job or may have few or no friends. And if they are very socially anxious, they may cut themselves off from the types of social encounters that previously they enjoyed.

Perhaps the most researched psychological approach to depression has been called the *cognitive* approach. This focuses on the way we think and interpret things. It was developed independently by the psychiatrist Aaron Beck and the psychologist Albert Ellis.

Many self-help books on depression have been written using this approach, and it will also play an important part in many of the suggestions for getting out of depression that appear in the second and third parts of this book.

The cognitive approach suggests that particular kinds of thinking go with particular kinds of problems. For example:

Problem	*Thoughts*
Panic	*I am going to die from these symptoms of anxiety.*
Social anxiety	*I will do something that will make me look foolish/stupid and I'll be rejected or shamed.*
Depression	*I am a bad/weak/inadequate person and the future is hopeless.*
Paranoia	*People are out to get me.*
Anger	*Other people are bad/unkind, are treating me unfairly, or taking advantage, and deserve to be punished.*

By focusing on the thoughts that are associated with certain types of problems, people can learn to test the evidence for their thoughts and learn to generate alternatives. Cognitive therapy is defined by this focusing on thoughts and attitudes. By helping people recognize how their thinking contributes to their distress (especially a sense of defeat), and by changing the way they think about their problems, they can experience symptomatic relief. But if they go further and change their attitudes and basic ideas about themselves, they will be able to obtain more control over their feelings and thus be less vulnerable to anxiety and depression.

When we are depressed, we usually have a mixture of internal problems (negative ways of seeing ourselves, the world and the future) and external problems (e.g. money worries or relationship difficulties). By learning how to come up with alternatives to their internal problems and avoid damaging negative beliefs about the self (e.g. 'I am useless'), depressed people are often better placed to work on their external problems.

So being depressed often goes with thinking in certain ways. However, this suggests another question. How did we get into thinking negatively in the first place? According to the cognitive approach, when we are young we develop basic beliefs about ourselves, others and the world we live in that are built up according to how others treat us. Over time, these basic beliefs come to control our feelings and attitudes towards various things. If, for example, we are constantly told that we are unlovable or failures, we can develop a basic belief that we *are* unlovable or failures. For example, if children are consistently told that they are no good at sports, this is the view they may have about themselves. Consequently, they may tend to avoid sports, and because they avoid sports, they will, of course, never get better at them, thus confirming the idea that they are bad at sports. And when these children become adults, they may continue to avoid sports because, when they try to play, the *feelings* of looking silly or being no good can come back – even though as adults they may be very graceful. Thus early beliefs and experiences may have strong effects on people's current behavior and feelings.

Negative beliefs about the self can become subdued and even buried as we grow up – 'latent' rather than 'active'. But if some major life-event happens – say, an important relationship breaks up – the early beliefs and ideas we may have developed in childhood come back. So, in our grief over the loss of the relationship, we may explain the break-up to ourselves by referring to the beliefs and ideas we developed as children – for example, 'This relationship broke up because I am unlovable.' A negative belief/idea now influences the way we interpret events. So whenever something bad happens to us, especially if it generates strong feelings, instead of seeing it as bad luck or just life, we tend to see it as further evidence of being a failure or unlovable. Because we are interpreting information negatively, to fit with the belief of being, say, a failure, the belief is maintained.

Let me give an example. Sally had a fairly neglectful upbringing. When she was still relatively young, her mother told her that she had got married when she became pregnant with her. Unfortunately, the marriage was unhappy and her mother would ponder on how things might have been different for her had she not got pregnant. She would often say, 'If it hadn't been for you, I would have done such and such.' Sally felt that her mother saw her as the reason she had not done more with her life. Generally, these discussions were not carried out in anger but with regret and sadness. At times, her mother had also strongly hinted that she felt like leaving home. Sally had taken these 'hints' as serious threats of abandonment. She gradually developed certain beliefs and ideas: 'I am a nuisance to others. I stop people doing what they want to do. People don't really want me around. I must not do anything that might push them away. Others might leave me at any moment.'

She carried these basic beliefs inside her throughout her life. Whenever there were conflicts, she would feel anxious and think, 'Maybe I'm being a nuisance' or 'I must let others do what they want to do.' If she ever felt that she was putting others out, or letting them down, she would feel very guilty. As a result, she found it difficult to assert herself and was constantly on the look out for clues showing that she was being a burden to others. When an important long-term relationship with a boyfriend broke up, her automatic thoughts were: 'Well, I guess nobody really wants me. I am just a nuisance. I will never be loved for myself.' It is important to note that these beliefs were not cold and emotionless, but highly charged with emotion and feelings.

However, as you might guess, underneath this surface set of beliefs was another set. Here lay a high degree of anger. Having to give in to others all the time (in effect subordinate herself to the needs of others) had led to feelings that this was unfair. After all, Sally hadn't asked to be born. Why should she have to keep doing what others wanted? Why was she so unlovable? But, of course, she thought that if she asserted herself, this would threaten her with abandonment and feeling a nuisance. So these beliefs and feelings had to be 'repressed' and avoided. And, she felt, since her mother had done her best for her, she had no right to be angry with her mother. Even thinking about her anger towards her mother for threatening abandonment made Sally feel like a traitor and bad.

So, it is how we interpret things and give meaning to events and situations that produces, or at least maintains, depression. As we shall see later, our thoughts can take us on a downward spiral into depression: as we become depressed, we have more negative thoughts; and as we have more negative thoughts, we become more depressed. Here is an overview of Sally's beliefs and feelings and how they affected her:

Early childhood experiences
Mother said that had it not been for me she would have done more with her life. Worried that mother might leave one day.

Basic beliefs
I am a nuisance to others. I stop people doing what they want to do. People don't really want me around. I must not do anything that could push them away. I must be to others what they want me to be. Expressing anger and/or asserting my needs could lead to rejection. I must be grateful for love. I am a bad/ungrateful person if I express my dissatisfactions.

Basic behaviors
Non-assertive.
Avoid conflicts.
Not initiating things she wants to do.

Depression triggering event
Break up of a relationship. Loss of a valued person who blamed me for being rather boring.

Typical thoughts
I am a nuisance to others.
I can never get it right.
It would be better if I weren't here.
Relationships are just too difficult.
Can't bear to be alone.

Symptoms
Poor sleep and exhaustion
Constant thinking about loss and self-blame
Feelings of worthlessness
Loss of pleasure or capacity to enjoy things
Feeling that future seems hopeless
Weight loss
Inner feelings of emptiness
Increased fear and general feelings of disorientation

You may have noticed two things about Sally. First, there was a clear problem in her attachment system. She was very anxious about forming close relationships and felt vulnerable to being left and abandoned. But the way she *behaved* and coped with this – in effect, her strategy to stay in contact with others – made her act like a subordinate and, at times, even a servant. Her relationships did not boost her self-esteem. Indeed, apart from making herself 'fit in with others', she felt that she had no power to hold on to good relationships. So when it came to asserting her own needs and opinions, she felt that she had neither the right nor any justification for doing so. As a result, her confidence was always dependent on being in a relationship. Without one, and a lot of reassurance, she felt empty, and vulnerable, and often felt inferior and subordinate to others.

The Role of Early Traumas

One powerful way that some individuals learn their values and how to judge and rate themselves is through having very painful experiences in childhood. For example, if they have been sexually abused, they might come to feel that sex is bad, dirty or dangerous – and that they themselves are in some way bad or dirty and their sexual feelings are dangerous. In effect, the trauma robs them of their sexual lives and feelings of goodness.

Sometimes parents are unable to cope with frustration, and when things get tense, they lash out at their children or call them names. This is intensely painful for the children, who find it difficult to recognize that their parents have a low tolerance for frustration. The children on the receiving end of this rage might blame themselves and think that they really are very bad. And sometimes parents are unable to give their children physical affection, perhaps because they don't know how or because they feel very awkward about it. One of the saddest things today is that some parents still think that being physically affectionate towards their children, especially their sons, will turn the boys into sissies.

Many depressed people can look back and see that their early life was often rather barren of affection and, at times, very harsh. Perhaps the time has come to consider what value judgments about yourself you still carry from those days, to re-examine them and to reject those that are no longer useful or helpful to you. If others have treated you harshly, isn't it time to learn how to treat yourself better?

Because, as children, we are often unable to see our parents as flawed individuals with problems of their own, we tend to think that the way they treated us was our own fault – there was something about us that made them behave in the way they did. If they were very critical of us, we tend to carry on the tradition and be critical of ourselves. However, with understanding, insight and hard work, we can learn to change these habits and learn to be compassionate towards ourselves.

Social Aspects

Depressed people often have a mixture of problems, both internal (styles of thinking, negative feelings) and external. Social approaches have looked into these external problems. Indeed, social researchers (e.g. George Brown and Tirrel Harris) have found that (external) social factors play a large role in the onset of some depressions and in the recovery from them. In addition, there are things that make us vulnerable to depression (vulnerability factors) and things that push us into it (provoking agents).

As evolutionary theory would predict, vulnerability to depression is related to having no close relationships with people in whom one can confide, feel close to and supported by. Low self-esteem – feeling inadequate, inferior, worthless or of low rank or status – is also a vulnerability factor. But, importantly, some of our self-esteem comes from having roles that give us a sense of meaning and accomplishment, and from having friends who value our company.

Some people think that being a parent and looking after children should be enough of a role, but the evidence suggests that this is not true. Although we may love our children, and they can give us many pleasures, we did not evolve to live enclosed in houses with restless, demanding young offspring – frankly, they can tax us to our limits! Young children need a lot from us, but we cannot, on the whole, confide in them or turn to them for support and the emotional sharing of problems. Nor, on the whole, do children boost our self-esteem, at least not in the same way that adults can.

However, the straw that breaks the camel's back is often some event that just overwhelms us. This may be finding out that our partner is having an affair, or the loss of a job that threatens us with major financial hardship, or the discovery that one of our children has a serious illness – or it may be a personal failure. Events with *long-term implications* can take us that one step too far and we fall over the edge and spiral down into depression. It is as if we suddenly become exhausted, feel out of control and trapped.

Social Roles
A number of social psychologists today recognize that much of our self-esteem is taken from our roles – what we *do*. These roles also give us a sense of status and some rank in society. Sadly, today bringing up children and saying that one is 'a housewife' are not seen as roles worthy of much status, despite these being some of the most important and emotionally taxing activities that people can tackle.

A major concern with depression in young people is that they may lack clear roles, such as jobs, and may not feel part of their communities. Yet feeling that we have something to offer to others and that we are appreciated and valued for what we do are important sources of self-esteem and social status. Jobs also give us some direct control over our lives, as well as allowing us to plan for the future and providing opportunities to interact with other people. Without jobs, we can feel unwanted by society, feel deprived of an identity, and find it difficult to make plans. We can also feel socially isolated.

Consider Kath. She had always wanted to get married but had never met the right person. However, she had dedicated herself to nursing and this had become her life. Then, at the age of 54, she developed a serious illness, which meant that she had to take early retirement. Grieving for the one thing in her life that had given her meaning, she slipped into depression and gradually lost contact with her friends, especially those who were still working.

Many who come to therapy have, as part of their depression, problems in being able to find work or some other meaningful status-boosting role outside the home. Sometimes they are too anxious to try, sometimes their partners won't let them, and sometimes it is simply too difficult. In addition, many current Western lifestyles are not those that humans have evolved to cope with, and these unnatural lifestyles cause problems. We evolved to live in close-knit communities where children were not enclosed in small homes, but were mostly active out in the open where friends and relatives could keep an eye on them. Women were certainly not segregated from the working of the group as they are today. In my view, some of the high rates of depression are due to our abnormal social patterns and lifestyles.

The main reason for exploring these social aspects of depression is to highlight the fact that suffering from depression does not prove that you are a bad or weak person, and there may be things in your life that make depression more likely. Once you give up self-blaming and feeling inadequate, you might begin to see how to make changes. It is also important to note that a life looking after children on your own does not necessarily lead to happiness. Indeed, it has been shown that the arrival of children can lead to a reduction in happiness in the relationship of the parents. This is not to say, however, that children can't bring great pleasures and that some people become depressed when they lose this role, as children 'fly the nest'.

Why are Women More at Risk From Depression?
It has already been noted that, in general, women are around two to three times more likely to suffer from depression than men. There are various theories about why this should be so.

Biology This view holds that the higher rates in women are due to differences in reproductive biology (e.g. the levels of certain hormones). In other words, there is something different about the female brain compared to the male brain, which increases the risk of depression. Recent research suggests that emotional information may be processed slightly differently in the brains of men and women – although whether this increases the risk of depression is unknown.

Psychology This view holds that the higher rates of depression in women are due to differences in the way they are 'socialized' as they grow up. Women are brought up to be more accepting of subordinate positions, schooled to be carers and, compared to men, to be less assertive or competitive. The incidence of sexual abuse is higher in women than in men. Also, the ways that men and women recognize and cope with distressing life-events may be different (e.g. women are more likely to focus on feelings and blame themselves if they have relationship problems). Women then are more in touch with their feelings and more able to express sad and unhappy ones and may have a greater need for closeness. Women may also brood more on unhappiness – although this can be because they are more socially isolated. Men, however, are more likely to blame others for problems and are less able to recognize and express sad feelings (e.g. 'big boys don't cry', and the need for affection and closeness is seen as a sign of being a wimp). They are more likely to turn to drink or become aggressive if they have emotional problems.

Social   This view holds that variations are due to differences in social opportunities and gender roles. Women are more likely to occupy subordinate positions in society and the family, to be restricted to the home and to be subjected to male dominance (e.g. abuse). Marriage particularly may not always be that helpful for women if it maintains them in subordinate positions with reduced opportunities to socialize with others and to engage in meaningful social roles outside the home.

My own view is that the differences in rates of depression are, on the whole, due to a mixture of these factors.

Key Points
- Depression is a powerful state of mind that is related to biological change. Your brain is in a different physical state when you are depressed from when you are not.
- Sometimes depression results from something that has been 'turned on' in us. Just as a painful state of grief can be turned on by the loss of a loved one, so too depression can be turned on by the problems we have in our lives and how we come to view them.

continued on next page

- Learning to exert more control over our lives and our thoughts can help us in many ways, not least by giving our brain chemistry a chance to recover.
- Depression tends to focus our minds on certain kinds of thoughts – e.g. unlovability, inferiority or entrapment.
- Once depression starts, our thoughts can play a powerful role in whether the depressed state remains 'turned on'.
- Vulnerability to depression might arise because we carry a number of latent negative beliefs/ideas/views about ourselves (e.g. as unlovable or a failure). We develop these in childhood.
- These basic beliefs can become activated again when negative events happen to us.
- As a result, we tend to explain or interpret the reasons for the negative events with our negative beliefs – e.g. 'This relationship broke up because of me – I am unlovable.'
- We then start interpreting many things by using the explanation of, say, unlovability, and this makes the belief seem more true. Moreover, because we blame ourselves, we may begin to see the future as unchangeable and therefore beyond our control.
- It would be incorrect to say that all depressions are due only to how we interpret things. A significant contribution can come from our social environments.
- Having no, or only a few, social roles that give us a sense of self-esteem (and feeling that there is not much that we can do that is useful) can also bring on depression.

3

Negative Thinking and Relationships with Others

When we are depressed, we feel tired a lot of the time, don't sleep well, don't look forward to things, lose interest in sex and food, and so on. Another of the major changes that take place is in the way we think. Negative thoughts, interpretations and memories become much more common. Whereas, before, we might have felt reasonably successful, when depressed we feel like failures. Whereas, before, we might have looked forward to going on holiday, now it seems an ordeal. Whereas, before, we might have taken pleasure from being with the family, now we are not sure what we feel for them, or even if we feel anything at all. When we are depressed, there is a change in the way we see ourselves, the world and our future.

> Before I was depressed, I thought I was getting somewhere, but now I think I was just deluding myself.　　　　　　　　　　　*Joe*

> Before I was depressed, I used to think others liked me and I was an all right sort of person, but now I doubt that.　　　　　*Karen*

> Before I was depressed, I could think about many things at once and solve problems easily, but now I get easily overwhelmed and can't concentrate. My mind is too full of small worries that seem to have become blown up out of all proportion.　　　　　　*David*

These people are experiencing the effects of depression on their thinking and feelings. Before we look at the typical types of biases in our thinking that depression can bring, let's consider why the brain does this. Why does it cause us to think so negatively? At the time we feel most down, why does our thinking change to make matters worse?

32

The Role of the Brain

There are various possible reasons why we become more negative in our thinking as we become depressed. One view is that we all have, to a greater or lesser degree, various negative beliefs about ourselves (such as being unlovable, a failure or inadequate). The kinds of events that can activate these negative beliefs are usually major losses or frustrations, including the break-up of a relationship, difficulties in a relationship that increase conflicts, and great disappointments of some kind. The events trigger the negative beliefs (e.g. of being unlovable) and begin to impose a negative meaning on situations. This vicious circle is outlined in Fig. 1.

Fig. 1

So our thinking starts to take us on a downward spiral and we start to look for evidence that confirms or fits with our negative beliefs rather than looking for evidence that does not fit them. As we remember other failures, our depressed feelings start to spread out like a dark tide rolling in to cover the sands of our positive abilities.

There is however another view that does not contradict the above but adds, in my view, quite a bit to it. This view suggests that our brains *evolved* to think differently when we are under threat compared with when we feel safe.

Consider, for example, an animal feeding in an open field. Suddenly its attention is drawn to a movement in the grass. What should it do? Should it ignore it, wait to find out what it is or get the hell out of there? Now, in many cases in the wild, the best thing to

33

do is 'get the hell out of there,' for the movement could be a predator and delay could be costly. In fact, it only has to make the wrong decision once and it's dead. It would be far better to run away when there was no need to than stay and take the risk. If it runs away it has lost some time feeding but is still alive.

What this means is that, when we are under threat, our brains have been designed to work on a 'better safe than sorry' principle. That is, our brains were not designed to think rationally in all situations, but at times to jump to conclusions and assume the worst, which allows a rapid response if needed. It does not matter that this jumping to conclusions could be wrong, only that it works and protects us. The strange thing about this is that it means that the *brain is designed to make mistakes*, especially when we are under stress – of assuming the worst and taking defensive action. Today, jumping to conclusions and assuming the worst can lead us to feel pretty miserable, so we need to bring our rational minds to bear on the situation to help us get more control over our feelings.

When we think about the nature of many of our fears – of the dark, unfamiliar places or people, becoming ill, being rejected, creepy-crawly things and so on – we can see that, over millions of years, they led us either to avoid them or to become highly defensive and on our guard. When a child or someone else we love does not come home when expected, it does not take much for the first pangs of anxiety to occur in the stomach, even though rationally we know that the chances of anything bad having happened to them are slim. In certain contexts, the rational judgment of probabilities only goes so far in helping us with our anxiety.

But how does this kind of understanding apply to depression? With insight and effort, we can learn to go some way towards correcting the false assumptions the brain has made. It also helps to know that, when we make such mistakes, this is in no way evidence that we are stupid or particularly irrational; rather, we are experiencing a natural function of the brain.

Social Threats

In many of our social behaviors, we tend not to follow rational rules. Why do we fall in love? Why do we choose a career in nursing or social work when we could make lots more money in business? Why do some people like working with computers but others prefer working with people? Why do we want to have children? The answer is that these things appeal to us emotionally, and although rational thinking may play a part in our decision-making, it is only a part. The science fiction series *Star Trek* used this fact to good effect. Mr Spock was highly rational whereas the human crew were much more 'emotional'. Therefore, to be emotional is to be human. But this is not to say that emotional reasoning is better or worse than rational reasoning – for each has its place. It is just that emotional reasoning can at times lead us astray, and we have to learn to contain or challenge some of the thoughts and feelings of our more emotional side.

But it is when things threaten us that we are most vulnerable to losing our rationality. So let's return to thinking about threats. Now, of course, the kinds of things that threaten us when we become depressed are not spiders and snakes. It is fear of being inferior or failing, of disapproval or being abandoned, of becoming trapped in unpleasant situations, of losing control of one's plans and goals and so forth. The key point is that there are certain types of events or cues that naturally increase our sense of threat and shift us to less rational ways of thinking. The more threatened we feel, the more the primitive parts of our brain take over and start to feed in feelings that impel some action to defend ourselves. Our automatic thoughts and feelings become more and more controlled by our primitive brains and less under the control of the rational brain.

If we have a basic belief of, say, unlovability, or that we are inferior, or that others are untrustworthy, the threshold for switching into perceiving threats is lowered. But, and this is important, we can be threatened by feelings of failure, rejection and loss without ever having developed strong negative beliefs. True, negative, early life experiences can lower the threshold for activating the primitive brain to deal with these threats, which will bring back all kinds of negative feelings, but most of us have some threshold that can be crossed. After all, even though we may never have experienced grief, the moment someone close to us dies, we can be overwhelmed by it – it is a natural response, common to all humans. Even some animals seem to experience forms of it.

Social Threats and Human Needs

On the whole human beings throughout the world tend to be happier in some situations and unhappy in others. We have already mentioned grief; that is, we can all be thrown into profound states of mental anguish if someone close to us dies. We do not learn to experience grief – it is a natural feeling and experience. Of course, our beliefs may affect how much grief we feel. For example, if we believe that we may see our loved one in heaven this may help us a little. And we may believe that we must be strong and not show or share our grief, or we can believe that we are entitled and need to share it.

But we can go further than this. On the whole humans feel either happy or unhappy in the following situations:

Happy situations	*Unhappy situations*
Loved and wanted	Unloved and unwanted
Close to others	Abandoned
Accepted and belonging	Not accepted and rejected
Have friends	Do not have friends
Accepted member of a group	An outsider or ostracised
Having something of value to offer others	Have little of value to offer others
Appreciated and valued by others	Being taken advantage of
Feel attractive to others	Feel unattractive to others
Have status and respect	Do not have status and respect
Winning	Losing

What this table suggests is that there are some common situations the world over that increase our happiness and some that reduce it. Or to put this another way, those things in the right-hand column make us feel threatened. The reasons for this are complex, but in general humans have a number of very social needs, and if these needs are met we tend to feel happier than if these needs are not being met. There is a good reason for this, which is that the brain is wired up to want these things. Those who were able to have these needs met – who were 'socially successful', in evolutionary terms – did better than those who did not. By 'better' we mean that they tended to survive better and leave more offspring. So we are biologically inclined to try to achieve the things in the left-hand column of the table and avoid the things in the right-hand column. Social success is wired into our emotions. The more our beliefs begin to shift towards the things in the right-hand column, the more threatened and unhappy we are likely to become.

Relationships with Others

No person is an island, they say. At times we need to feel cared for by others. If we are sick or go into hospital, we need others to look after us physically. If we feel sad, we might turn to others for a cuddle or reassurance. We can have both a physical and an emotional need for care. Close, reassuring contact releases chemicals in the brain called endorphins, which help us feel better.

If all goes well, when we turn to others we can feel uplifted, calmed, helped and so on. However, suppose we have negative beliefs about our emotional needs. These might include:

- Nobody could care for me.
- My needs are a nuisance.
- I am a burden to others.
- It is pathetic for me to need love and reassurance.
- I can't survive on my own.
- I will always be alone.
- It is childish to need reassurance from others.
- A needy person is a weak person.
- A needy person is a greedy person.
- My needs are far too much for anyone to cope with.

These beliefs can make our needy selves difficult to handle. In consequence, we don't work through our feelings or learn to distinguish between what we really do need from others and what we can look after ourselves. In such situations, we might close down our emotional needs and become more depressed. Talking to friends can be helpful because in this way we are making attempts to reach out to others and 'owning' our needs. Indeed, knowing what our needs are and being able to express them is important for mental health, especially if we are successful in eliciting supportive signals from others.

We can, of course, also have beliefs about others. These cover two broad concerns: the refusal or inability of others to care, and the availability or absence of others to show care. Examples of the first type are:

- Others are too busy to bother with me.
- They are not up to caring for me.
- They will punish me for needing.
- They don't understand.
- They will like me less for needing.
- Getting only a little is not enough.

Examples of the second type are:

- Others should give me what I want when I want it.
- My needs are more important than others'.
- If they don't give me what I want, they don't love me.

It is part of human nature to need others, and when we are under stress, it is natural for these needs to increase. When we are adults, it is also common for all our needs not to be met. It may also sometimes be true that others do not understand what we are feeling and so fail to meet our needs.

Sometimes we turn away from our own needs and focus on those of others. Typical beliefs here are:

- I must always put others first.
- To put my needs before theirs means I am a selfish person.
- I must be what the other person wants me to be.
- Self-sacrifice is good.
- I need to be needed.
- If I give lots to others, they will give to me.

The central issue here is that giving and receiving is always a matter of balance. If we move too far in one direction, we will suffer – perhaps giving a lot but feeling that others don't give much back. And if we are honest with ourselves, we sometimes care for others to make ourselves feel good: 'I am a good person because I care so much.' As long as we are honest and recognize that we are giving care to others to make ourselves feel good or better, fair enough. But if we deceive ourselves – that our caring really is purely for the other person with no strings attached – we can feel very let down when others do not return our care.

Sometimes, in order to feel good about ourselves, we try to turn ourselves into very caring individuals and then find that we feel swamped by the needs of others. We have, in effect, made a rod for our own backs. We may have a desperate wish to escape from the burdens of caring. But if you are heavily into self-sacrifice, this need to escape is not seen as a signal to pull back a bit and look after yourself more, but becomes a source of guilt and bad feeling.

If you behave like a servant, others may well treat you like one. A caring–sharing relationship is difficult unless you are up-front about your own needs. We all have social and emotional needs because we are human beings, but some people become either overly needy as adults or develop strong beliefs that their needs cannot be met and/or that they are in some way weak or inadequate for having them.

Exploitation
When we are depressed, we often become very sensitive and concerned about what others think about us. And this may be because humans in general have evolved in such a way that they are very sensitive to being exploited and cheated.

Just think about how common it is for humans to feel angry at being cheated. Finding that your lover has been unfaithful, or that your friends have let you down, or that a promise has not been kept – all these tend to activate strong negative feelings, because we feel cheated.

We are born with a sensitivity to cheating (because being cheated is a threat). However, when we become depressed we can see deceptions almost everywhere because, once again under threat, the brain jumps to conclusions. When Jane returned to work after being off sick, her colleagues asked her how she was. But Jane thought, 'They are only asking this to make themselves feel better and not because they really care about me.' In effect Jane was saying that her colleagues were actively trying to deceive her.

When we are depressed, we become far more sensitive to the possibility that others are only pretending to be nice, that they are cheating us. And if we receive mild put-downs or people ignore us for whatever reason, we can read all kinds of things into that. This is because, when we are depressed, we are on the look-out for various kinds of social threat.

Depressed people often feel that they give a lot to others but receive less back in return: 'I always phone others but no one phones me.' When we are well, we may well recognize that other people don't give us the attention that we want, but 'That's life,' we say, or 'That's them.' The fact that they don't care to the degree we would like does not mean that they do not care at all. But when we are depressed, this really irritates us and we start to think that other people are not sharing enough of their time and concern with us.

It is important to recognize that this may well be the brain jumping to conclusions again. Although you may feel that others are only pretending to care or that you don't deserve better, this does not make it true. When we are depressed, it is natural for us to think like this, but as we shall see, there are ways that we can challenge these ideas and not let the depression fool us into seeing threats that aren't actually there or exaggerating those that are.

Status
Many beliefs in depression focus on our internal sense of status and self-worth, which invariably means our feelings of inferiority. When we are depressed, we tend to compare ourselves with others and come to the conclusion that we are inadequate, defective, a failure, undesirable in some way – there is always something about us that marks us down.

When Mary lost her lover to another woman, it was not so much the loss that upset her (she had had doubts about the relationship and had wondered whether she wanted it to continue). Instead, her distress was focused on the 'status thought', 'What does she have that I don't. Maybe my love-making wasn't so good. Maybe I'm less attractive than I thought.' It was these concerns, of why she had lost out to another woman, that made her feel most depressed.

Inferiority beliefs show themselves most clearly in our feelings of shame and inadequacy. When we become depressed, the brain sees threats in our ability to compete and show ourselves confident. One failure or setback becomes evidence to the brain that other challenges we might meet will also end in failure.

John lost an important argument at work, and thought, 'I didn't put my point of view carefully enough. I'm inadequate. I'll never be able to win when it matters to me.' As he said later when he felt better, although normally he would have been disappointed by the defeat he had always lived by the motto: 'You win some, you lose some.' In this case, however, the disappointment and stress of losing had led him to start jumping to conclusions. Interestingly, at the time his love relationship was not going well, and this background stress probably elevated his stress hormones and made it much easier for his brain to switch to feelings of defeat and inadequacy.

We now know that animals do not fight or challenge each other all the time, but only in situations when, after evaluation, they think that they have a chance of winning. Thus we have, in our brains, innate mechanisms that help us to judge when the chances of winning are good and when they are not. All kinds of things can affect this system – for instance, being very tired or exhausted, recovering from flu, not being able to sleep, being under various other stresses. The problem here is that, when we become depressed, the demands on us seem to exceed our ability to meet them. When this happens, the system starts to go for a 'better safe than sorry' option and gives us the feelings and ideas that we can't win at anything, that we will always fail, and are bottom of the pile. Although this system is designed to inhibit us from becoming challenging in situations in which we are unlikely to succeed, when we are depressed it saps our energy and tells us: 'Don't even try.' In one sense, this system is trying to protect us from yet further defeats. However, in the modern, human, depressed brain, the brakes are applied too hard. Moreover because, as humans, we can brood on our defeats and use them to make judgments of ourselves, we can increase our own depression.

Key Points

- When we become depressed, we become sensitive to various real or imagined threats.
- Nine times out of ten, our brains go for a 'better safe than sorry' option – that is, they say: 'Whatever we try to do, it won't work so don't take the risk.'
- When we are depressed, we can become irrational in certain ways.
- This shift in our thinking happens not because we, as human beings, are irrational in the sense that we are stupid; it is to do with how our brains work when we are depressed.
- The shift to more defensive thinking can be increased if we hold negative beliefs (acquired in childhood) about our lovability or sense of worth.

PART II

Learning How to Cope

Part II lays out some self-help approaches that people suffering from depression have found useful. My advice would be to read through the whole section first – to give yourself an overview – then go back to the beginning and, step by step, work through the chapters that you feel are most appropriate to you, doing the exercises at the end of each one.

Be your own adviser, and test out whether these ideas are helpful to you and decide which best suit you.

4

Initial Steps

There is really no 'one thing' that is depression. There are many types and many causes. Depression is not like having the flu or a cold. Instead, a diagnosis of depression can be applied to a varied array of people who suffer from multiple problems and difficulties in unique ways, and whose depression has detrimental effects on their confidence and energy level. For some people, depression is triggered by a major life-event such as unemployment, housing problems, poverty or serious financial loss. For others, there seems to be a high genetic loading. Still others are sensitive to depression as a result of negative early life experiences, and for yet others, depression arises in the context of difficult family and close relationships or social isolation. And, of course, people can have one or many of these various difficulties. Not surprisingly then, we will need a whole range of approaches and treatments to deal with depression. What is helpful for one person may not be to another.

In this section of the book, I will outline some of the approaches that you might be able to use for yourself, to help you cope with any difficulties you may be experiencing or at least feel less over-whelmed and pessimistic about them. Because it is the nature of depression to think negatively about ourselves and the future, it is possible that these symptoms of depression may be stopping you from taking steps which may offer solutions to some of life's problems.

Changing Your Behavior

When we are depressed, all the activities we have to perform each day can seem overwhelming. However, it is useful to try to organize them in such a way that they can be approached *step by step*. Take staying in bed. Now, if staying in bed helps you feel better, all well and good, but often in depression it does not. We simply use bed, not to rest and regenerate our energies, but to hide away from the world. Then we feel guilty and attack ourselves for not doing the things we have to do. Also, when you are lying in bed, you may tend to brood on your problems. Although bed can seem like a safe place to be, it can actually make you feel much worse in the long run. So the most important step is to try to get up and plan to do one positive thing each day. Remember, your brain is telling you that you can't do things and to give up trying. So you have to slowly convince that part of yourself that you *can* do things – bit by bit.

Occasionally, however, because depressed people often bully themselves out of bed with thoughts such as 'Get up, you lazy bum. How can you just lie there?', it can sometimes be useful to try the opposite tack. This is to learn to stay in bed for a while, at least one day a week and enjoy it – read the newspaper or listen to the radio and tell yourself how pleasant it is. To be able to lie in bed without feeling guilty can be helpful for some people. So when we talk about getting up to do things, this is not to 'bully you out of bed' but to encourage you to get up because lying there and brooding on problems may only make you feel worse.

Breaking Down Large Problems into Smaller Ones
Suppose you have to go shopping. Try not to think about all the hassles before you start. Instead, first look in your cupboards and make a list of what you need. When you've done this, give yourself some praise. After all, you are one step further ahead than you were before you made the list. Next, get your bags and other things together to go to the shops. On the way, focus on the fact that you are now well prepared for shopping. Again, try not to think about the hassle of getting around the shops. When in a shop, work your way slowly around until you have everything on your list.

If this all sounds a bit like following a recipe, then in a way it is. The key thing is to try to avoid being distracted by thoughts of 'It will all be too difficult and can't be done.' The evidence suggests that, when we are depressed, we lose the tendency to plan things in an ordered way and are easily overwhelmed. Challenging depression can mean deliberately planning activities step by step. I agree that this may seem a boring thing to have to do, but remember you are training your brain to think differently. If you have broken a leg, you would have gradually to learn how to put weight on it and walk again. Challenging depression step by step is simply the mental equivalent of this.

Planning Positive Activities

Often, when we feel depressed, we think we have to do all the boring things first. Now, sometimes, boring chores are unavoidable, but you should also plan to do some positive activities – simple rewards that give (or used to give) you pleasure. For example, if you like sitting in the garden with a book, going to visit a friend or taking a walk, plan to do these activities. Sometimes depressed people are very poor at including positive activities in their plans for the day. All their time is spent struggling to get on top of the boring chores of life. They may feel guilty going out and, say, leaving the washing up undone. But we need to have positive activities. If we don't, it is like drawing on a bank account without putting anything into it. The positive things you do can be seen as depositing money in your account. Each time you do something that gives you pleasure, no matter how small that pleasure is, think to yourself: that's a bit more in my positive account.

Coping with Boredom

Some depressions are related to boredom. The lives of some depressed people have become repetitive and boring. Sometimes this appears unavoidable. However, again the key issue here is to diagnose boredom and then take steps to challenge it. One of my patients had gradually slipped into a lifestyle that involved going to work, coming home, watching TV and going to bed, having given up meeting friends and planning activities with them. Slowly, step by step, he began to think of things he would like to do, and then tried to see if he could do at least some of them. One of the things was joining the local football club and getting involved as a social member. Another was joining a local charity group and helping with fundraising.

Some depressions are related to feeling socially or emotionally isolated, lonely and understimulated. The problems are social and environmental ones, and low moods may be a natural reaction to boredom and a lack of social stimulation.

Women who are trapped in the home with young children are particularly vulnerable to boredom. Again the main thing here is for them to recognize that they are bored and begin to explore ways of getting out more and developing new contacts. They could perhaps contact mother-and-baby groups, and ask their friends about other activities. If social anxiety is a problem, people who are depressed like this could try to do a little more each day in making outside contacts and/or contact their family doctors to ask if there are any local groups who might be able to help them with social anxiety and getting out more.

Increasing Activity and Distraction

Sometimes, when people feel very depressed or uptight, they can also feel agitated. At these times, trying to relax does not work so well. The mind just won't settle down to it. Then they need to distract themselves with a physical activity. There are various options here. Anything that involves physical activity – digging the garden, jogging, aerobic exercises, decorating – can be helpful. Physical activity can be especially useful if you are tense with anger or frustration.

In depressed states of mind, we tend to ruminate on all the negatives in our lives and, at times, lose our perspective. If you find your mind swirling around a number of negative thoughts, try to find something to distract you. You have probably tracked through some of these thoughts over and over again. They don't take you anywhere except to feeling worse.

Now your thoughts do affect the way your brain works. For example, suppose a group of non-depressed people decided to carry out this experiment. At eight o'clock each night, they would start to dwell on sexual thoughts and fantasies. What do you think would happen to their feelings and their bodies? What they may well find is that, when they make themselves dwell on these fantasies, their bodies begin to become sexually aroused as a result of special hormones released in the brain to prepare them for sex.

You are probably well aware that people's bodies can be changed (aroused) by the fantasies they engage in. But what you may not have considered is that depressing thoughts may also affect the types of arousal that take place in your body and the chemicals released in your brain. So just as people might try to control their sexual thoughts by taking cold showers or otherwise distracting themselves to avoid getting too aroused when they don't want to be, so also with depression. Try to find ways of distracting yourself, to avoid feeding depressive feelings by dwelling on the negative. We will later explore how you can challenge some of these thoughts, but the first step is to recognize how thoughts themselves can have an effect on how our bodies (and brains) operate.

Creating 'Personal Space'

Occasionally there may be a problem in creating 'personal space' – that is, time to be spent on oneself. We can feel so overwhelmed by the needs of others (e.g. the family) that we allow no 'space' for ourselves. We become overstimulated and want to run away. If you find that you need time on your own, try to talk to those close to you and explain this. Make clear that this is not a rejection of them. It is, instead, a positive choice on your part to be more in touch with yourself.

Many people feel guilty if they feel a need to be alone doing the things that interest and are important to *them*, but it is important to try to negotiate these needs with loved ones. Most importantly, do not assume that there is anything wrong with you for wanting space or that there is anything necessarily wrong with your relationships. Relationships can become claustrophobic from time to time. If you know that there is space for you within your close relationships, this may help to reduce possible resentments and urges to run away.

Knowing Your Limits

Various patients of mine have become exhausted from overwork and then couldn't cope with the demands placed upon them. They noticed that they are failing and becoming overwhelmed, felt ashamed about their failings and became depressed. Now most depressed people are real battlers. Very rarely do I see depressed individuals who put their feet up, enjoying having time off, and who know their own limits. Sometimes this problem is related to perfectionism (*see* Chapter 16). A term that some professionals use is *burnout*. 'Burnout' means that an individual has reached a state of depletion. Burnout can be a trigger for depression in some people. Whether you are a parent struggling to bring up children at home or someone trying to cope with too many tasks at work, try to acknowledge that you, like all the rest of us, have limits to the amount of work you can do.

Try to think of ways that you might try to replenish yourself, but most importantly, don't criticize yourself for feeling burned out – acknowledge it honestly and think through steps that might help. Are there enough positive things in your life? Can you do anything to increase them? Can you speak with others about your feelings and seek their help? Burnout can occur if we have not created enough personal space. For example, young doctors can become depressed because they have not been able (or the system had not allowed them) to create personal space and they can suffer from overwork and burnout.

All of us vary on this. Although some may seem to be able to cope with anything and everything (and make us feel that we should be able to do so as well), this does not mean that we should. Limits are personal things and they vary from person to person and change from time to time and situation to situation.

Dealing with Sleep Difficulties

Sleep varies from person to person. My daughter and I have never been particularly good sleepers, whereas my son and wife can fall asleep almost anywhere. In addition, the ease of getting to sleep and a person's need for sleep change as people grow older, so our sleep patterns are personal to us. Don't worry about not getting enough sleep. Margaret Thatcher only slept for fours hours a day! Sleep problems can take various forms. Some people find it difficult to fall asleep, others wake up after being asleep for just an hour or two, still others wake up in the early hours, and there are also those who sleep extremely lightly.

Think of sleep as another behavior that needs managing. A milky drink before bed may help. Make sure that your bed is comfortable and the room well-ventilated. Plan for sleep. Don't do what I used to, which was to work late into the night and then find I couldn't sleep because my head was buzzing with the things I had just been working on. In planning for sleep, think about relaxing (and try to relax) half an hour to an hour before bedtime. Listen to relaxing music and/or do a relaxation exercise. If possible, read a book that takes you out of yourself (but not one that scares you or is particularly mentally involving). If appropriate, ask your partner for a soothing massage. Take gentle exercise during the day.

Among the things to avoid is alcohol. Having a drink (or two) may seem helpful but usually is not. It leads to disturbed sleep patterns, and you can wake early in the morning with mild (and, if you drink heavily, not so mild) withdrawal symptoms. Also don't catnap during the day. If I sleep for longer than fifteen minutes during the afternoon, this can really mess up my night's sleep. If you wake early, get up and avoid lying in bed, ruminating on your difficulties. Frankly, as a poor sleeper, if I wake early I tend to get up and work. Of course, at times this leaves me feeling tired, but I have come to accept this as my style. If your sleep pattern is very disturbed, you may find an antidepressant very helpful (*see later*). Also some people have found that going without sleep for a whole night and not catnapping the next day can help lift mood. This, however, is best done under supervision. There are some good self-help books on the market for sleep problems.

Body Work

An important consideration is the state of one's body. Your body is like a garden, and to function well, it needs looking after. It can become exhausted and need pampering. Learn to care for your body and treat it with respect. Teach it how to relax, exercise it and feed it good things.

I would advise trying to find a sympathetic family doctor with whom you can have a frank and open discussion about your depression. In 1992 the Royal College of Psychiatrists in Britain mounted a 'Defeat Depression' campaign to increase the awareness and skill of family doctors in this area of psychological problems.

Very occasionally, depression can arise from a number of physical conditions. These include:

- problems with the thyroid gland
- anemia
- vitamin deficiency (e.g. B_{12})
- hormone problems
- stroke
- complications with other medications

So it is obviously a good idea to have these screened out as soon as possible. However, one should also recognize that the vast majority of depressions are not triggered by a physical condition.

Antidepressant Drugs

The next thing to consider is whether or not to take antidepressant drugs. Many people worry that these drugs are addictive, but they are not. They work in a very different way from the minor tranquillizers such as diazepam (Valium). For one thing, they take between two to six weeks to affect mood, although they may improve some of the symptoms (e.g. sleep disturbance) before this. Some people do not like the side-effects of these drugs – which include sleepiness, dry mouth and weight gain – although these usually pass after the first few weeks. There are a number of different types of antidepressants, and if one does not suit you, another one might, although most have some side-effects and work in similar ways. Any disadvantages have to be balanced against the beneficial effects that medication may have on your mood.

You should discuss these issues with your family doctor and consider the pros and cons of taking medication. However, if you are very depressed and have become exhausted by poor sleep, very withdrawn or lost interest in everything around you, one of the antidepressant drugs may be extremely helpful to get you started on the way up. In addition, there are some forms of depression that are extremely difficult to get out of without drugs.

Your doctor may also recommend that you see a psychiatrist. There is nothing shameful about this. Psychiatrists are medically trained, and although some may over-medicalize depression, their opinions can be useful. Be as open as possible about your depression and set out to get the best advice you can.

It is difficult to offer general advice here because so much depends on the type of depression you have, how severe it is and how long it has lasted. But whether you choose to take medication or not, there is now increasing evidence that working on thoughts and basic beliefs can help to alleviate many of the mild to moderate depressions and can help prevent relapses. There are also issues that drugs cannot address. After all, they can't retrain us, teach us how to manage our thoughts or solve social problems.

Seasonal Affective Disorder

Some depressions seem to come on as the longer days of summer shorten in autumn and winter. This is called 'seasonal affective disorder', or SAD, and is caused by a sensitivity to a lack of natural light arriving through the eyes to the pineal gland in the centre of the brain. One tell-tale sign, apart from the depression coming on at a certain time of year, is sleeping heavily (over ten hours in some cases) and finding it difficult to wake up in the morning.

If you suspect that your depression is related to seasonal changes, you may wish to talk to your family doctor about this. Some people find that exposure to bright light early in the morning can be very helpful, as can light boxes that give out bright rays of light at a particular wave length; you must sit near them for up to two hours a day. At the back of this book, I give the addresses of societies dealing with seasonal affective disorder, which you can contact to find out more information about the nature of this condition and where you can buy light boxes.

Changing the Way You Treat Your Body

Eat a healthy diet   People who are depressed often eat very poor diets. Try to work out a balanced diet including fresh fruit and vegetables and a high percentage of carbohydrate (e.g. pasta, bread, potatoes). This is because these foods release their energy slowly and may help to boost certain chemicals in the brain that are depleted when we are depressed. You may wish to take advice on this. A good book is Dr Alan Stewart's *Tired All the Time* (see Useful Books for details). There is increasing evidence that weight loss itself can affect various brain chemicals. So consider if your depression came on or got worse as you lost weight. Some research has also shown that eating large amounts of sugar and other refined foods might increase irritability in some people, so try cutting out cakes and other sweet things. Some people like to take extra vitamins. Now the evidence for these helping depression is very unclear, but provided you are not doing yourself any harm (e.g. too much vitamin A can damage your liver), these may work as a placebo if nothing else – that is, you may become less depressed simply because you believe in the vitamins, not because they have actually had a direct effect on your brain chemistry. A sympathetic family doctor will advise you on this.

Take exercise   There is increasing evidence that, for the mild-to-moderate depressions, exercise can be very beneficial because it tends to boost the production of certain chemicals in the brain. A patient of mine, who had a bipolar illness (and was taking lithium and an antidepressant), found that, if he awoke in the morning feeling down, a vigorous swim in the local pool helped to lift his mood. When we become depressed, we tend to do less, and if you can encourage yourself to take exercise, this can be helpful. It may give you a sense of achievement – in addition to being good for you and boosting certain brain chemicals.

Reduce your alcohol intake   Alcohol can have a depressant effect, and it is usually helpful to reduce your intake, especially if you tend to drink to control your moods. Sometimes people use it to get to sleep; as we have seen, this can be detrimental. Alcohol is a bad way of managing stress and depression.

Stimulants and other drugs   If you are taking stimulants, try to get off them. This applies even to mild stimulants such as coffee. Occasionally, I've found that some of my depressed patients drink vast amounts of strong coffee – sometimes over ten cups a day. Many stimulants can have depressant and/or anxiety-increasing side-effects.

And if you are using illicit drugs, try to get off them as they will not be doing your body any good. Some cannabis smokers lose motivation and become depressed and apathetic with this drug, and if there is an underlying sensitivity, it can also lead to mild paranoia. In fact, abuse of all drugs needs to be considered here, including painkillers. If you are taking a lot of painkillers, you should see your family doctor and plan to reduce your intake.

Tranquillizers Taking the odd tranquillizer from time to time can be helpful. However, if you have been using tranquillizers for a long time, you should think about getting off them. You must not try to come off them too quickly, but rather reduce your intake slowly. It is important to obtain medical advice from your family doctor, who might refer you to a psychiatric nurse or psychologist. There are also self-help groups and books to help with tranquillizer withdrawal.

Learning to Relax

Sometimes this is easier said than done. However, there are a variety of books on relaxation and self-help tapes on the market, as well as classes and groups. Explore these and see if you can find one that suits you.

There are some key elements in relaxation. Here is a quick guide.

Breathing First, learn how to control your breathing.

- Sit comfortably in a chair, or lie down, and focus on inhaling and exhaling. The key thing is rhythm.
- Inhale by slowly taking the air down into your lungs (try to feel the air going down to your diaphragm), hold the breath for a couple of seconds and then exhale slowly.
- Try breathing in and out, counting slowly: IN (*one, two, three four*), HOLD (*one, two*) and OUT (*one, two, three, four*).
- When you have found the rhythm that suits you and is comfortable, focus on the words 'in' and 'out'. In your mind say, 'In–Out, In–Out, In–Out' – in line with your breathing.

Don't strain but try to breathe reasonably deeply and slowly and make the rhythm as comfortable and as easy as possible. Once you feel happy with the basic rhythm, consider the fact that you are attempting to slow your body down and bring it to a state of relaxation. Each time you exhale, say in your mind 'RELAX' – or, if you prefer, 'CALM'. Imagine that each time you breathe out, your body is relaxing, letting go of its tension and becoming heavier, floppier (like a rag doll) and warmer.

Muscular relaxation   Once you are comfortable with this style of breathing, you can focus more on your body. There are a number of ways of doing this. First, you can focus on one part of your body at a time. As you breathe in, slightly tense one part and then, as you breathe out, focus on releasing the tension and relaxing.

- Let's start with your feet. As you breathe in, tense your feet and feel the tension. Now, as you breathe out, say 'Relax' and let go of the tension in your feet. Repeat.
- Now move on to the calves of your legs and do the same thing. As you breathe in, tense your calf muscles and feel the tension. Now as you breathe out, say 'Relax' and let go of the tension in your calves. Repeat.

Note how the muscles feel different when tense and when you let the tension go. Imagine them becoming warm and heavy. Using the same method, focus on one muscle group at a time, moving up gradually to the muscles in your thighs, lower back, stomach, chest, neck and shoulders, arms and hands, and face. When tensing your face, screw it up a little and then let go. When you have been through all the major muscle groups, focus on your whole body, allowing it to become heavier and more relaxed as you breathe in and out.

Repeat this for a while until you are familiar with the technique and what it feels like to relax. Each session should last about ten minutes or so – longer if you prefer. You can perform these techniques at any time of the day or night – you may find them particularly helpful just before bedtime. You can also use relaxation techniques when you are sitting watching the television or on a bus or in a meeting. The idea is to bring your body under more control and teach it how to relax. It is not just something you can do when you are alone or sitting comfortably, but something you can learn to do at any time throughout the day.

Next, try to use your relaxation techniques while you are walking around.

- Stand up straight but not rigid.
- As you walk around, focus on your breathing.

- Breathe in gently and reasonably deeply (but do not strain).
- As you breathe out, focus on the word 'Relax'.
- Notice how your body feels. Explore it for tension and try to relax any part that feels tense. Let your body go loose and heavy. How do your shoulders feel? Are they tense? If so, let them drop and go heavy. What about other muscles – e.g. those in your neck or forehead?
- Make a conscious effort to relax your body.
- Learn to attend to your body and get to know when you are holding tension in it. Like most things in life, this will take practice.

A key aspect of relaxation is to re-focus your attention away from your negative thoughts. The more you can concentrate on relaxing, the less your mind will dwell on other matters, and this can help to de-activate the depression syndrome.

Other Relaxation Techniques

Some people find they can deepen their relaxation by *creative visualization* – that is, bringing pleasant images to mind. For example, when listening to the sound of your breathing in and out, see if imagining the sea coming in and out deepens your relaxation. Focus on the smell of the sea, and how gently it laps against the shore in rhythm with your breathing. With each exhalation, your tension is ebbing out of you, taken away on the tide. Other people prefer images of a cool garden or woods or being by a river or watching a hot-air balloon sail up into a clear sky, or even snuggling up next to a warm fire. Each of these images are personal to the person who visualizes them. Think of images that tend to be associated with relaxation for you. In your mind, create a place of peace and healing and return to it when you relax.

Once you have the basic relaxation techniques, you might experiment with different approaches and see which one suits you. Some people find it helpful to listen to relaxing music. Meditation, too, can be beneficial. This can be done alone or in a group. Not only might such a group teach you some useful ways of relaxing, but it will bring you into contact with others and give you a focus for a shared activity.

Key Points
- There are many forms and causes of depression.
- Because of these differences we need to have a variety of different approaches to depression.
- It can be helpful to plan activities step by step. Break problems or tasks down into simple steps and follow them one at a time.
- Try to include some positive activities in your life. At times, you may need to increase your social contacts, at other times reduce them (i.e. create personal space). Much of this is about working out your own needs.
- The type of thoughts we have can affect the way our brains work. Sometimes, certain thoughts can be controlled via distraction.
- Don't assume that you have become an inexhaustible supplier of good works. No one can be. Learn to work out your limits. If you think that there are very few things that you aren't able to cope with, the chances are that you are not working within your own limits.
- Finally, treatment often needs to be aimed at how our bodies are working. It may require us to take seriously the possibility of using an antidepressant to help us get going again. We may need to change our life styles (e.g., take more exercise, improve our diets, cut out the coffee, learn how to relax, distract ourselves).

Exercises
- Make a list of the points in this chapter that you think are relevant to you.
- Clarify in your mind:
  (a) How are you treating your body?
  (b) How are you organizing your activities? Can you plan to do things step by step?
- Make a list of the positive things you would like to include in your life. These can be quite simple – e.g. I would like to see my friends more, go to the movies more, have more time to myself. Consider ways that might make some of these things happen.

5

Thoughts and Feelings

In this chapter we are going to explore how our thoughts and feelings are often linked together, and how together they can push you down into depression. Let's begin with a hypothetical situation. Suppose you are standing in a crowded train and someone steps back onto your foot. It's quite painful. Your first thought might be: 'Clumsy idiot!' and your feelings are of irritation or anger. However, if the person turns around and you see that he or she is carrying a white stick, indicating blindness, not only might your thoughts change (i.e. it was not clumsiness) but so will your feelings. You might feel sorry for the other person, and even guilty for having felt so angry and for not realizing the situation.

The point is that, when an event happens to us, we must decide what the event means *before* we can respond to it emotionally. Change the meaning and the emotions change. Now one way of capturing this is to distinguish the *event* from the *meanings* we give to it and the *emotions* and other reactions that we may have to it. We can explore this by using three columns:

A	B	C
Event	Meanings	Consequences
Triggering event	Beliefs and key thoughts	Emotions
	Interpretations	Behavior
		Physical reactions

Suppose a good friend or lover promises to phone you at 11 pm and asks you to wait in for the call, but then the time comes and goes and there is no phone call. What are the various possibilities for the consequences – what might you feel? Well, you could feel many things: anxiety, anger, sadness or even relief. And you would be absolutely right to say that it all depends on what you think the reason is for the person not phoning. That's the point. We can see this below using the three columns.

A	B	C
No phone call	Something has happened to him/her —e.g. an accident.	Anxiety
	He/she went to a party and forgot about me.	Anger
	He/she doesn't care enough to remember.	Sad
	He/she will phone tomorrow so I can just go to bed now.	Calm/relief

Automatic Thoughts

As we have already seen, jumping to conclusions is a very common response when we feel threatened in some way. In the above example, the negative emotions indicate that the lack of a phone call from the friend/lover is taken as some kind of threat. Jumping to the conclusion that, for example, your friend/lover has had an accident is called an 'automatic thought'. You can't know what has happened or the reasons why he or she did not phone until you have the *evidence*. So all other thoughts are guesses or theories. None the less, you may feel anxious or worried. Now as the term implies, automatic thoughts are those interpretations/ideas/thoughts that seem to come automatically to mind; they are our 'pop-up thoughts'. They are immediate, consciously available thoughts that require little or no effort and can seem plausible. They are not arrived at through much in the way of reflective reasoning.

Let's consider these thoughts a little more, this time using the example of anger over the lack of a phone call. The first thing to note is that you probably don't often think in words like, 'Oh, I think my friend/lover has gone to a party and has forgotten to ring and left me waiting in for the call.' More likely, you have flashes of pictures in your mind. Can you answer these questions? Is he/she having a good time? Is he/she talking with other people? Is there music playing? Is it classical or disco music? Now I would imagine that you can answer these questions fairly easily. This is because we often create images in our thoughts.

Sometimes automatic thoughts are difficult to catch because they happen so fast. Had I not asked you about the party, those thoughts might have gone relatively unnoticed or been only semi-conscious, but when I drew your attention to them, you may have become aware that you had had them. So, sometimes, when we feel a change of emotion, we have to focus on our thoughts and what is actually going through our minds.

It is common for automatic thoughts to occur in images, daydreams and fantasies. As in the example above, we may con-struct scenarios of seeing the friend/lover in some particular place (e.g. the party) and imagine him/her having a good time, laughing, drinking and so on. We may also enter into a kind of discussion with ourselves as a result of our automatic thoughts and fantasies. For example, having decided that the friend/lover is out having a good time while you are waiting for his/her call, you may start to rehearse in your mind an argument or what you intend to say the next time your friend/lover does phone. You might even rehearse something that you know that, in reality, you would not carry out due to fear of being rejected/disliked or because of moral concerns.

Sometimes we may not be fully aware that we are constructing such scenes in our heads but experience only emotions and feelings. For example, when the phone does not ring, you may find yourself becoming more sad or irritated, but your awareness of your thinking processes may be hazy. Sometimes we just let the scenes in our minds run on, as if there is some 'inner director' in our heads feeding our minds various ideas and pictures that are full of meaning. Hence, we may need to train ourselves to sharpen the focus of our automatic thoughts and make them more easily known, recognized and challenged. We may need to use active imagination – that is, to allow ourselves to tune into the thoughts so that we can examine and deal with them more easily.

One Thought Leads to Another

You may have noticed something important in the examples given above – one thought leads to another. Humans are highly creative in their thinking and we are usually not happy with just one or two thoughts. At times, especially when we are heading into a depressive spiral, our thoughts spin down into catastrophes. For example, let's consider how someone heading into a depressive spiral might think about the friend/lover who didn't phone. The sequence of thoughts might go like this.

He/she hasn't phoned.
This is because he/she has forgotten about me.
Maybe he/she had better or more fun things to do.
If he/she cared about me, he/she would have phoned.
Therefore, he/she doesn't really care.
I don't ever seem to be able to find someone who cares about me.
What's wrong with me?
Maybe I am just too boring and unattractive.
I'll never have a good, long-lasting relationship.
I'll always end up abandoned.
Life is completely pointless and empty.

This cascade of thoughts can be so rapid that we hardly notice it. But rather than just being disappointed or slightly irritated by the phone not ringing, we end up feeling much more depressed because our thoughts lead us to the conclusion that we are boring, not cared for, are going to be abandoned or are being used by others. When we enter into depression, we often experience such rapid cascades of thoughts like those above. When we are depressed, our thoughts can literally run away with us and take us to the worse possible scenarios. And this can happen very quickly – sometimes within seconds.

Downward Spirals and Emotional Amplifiers

Usually thoughts like these provide feedback for each other. For example, when we are depressed we often don't feel like doing much; when we don't achieve much, we tell ourselves how useless we are; and when we tell ourselves how useless we are, we feel more depressed.

Figure 2

Now you can probably see that, if you are caught up in this type of spiral, it will be very difficult to get out of it, unless you take steps to stop it. These thoughts might be called *emotional amplifiers* because, as they go around and around, they become more intense. There is nothing in the spiral that dampens them down. So you need to build in *emotional dampeners* – ways to break the cycle. You may also see that there are some key links in this spiral that you could challenge. You could do just a little bit of some activity and then give yourself a lot of praise for doing something even though you are depressed. You could learn to praise your efforts rather than the results. The problem here is that, when we are depressed, we often discount the small positive things we do. Unless we make big strides of progress, we tend to be dissatisfied.

Another way that you might break the circle is to say, 'Even though I'm not achieving much right now, this doesn't make me a worthless human being. There is more to me than just my uses or achievements.' Now if you are depressed, don't be surprised if these arguments don't impress you. You can be expected to discount them – after all, you feel depressed and that's what we all do when we are depressed. We stick rigidly to what *we* think and the way *we* see things – we are not easily persuaded by rational arguments, especially from someone else. We can also become pretty arrogant and believe that only *we* know the truth – and thus ignore other people's point of view about us. We say that they don't understand, or can't really know – we do all kinds of things to ensure that we are correct in our negative views and others are wrong. I will explore ways to challenge these ideas shortly.

Thoughts About Feelings and Behavior

Although it is often situations and events that spark off negative thoughts, this is not always so. Sometimes, we can have inner feelings such as anger and then have thoughts about those. For example, you might think it is bad to have intense feelings of anger. Or you might have sexual feelings about someone and feel very guilty because you tell yourself that such feelings and fantasies are bad. Or you might feel anxious about something and then think that you are stupid or weak for feeling anxious. You may just wake up feeling tired and think, 'Oh, God, another bloody day! How am I going to get through it?'

We may also have negative thoughts about what we have done or failed to do. We may dwell on our actions and start to judge ourselves negatively. For example, because we are anxious, we might not go to a party or some other function to which we have been invited. We might then think that we have behaved badly and let other people down. We become preoccupied with guilt.

Because he suffered from social anxiety, Colin did not go to a friend's leaving party at work. He had the following thoughts:

I should have gone.
I've let my friend down.
He will be angry that I didn't go and will lose interest in me.
Others will wonder what's the matter with me.
I have missed out on a good time again.
I'm useless in social situations.
I'm pathetic to get anxious.

The more that these thoughts took hold, the more anxious and depressed he became.

And sometimes it is what we feel within our bodies that generates negative thoughts. For example, people who have panic attacks may notice that, when they become anxious, their heart rate goes up. This leads to the thought: 'There must be something wrong with my heart for it to beat like this.' They then focus attention on their heart rate, and because they are thinking that there is some-thing wrong with their heart, they become more anxious. And, of course, as they become more anxious, their heart rate goes up even further. Even though the heart is basically a pump and is designed to increase and decrease its beating as circumstances require, the idea that an increased heart rate signals an oncoming heart attack produces an intense anxiety spiral.

Figure 3

Hence we can see that we can have negative thoughts about ourselves, others and the future, all of which can increase our depression, and that these can be sparked off by events, our inner feelings, things we notice in our bodies or past actions.

Writing Down Your Thoughts

In Monitoring and Challenging Your Thoughts (see p. 279), I give an example of a form that can be used to write down automatic thoughts. This is similar to the one we used with the phone call example on page 60. However, in this form you will see that, in the first column, various things can spark off negative thoughts and lead to various negative evaluations and conclusions. You can include events such as people criticizing you or things not working out as you would like (like not receiving the phone call). We can also make negative evaluations of our *feelings* (e.g. I am a bad person for feeling angry; it is wrong to feel sexual towards someone else who is not my partner), our *behavior* (I should not have acted like that; I am a bad person for losing control) or our *bodies* (when my heart rate goes up, this means there is something wrong with it and I might die). Then you can fill in the other two columns as before – that is, the beliefs and key thoughts of the 'triggering' event and its consequences.

The key thing is to choose what you want to focus on, then write down the thoughts that go through your mind. If you habitually write these down, you will get better at identifying them. Writing thoughts down helps to clarify them and allows you to concentrate on them, thus avoiding having them slip in and out of your mind in a rather chaotic fashion. A good way to start is to try to notice how your moods and feelings change. Try to remember what might have been happening to you at the time they changed – for instance, a criticism, or something that did not work out as you wanted it to, or something you hadn't done or thought you ought to do. Next, write down the thoughts associated with these situations.

Another useful way to begin is, if you notice a change in your feelings, or even if you notice that you are feeling something that you can identify as anxiety, depression or sadness, ask the question: 'If my feelings could speak, what would they say to me?'

You will notice that there is a fourth column for writing down alternative thoughts. Some worked examples (p.281–3) follow the blank form. As you go through this book, I hope that you will get better at not only identifying what goes through your mind and noting your own depressive spirals (and emotional amplifiers), but that you will also be able to challenge some of your more negative thoughts and not let that 'better safe than sorry' and 'assume the worst' type of thinking run away with you. If you find such a challenge difficult – don't worry. It takes time and practice. We are going to work on it in later chapters.

How to Identify Your Thoughts

Sometimes it is difficult to know what we are thinking, so how can you help yourself work out what is going on in your mind? Well, one way is to ask yourself some questions. For example, let's suppose that you tried to do something and it did not turn out right. You feel disappointed and your mood takes a dip. You could then ask yourself:

Question	**Possible Answer**
What do I think are the implications of this event?	I won't be able to achieve what I want to achieve.
What does that lead me to think/believe?	I tend to fail at most things I try to do.
What conclusions am I drawing from this situation?	I am not going to succeed in what I want to achieve.

You can also ask questions about what you think others will think or how others will react.

What do I think they will think about my failure?	They will think I'm not capable of much.

Another set of questions asks you to think about the conclusions that you might be drawing about yourself as a person. Ask yourself:

What does this say about me?	If I fail at this, it means I am inadequate.
What do I think this means for my future?	I will never get anything right.

In general, there are three basic types of question to ask yourself. These are:

1 Questions about how you see yourself as a person.
2 Questions about how you think others see you.
3 Questions about implications, including for the future.

So then, if we take our example of 'trying to do something that does not go well,' we might have a set of thoughts that are something like this:

• I have not succeeded in this task.
• Failing at this means I am an inadequate person.
• Other people will think I am not capable of much.
• I am not going to succeed in anything I want to achieve.

These thoughts might not have been obvious before we asked ourselves the questions. Moreover, taking the time to consider these questions allowed us to focus on our thoughts. By asking certain questions, we can get some insight into what we think about certain situations and events.

Like many things in life, doing this will take practice and it may seem odd at first, but after a while, you might notice that there are some repeating themes in how you think. For example, in depression, we often make negative conclusions about the future, about what others will think about us and what we think about ourselves.

Basic Beliefs and Attitudes

You may well ask: Where do these negative thoughts come from? One answer is that they are generated by the state of depression itself. But it is also often the case that automatic thoughts are generated from the various attitudes and basic beliefs we have about ourselves, others and life in general, and these predate the depression. They include such things as:

- If people make mistakes, they are inadequate.
- People who show strong anger are unlovable.
- You can never be happy if you do not have a conflict-free, close relationship.
- If you have strong arguments with someone close to you, they don't love you.
- If your parents did not love you or treated you badly, you are unlovable.
- Sex is dirty.

There are many types of attitudes and basic negative beliefs like these that tend to lead to negative conclusions. In my own case, I was bad at English and I developed the negative belief: 'Being poor at English equals being stupid.' When I was depressed, this belief seemed very true to me – and I therefore felt not very bright or able. When I noticed poor spelling in my work, or I was criticized for my poor English, I would have a particularly uncomfortable 'sinking feeling'. It was only later that I realized that this belief ('I am stupid') was untrue and that I only applied it to myself and not to others. But that's the way with basic beliefs – we often don't realize that we have them. It is how our feelings react to certain situations that tells us that we should be alert to the possibility that we may have some basic negative beliefs that need identifying and changing.

As a rule of thumb, negative automatic thoughts are triggered by situations at specific points in time. They may often include basic negative beliefs, but these are also key ideas we have all the time – like our basic views about life. Have another look at Sally, who we discussed in Chapter 2. Here are her basic beliefs again.

I am a nuisance to others. I stop people doing what they want to do. People don't really want me around. I must not do anything that could push them away. I must be to others what they want me to be. Expressing anger and/or asserting my needs could lead to rejection. I must be grateful for love. I am a bad/ungrateful person if I express my dissatisfactions.

Although these thoughts and beliefs were not active all the time, it did not take much to trigger them.

Dwelling on Thoughts

There is a difference between thoughts that are indeed automatic and thoughts that we dwell on. Automatic thoughts are those that are related to fast reactions and come with emotions and feelings. For example, someone jumps out in front of your car and you immediately go into a stomach-churning panic associated with the thought, 'I might hit them.' Someone phones you up and says your lover is sleeping with someone else, and again this 'hits you' almost immediately. In these examples, personal meanings are made extremely rapidly. In the case of the phone call, you might reflect on what was said and then decide that the information is not true and that someone is trying to stir up trouble between you and your lover. In other words, you backtrack and start to 'undo' your first emotional reaction. Alternatively, you might assume the information is true and start to dwell on it.

When we dwell on something, we turn an idea or set of beliefs over and over in our minds. A common situation is to lie in bed and worry, your mind focusing on a particular train of thoughts. This is not the same as having an immediate reaction to something and then pulling back and seeking out the evidence. When we dwell on things, we are allowing ourselves to think along a certain path for many minutes or even hours. When we respond rapidly and emotionally to something, we may need to stop ourselves and focus on what we are thinking. When we dwell on something, we are more clear about what we are thinking. The important thing here is to recognize that dwelling on negative thoughts can have the effect of making negative feelings become more entrenched.

Depression involves not just automatic thoughts and immediate reactions to situations, but what is called 'ruminating' – that is, dwelling on the same negative thoughts. This type of thinking is the most important to recognize and interrupt. You could try distracting yourself. Or you could try asking yourself: Where are my thoughts taking me? Is this helpful? Am I going over old ground and will only end up feeling worse? If this is the case, writing your thoughts down – rather than allowing them to go around and around in your mind – can be one way to interrupt them. Or you could say to yourself, 'I know where these thoughts are leading, and if I let them go on, my mood will go down.' Once thoughts are written down, they may be easier to dispute and challenge.

By now, you will probably be aware of the kinds of things you dwell on. These may be thoughts of inadequacy, injustice and unfairness, revenge, loss, and/or negative predictions of the future – in fact, just the kinds of thoughts that everyone has from time to time. Try to identify the things that you usually find yourself dwelling on and try to become more aware of any common 'themes' in your thoughts. If you find it difficult to recognize when your mind is dwelling on things, you can leave notes to yourself around the house that remind you to check on what you are thinking. Or you could carry a stone (or some other small object) in your pocket so that, each time you feel it there, this will be a signal to check on your thoughts. If you have been dwelling on certain things, gently remind yourself that you can break off from these thoughts. Indeed, do whatever works for you to stop yourself from dwelling on and indoctrinating yourself with negative thoughts.

Of course, this is not to say that we should never have sad, anxious or negative thoughts and feelings or that we should always try to distract ourselves from things that are painful. In fact, some of these can help us to develop solutions to problems or to work through painful feelings such as grief. Rather, the thoughts and feelings you should avoid are those that lead to downward spirals and do not serve any purpose other than to increase depression.

Key Points
- When things happen to us, we often have various thoughts about what the event means to us. These are our interpretations.
- These thoughts can be automatic and just pop into the mind.
- One automatic thought can lead to another and spiral us down into deeper, more depressed feelings.
- We can have negative thoughts not only about particular situations but also about our inner feelings, fantasies and past actions.
- Our thoughts may be difficult to pin down, but if we ask ourselves certain types of questions, they might become clearer.
- We may ruminate and dwell on these thoughts and ideas, and so spiral down into deeper, more depressed feelings.
- We often need to train ourselves to become more aware of our automatic thoughts and the themes we tend to dwell on.
- One way to begin to gain more awareness of your thinking is to make a habit of writing down your thoughts.
- Some of our negative automatic thoughts are triggered because we have underlying basic negative beliefs. Until we recognize our automatic thoughts, we may not be aware of these basic beliefs that could be guiding our lives.

Exercises
- Think about and try writing down your thoughts. At first, you might use a notebook that you keep handy. Draw up three columns that allow you to separate out triggering events, beliefs and key thoughts, and feelings. Look up Monitoring and Challenging Your Thoughts (pp. 279–83) to explore some worked examples.

continued on next page

continued from previous page

- Write down whatever comes into your mind – even if, at first, it does not make much sense.
- Start to consider your thoughts when your mood changes. Learn to 'catch' your thoughts. Give yourself time and space to focus on them.
- To gain more insight into your thoughts, ask yourself some questions. These can include:
  1 Questions about how you see yourself as a person.
  2 Questions about how you think others see you.
  3 Questions about implications, including for the future.
- Make copies of the Thought Monitoring and Challenging form on p. 280, familiarize yourself with it, and try using it.
- As you become better at catching and noting your thoughts, work on the fourth column – to challenge your thoughts. To do this, read the next few chapters.
- Watch out for negative thoughts such as 'This can't work for me.' Instead, say to yourself: 'Maybe this won't help, but what have I got to lose from trying?'

6

Challenging Negative Thoughts and Feelings

In the last few chapters, we noted that, when we become depressed and feel so low and tired, our thoughts tend to take us downward. They rarely encourage us or offer uplifts – just when we need them. If anything, our thoughts are rather bullying and critical. In this chapter, we are going to explore ways of breaking out of the downward spiral. Look at the fourth column of the Thought Monitoring and Challenging form on p. 280. We are now going to learn about how to use this – how to challenge and dispute negative thoughts.

Start by looking at things from different angles. Just as when we want to buy something – say, a house or a car – we like to have some alternatives to choose from, so too with our thoughts; we need to try generating alternatives. Now, the voice of depression is often a bully and it tends to block out alternatives. Depression is like the car manufacturer Henry Ford, who once said, 'You can have any color you like as long as it's black.' Depression likes us to believe that what it says is the way things really are, and it can be terribly arrogant in this respect. Depression is very keen to tell us what we can't do, what we shouldn't do and how bad things are. But it is a primitive part of our brains speaking, and there are two basic orientations that we can take that will help to control it: insisting on rational questioning and alternatives, and developing basic compassion.

Rational Minds to the Rescue

To get out of depression, we need to encourage our rational minds to do more work. But a word of caution first. Although learning to think in a different way can be extremely helpful in overcoming depression, this is not all there is to change. Sometimes depressed people need to form relationships with others who can help them grieve, remember things forgotten or face things they can't face alone, or even to help them mature. Sometimes people become so depressed that they will benefit from medication to kick-start the system and/or help with sleep. But when thoughts are stacked against you, gaining more insight and control over them can be a tremendous help. One way of doing this is to be more rational about them. So let's look at the functions and qualities of the rational mind – since we want to recruit it to help you.

- The rational mind likes to look at the *evidence*. It is a scientist or detective and treats ideas and thoughts as theories that can be proved incorrect. The rational mind does not settle for simple answers; like a Sherlock Holmes, it observes carefully and wants to know more before coming to a decision.
- The rational mind likes to have *alternatives* to choose from. It does not like to have few choices because it tends to assume that there is always more than one way of seeing things.
- The rational mind likes to *test things* and run experiments.
- The rational mind does not like being overly influenced by emotional appeal or hasty conclusions.
- The rational mind knows that knowledge develops slowly. Things become more complex as we know more, and this is a source of fascination and deepening understanding.
- The rational mind knows that sometimes we learn most from trial and error – that, in fact, we often learn more from our errors than we do from our successes.
- The rational mind will attempt (if given the chance) to weigh up the *advantages* and *disadvantages* of a particular view or course of action.
- The rational mind likes to take a long-term view of things and recognizes that we often get to where we are going step by step. It realizes that it is our long-term interests that are important, regardless of short-term setbacks or benefits.

So the 'rational, testing approach' is one side of ourselves that we need to cultivate. However, the rational mind works best at combating depression when it has a friend. This friend and ally we can call the compassionate mind. Thus, we need to develop a compassionate/friendly rationality – not a cold impersonal one.

The Compassionate Mind

We have evolved the capacity to care for other people, animals and things. For example, if children are hurt, parents often know that rationalizing with them is not enough. The children will often need a cuddle and a bit of tender loving care. We recognize that other people often need looking after and caring for, and we have evolved the capacity to do this within our brains. We can empathize with others and feel sad for them and often want to help them. However, in depression, we often lose this inner capability. We often fail to look after or nurture ourselves, and we may not even recognize that we need to become more inwardly caring. To heal often means we have to learn to reactivate the caring–healing part of ourselves that depression has knocked out.

The compassionate mind, like the rational, has certain qualities:

- The compassionate mind is concerned with growth and helping people (and things) reach their potential.
- It is concerned with supporting, healing and listening to what we and others need.
- It listens and inquires about problems in a kind and friendly way.
- It is quick to forgive and slow to condemn.
- It does not attack but seeks to bring healing, repair and reunion.
- It recognizes that life can be painful and that we are all imperfect beings.
- It does not treat ourselves or others simply as objects with a market value. Self-worth/acceptance is not something that can be earned; it is not conditional or based on fulfilling contracts.

We can learn to train our thoughts to be warm and friendly and cultivate the qualities of the compassionate mind. For some of us, especially those who have not received much in the way of warmth and kindness when they were young, this can be a most difficult but important step.

Bonds, Tasks and Goals

When people seek therapy, they want to find a compassionate therapist who will try to: (1) understand them and not condemn them; (2) show warmth and friendliness; and (3) help them see things in a different way, and to mature and grow. In seeking these things, people are showing an inner wisdom – recognition of what heals.

When therapists are trained, they are often taught to focus on three things: the *bonds* and relationships between patient and therapist, the *tasks* that need to be undertaken and the *goals* and aims of the therapy. In helping yourself to get out of depression, you can take the same approach.

Bonds

The bonds here refer to your inner relationship with yourself. The idea is that you may need to shift from a bullying and hostile relationship with yourself to a more compassionate, helpful, friendly and accepting one. This is not always easy, and you may have to work hard at it. Here are some pointers.

- If you are monitoring your thoughts and can detect that you are being overly critical or defeatist, imagine what you would say to people you cared for (e.g. friends or family). Imagine how you would encourage *them* to try out different things or to keep going. Write down what you might say. Concentrate on the tone of your voice, your manner, whether you might put an arm around them. Note how you might accept their crying or fear and how you can understand their pain. Recognize how, when someone else is in pain, you do not want to bully or ridicule them and kick them when they are down. Now the basic attitude and approach you have towards caring and helping someone else is what you are trying to develop for yourself. Come up with a motto such as 'Caring and forgiveness heals; bullying, criticizing and attacking hurts' or 'I intend to relate to my inner healer rather than my inner bully.'
- Imagine a caring, helpful person reaching out to you, perhaps someone who is both compassionate and rational – the father or mother you would like to have had. Sometimes depressed

people, when they are struggling to challenge their negative views, prefer to imagine what their compassionate helper would think and advise. And remember: your inner helper has no limit to his/her patience.

Tasks

Often, as we move forward out of depression, there are various tasks that we can set for ourselves on our step-by-step journey. The following are examples:

- Learn to tune into and monitor more accurately your thoughts and feelings.
- Write your thoughts, or record them on tape.
- Learn to be honest with yourself.
- Learn how to take big problems and break them down into smaller ones.
- Set yourself small pieces of homework to complete.
- Learn to be more assertive or less self-attacking.

Goals

These goals are the things you want to achieve. At first, depressed people usually just want to feel better. But this large goal needs to be broken down into smaller ones. These smaller goals might be:

- To do a little more each day.
- To be more assertive with some other person.
- To spend more time on something you enjoy.

It can be useful to set yourself a couple of goals at the beginning of each day or week. Start by setting small ones – the smaller, the better. Then think about the tasks involved to achieve these goals and how you might maximize your chances of success. If things are difficult or you don't reach your goals, ask yourself some questions.

- Were the goals too much?
- Could I have broken them down further?
- Did I run into unexpected problems?
- Did I put enough effort into achieving them?

- In my heart of hearts, did I think that achieving them wouldn't really help?
- If I failed am I being compassionate with myself?

Some Ways of Challenging Negative Thoughts

Getting the Evidence

When we jump to conclusions, we usually forgo much in the way of gathering evidence. We'd make very poor scientists or detectives. So we often need to train and strongly encourage ourselves to do this. When we have a negative idea about ourselves, others, our future or the world, we need to ask, 'Do I have enough evidence for this conclusion?'

Anne thought that she had ruined a dinner party by overcooking the food. She was clearly disappointed about the food, but in fact, there was no evidence that the whole evening had been messed up or that the guests had not enjoyed her party. So how might we help Anne not to dwell on the overcooked meal but focus on what was good about the evening? One way is to take a thought like 'I've messed up the whole evening with my overcooked meal' and dispute it. The kinds of thoughts that might go into the fourth column of the Thought Monitoring and Challenging form (p. 280) could be both rational and compassionate:

Rational mind

- Where is the evidence that the whole evening was messed up?
- Did your guests seem unhappy?
- Do you think they will come again?

- Ask people if they enjoyed it and see what they say.

Compassionate/friendly mind

- This is very harsh isn't it?
- How does being so critical help you?
- What's one overcooked meal between friends?
- You wouldn't judge your friends so harshly. What would you say to them?
- To overcook is human. Forgive yourself and let's plan the next party.

Getting the evidence is important when it comes to putting effort into things. When we give up on something too quickly, it is often because we have jumped to the conclusion that we could not do it. We focus too much on the bits of information that point to a negative conclusion and ignore the bits of information that point to a more positive one.

Generating Alternatives

Related to getting better evidence on which to make decisions is the need to learn how to generate alternatives. When we are depressed, it is quite difficult to do this. But we can begin by looking at the evidence that *does not* support a particular idea or belief.

Jane and Terry had an argument over money. Because the argument got rather heated, Jane concluded that Terry no longer loved her. If Jane had read this book, she might handle things differently by writing out her reasons for such a belief and considering alternatives.

We had the argument because:

Negative ideas	*Alternatives*
• He doesn't care about me.	• He's worried about money, too.
• He said hurtful things.	• He's prone to say hurtful things when he loses his temper. And, if I'm honest, so do I. Well, I *think* them even if I don't say them.
	• He's stressed out at the moment – we both are because he might lose his job.
	• It's difficult to be very understanding when you're stressed out.
	• If we weren't so worried about money, we probably wouldn't have gone at each other like that.
	• Our argument is more evidence of stress than of not being cared for.

Another way that Jane could have done this would be to write two columns of *evidence for* and *evidence against*. The main idea here is that, whenever you come up with evidence that points one way, try thinking about the evidence that points the other way. Don't allow yourself to settle for only one view.

When Jane went through some alternative reasons for the hurtful things that had been said, she still felt unhappy about the conflicts in her relationship with Terry. However, she recognized that there were a number of factors related to the argument and not just the idea that she was not loved. When the heat had gone out of the situation, she decided to talk to Terry about this. At first, he said that he thought that she didn't really understand how he felt and how difficult things were for him – in other words, it was not that he did not love Jane but that he felt misunderstood by her. Although they then got into something of a competition over who was the least understanding, eventually they talked about the fact that the shortage of money was the common problem. They agreed that both of them were under stress because of that and they needed to join together against the common problem rather than venting their anger at each other. This would have been difficult to achieve if Jane had hung on to the idea that Terry's anger was evidence of him not loving her. In fact, both of them tended to interpret arguments as evidence for a lack of love.

Now, of course, it may well be that, when you are angry, the person you are arguing with is not your best-loved person *at that moment*, but this does not mean that you do not love them, nor does it mean that they don't love you. And we all need to watch out for the terrible 'must': 'I *must* be loved all the time' or 'In a love relationship we *must* never be angry with each other.'

Sometimes, however, the evidence points in the other direction – that there may *not* be much caring in a relationship. Karen had been going out with Tim for about eighteen months. He tended to be demanding and rough sexually. At times, he would come to her flat drunk and often broke their dates. Increasingly depressed, Karen made excuse after excuse for him.

Positive ideas	*Alternatives*
• He'd change if we were married.	• I saw his last girlfriend last month and she said that he was the same

- This is typical of all men.
- When he's down, he always likes to talk to me.
- He is often nice and takes me out sometimes.

- with her and that I was welcome to him. All accounts I have read suggest that, on the whole, people don't change that much after marriage.
- I know many other men who are not like this.
- There is more to a relationship than just supporting people when they are down. I might be being used here.
- Even Hitler was nice at times. It's really what I feel about it over-all that counts.

It was difficult for Karen, but when she began to look at alternatives to her idea that he did care for her, unfortunately the evidence was that he did not – or at least not in the way that she wanted.

Generating alternatives means that we get more than one point of view. Sometimes we don't want to think about the alternatives because they lead to painful decisions. In Karen's case, she had a deeper belief that, if she gave up this relationship, she might not find another. It was this belief that had stopped her looking at alternative thoughts about whether Tim cared or not and really focusing on the evidence. When she did look hard at the evidence, she realized that, on the whole, this was not a good or supportive relationship to be in. There was more pain than gain.

When she tried to use her compassionate mind by focusing on how she might talk to a friend, Karen came up with these ideas:

I know I'm worried about being on my own. But I can learn to face this possibility. I might be more miserable if I stay in than if I get out. Even if I get out of this relationship, this doesn't mean that I'll give up trying to find a better one. I can think about the qualities I could bring to a relationship and not just focus on my bad points. I'm honest and very loyal. I try to consider other people's feelings. Of course, no one's perfect but I deserve better. In my heart, I know this. It has just seemed too frightening to end it. But then again I have survived on my own before, and rather than hoping that a relationship with a man will make my life great, I can start to work on relationships with other people who can give me some pleasure and closeness. Ending this relationship doesn't make me unlovable.

Karen both wrote this down and spoke these ideas on to a tape when she wasn't feeling too depressed. She was then able to read and listen to them whenever she felt down. She was encouraged to feel kind and compassionate when she offered herself these alternative ideas and words of advice. This helped her to stop sinking into depression and face up to getting out of the relationship.

One typical response at this stage might be: 'Well, okay, I can generate alternative views but I really don't believe them. I'm just trying to fool myself.' If this is what you think, consider that this is typical of depression – it always thinks it knows what's real and accurate. At this stage, the act of generating alternatives and avoiding concentrating on single ideas is the important first step.

Advantages and Disadvantages

By now, you will have got the idea that writing things down can be very helpful, enabling you to clarify, focus and concentrate. It helps to stop ideas and thoughts swirling around in your mind without any focus. It is especially important to do because, like physical exercise which helps you build up your muscles and get fit, you often need to put effort into building up your skills in challenging negative thoughts.

Writing things down can also help you to clarify conflicts and dilemmas. You can write down two columns: advantages (pros or gains) and disadvantages (cons or losses) of making a change. Kevin was in two minds about moving house, so he wrote out the pros and cons:

Advantages	Disadvantages
• Nicer district.	• Further to travel to work.
• Bigger house with more space for the family.	• Unfamiliar. I like my old house.
• Bigger garden that I could enjoy and relax in.	• Might not have the time to maintain it.
• Good investment.	• More expensive.

Kevin's next task was to weigh each pro and con. He did this with his family, and he and his wife put arguments for and against. Through discussion, it became clear that it was the unfamiliarity of a new house and district that was the biggest hurdle. Kevin realized that he did not like to leave the familiar. Once this was clarified in his mind, he was able to challenge this view and accept that it might take him time to adjust to a new home, but in the long term, it would be a good decision to move.

Sometimes we can feel very blocked in changing our basic views of ourselves or ways of doing things. There always seems to be a cost. In therapy, Karen realized that, if things went wrong in relationships, she tended to blame herself. Although she readily acknowledged that giving up doing this would be helpful, she found it difficult to do. So she wrote down the pros and cons of giving up self-blame to try and discover why.

Advantages		Disadvantages
I would feel better.	*but*	I would become more angry with others. I would become like my mother who always blamed others, and whom I disliked.
I would take more risks.	*but*	I would provoke others to be angry or reject me.
I would not feel inferior.	*but*	I might not see my faults, and might become arrogant.

By writing these down, it became clear that, for Karen, there were a number of unrecognized disadvantages to changing – not least the fear of becoming the kind of person she did not like. Now, of course, no one would change if they saw that as the possible result. So Karen needed to consider the evidence for the disadvantages that she had identified. What evidence was there that not taking the blame for everything would make her arrogant? Aren't there many people who do not blame themselves but are also not arrogant?

In therapy, people often see many disadvantages to changing. Of course, they don't want to be depressed – but getting out of depression may appear to involve rather difficult things. They have to try and identify what these might be. What would change involve? What might be the fear in that? Not every advantage of change has a countering 'but', although it is useful to think of such possibilities. They can resist change if their perceived disadvantages (and fears of change) are not explored. Once they can see more clearly what is blocking them, they may be better placed to start challenging some of those blocks.

Sometimes advantages and disadvantages are not always seen. For example, the need to be in an intimate relationship to be happy can lead to dependency and a tendency to stay in unsupportive relationships – as in Karen's case. The need to be strong and independent might have the disadvantage that a person can't ask others for help.

You can do these written exercises on pros and cons many times and can carry them out quite slowly, with self-reflection and/or discussion with others along the way.

Designing Experiments

It is useful to challenge depressive ideas by setting experiments, that is testing things out and rehearsing new skills. In this way, you are more likely to get evidence. A useful motto here is 'Challenging but not overwhelming.' Remember – try to design your experiments to take you 'step by step' rather than rushing into something that has a high risk of failing. Don't worry if the steps seem too small. As they say, a journey of a thousand miles begins with a single step.

If your experiment doesn't work out, try to find out why. Was there anything about it that was a success? Were you attempting too much? Were your expectations too high? Did your negative thoughts overwhelm you? Did you really put the effort into it that you needed to?

Charlie was very prone to dismissing his own work as inadequate. In therapy, we had worked out some ways that he could challenge and dispute his negative thoughts. These were written down on a card for him to look at. He decided that he was going to experiment with using the card to combat his negative thoughts when they came up. However, he would only occasionally get out the card and read the more rational/compassionate thoughts that were written down. And when he did read them, he would not really put the effort into *thinking seriously* about these alternative thoughts. He was very casual about it and looked at the words without thinking through their meaning. In the back of his mind, he thought, 'This approach can't work.' So he had stacked the experiment against himself before he had begun. Now, of course, challenging negative thoughts won't work by magic. It does take some effort to try to dispute them. So in this case, although the experiment seemed like a failure, it actually threw up the evidence that he had the constant idea in his mind that the approach could not work, and it was this that undermined his efforts. He had to learn to use his compassionate mind to tell himself in a friendly supportive way:

> *Look, I know this is hard, and yes, it is a shit being depressed, but let's not stack things against yourself. Let's give it a fair go. After all, what have you got to lose? If you were helping a friend, you'd know how tough it is but you'd also try to encourage them to give it a go. Let's go through this step by step.*

Getting out of depression takes effort, and this is especially true if you are trying to help yourself. It is the same with getting physically fit. It would be no good putting on your trainers and running to the garden gate and back – you have to push yourself more than that. Now some people find this tough going, and it may be that they need some extra help from professionals. There's no point in berating yourself if you've tried your best and have found it just too hard to do. On the other hand, if you design an experiment for yourself, try to put all the effort you can into it. For example, when you consider alternative thoughts, make sure that you *really* consider them rather than just 'look at the words.' Allow yourself to consider how you would feel if you accepted these alternatives.

Key Points
- To combat depression, we need to call on different parts of ourselves: our rational minds and our compassionate/friendly minds.

continued on next page

---

continued from previous page

- We can learn that there may be evidence for a negative belief but also evidence against it, which we often overlook.
- Generating alternatives involves trying to think about an issue, belief or problem from as many different angles as possible.
- By focusing on a situation or possibility for change, we can try to identify the key advantages and disadvantages. Once a block to change has been noted, we can try to challenge that block.
- We can do experiments to gain more information or more evidence and try things out. These experiments should have a chance of success. To do this, we might have to break large problems down into smaller ones.

Exercises
- Write down your negative thoughts about a particular situation. Now look at them carefully.
- As you think about challenging and disputing these ideas, try to take a rational/compassionate approach. If you have negative thoughts, try thinking about what you might say to a friend who is in a similar situation. You might also consider how you think when you are not depressed.
- To begin challenging negative thoughts, focus on two things:
    1 Explore the evidence for (the things that support your idea or belief) and against (the things that do not support your idea or belief).
    2 Practise generating alternatives to your negative thoughts and beliefs. Even if you do not have much faith in these alternatives at first, the act of trying to generate them is an important first step.
- Take a specific difficulty that you might have and consider the pros and cons of changing your situation. Not only focus on the advantages but also try to spot some of the disadvantages that might be stopping you from changing.

7

Styles of Negative Thinking

This chapter explores the types of thoughts you may have when you are depressed. If you can gain insight into the fact that some of your thoughts tend to lack perspective or balance, you will be in a better position to challenge them.

As we become depressed, the way we think changes. Negative thoughts, interpretations and memories become much easier to bring to mind and dwell on. There is a shift to what is called a *negative thinking bias*. As we have seen, there are two possible reasons why this happens. First, our brains tend to go for 'better safe than sorry' thinking in situations of stress and emotional arousal. We lose flexibility in our thinking, choosing to seek certainty and assuming the worst. This is a basic design feature of the brain, and without care and effort to keep our thoughts on a rational, more flexible track, it can be quite easy to lose perspective. The second reason is that negative beliefs and personal judgments (such as being unlovable, a failure or inadequate) developed in childhood may become activated by negative life-events. The latter may include the break-up of a relationship, difficulties in a relationship that lead to increased conflicts, or major disappointments of some kind. The events trigger negative beliefs from the memory, and these begin to impose their meaning on situations. A typical spiral is outlined in Figure 4 (overleaf).

As our thinking takes on a downward spiral, we start to look for evidence that confirms or fits the negative belief. We may start to remember other failures, and the feelings begin to spread out like a dark tide rolling in to cover the sands of our positive abilities. Such thoughts tend to lock in the depression, deepen it and make it more difficult to recover from. Recall the sequence on page 33.

7

Figure 4

Certain *styles* of depressive thinking are fairly common. To challenge them, we have to (*a*) recognize them and (*b*) make an effort to bring our rational and compassionate minds to the problem. Let's begin with jumping to conclusions, which as I have previously suggested is often a key to other negative thoughts.

Jumping to Conclusions

If we feel vulnerable to abandonment, or have the basic belief, 'I can never be happy without a close relationship,' it is natural that, at times, we may jump to the conclusion that others are about to leave us. This will often impel us to try to cling on to these relationships, unable to face up to our fear of being abandoned.

Our primitive mind tells us that we could not possibly cope with being alone. Now that might have been true if we were still living in the wild – being abandoned is a serious threat, especially to the young – but it is not true today. Of course, being abandoned might be terribly painful and we might feel very sad, but we could cope if we allowed ourselves to look at the evidence and plan contingencies, such as eliciting help from friends, or reminding ourselves that, before we had a relationship with this person, we had coped on our own, or that many people suffer the break-up of relationships and survive. There might even be advantages from learning to live alone for a while.

If you have a fear of rejection or of losing a relationship, one way of helping might be to write down that fear and see if you can dispute it and think of ways of coping with a break-up if it occurs. Of course, the break-up will be painful – you can't protect yourself from that – but you can teach yourself to cope with it better. Here we are using columns B and D from the 'thought form' presented in the first appendix, on page 280.

Negative thought	*Disputes and ways of coping*
If I were to stand up for myself I might be rejected.	First, do I have evidence that I will be rejected or that this relationship will end? What is the evidence for and against this idea and fear?
	But let's suppose the worst for a moment. How can I learn to face this?
	It would be painful, but I can't be held hostage to these feelings.
	I can face this risk and take steps to deal with it. These steps might include talking to friends and seeking their support, and planning and allowing myself to think about living on my own.
	Relationships do break up, and there is nothing different about me if this happens. A break-up does not mean that I am unlovable. It just means that this particular relationship has not worked out.
	Maybe the time has come to see how I might cope on my own and overcome this fear of abandonment. The benefit of this might be that I will see that I am a person in my own right.
	So I might be jumping to conclusions in two ways: (1) by assuming that the break-up is about to happen when it is not; and (2) by assuming that I could not cope with the pain of it if it did.

Another form of jumping to conclusions is 'mind reading'. We automatically assume that people do not like us because they do not give sufficient cues of approval of liking us. In 'mind reading' we believe that we can intuitively know what others think.

Now it is useful to know who your friends are and to be sensitive to being deceived by others. If we were not, we might put a lot of work into relationships but, when the chips are down, not get much back. However, as we start to spiral into depression, we become more sensitive to being deceived, being used or taken advantage of, because these are threats. We might start to think that people do not really care for us, that they are only pretending – they are unreliable allies and friends. We may also recall times from the past when we felt uncared for.

We can challenge these thoughts by considering the following:

It is only natural for people to look after themselves, and maybe they are not caring for me as much as I would like. But this does not mean that they don't like me at all. Perhaps there are aspects of me that they don't like: come to think of it, there are aspects I don't like about them. But who said that I have to like everything about them or they have to like everything about me? We are only human, after all, and people will let each other down from time to time. That's life.

Another challenge might be 'let's look at the evidence':

The other person might be having a bad day and does not understand how I feel. Is it possible that I am reading a slight or putdown into their actions when none was intended? Are there alternative explanations for their actions other than they don't like me? If, after careful consideration, I decide that they are exploiting me or really don't give a damn, then maybe I'd be better off without them, or at least expecting less from them.

Predicting the Future

We often need to be able to predict the future, at least to a degree. We need to have some idea about what threats, opportunities and blocks lie ahead to know whether to put effort into things or not.

How much energy/effort our brains devote to securing goals depends a great deal on whether we have an optimistic or pessimistic view of the future. It may be highly disadvantageous to put in a lot of effort when the chances of success appear slim. The problem is, as we become depressed, the brain veers too much to the conclusion that nothing will work, and continuously signals: 'Times are hard.' Depression says: 'You can put a lot of effort into this but not get much in return. Close down and wait for better times.' So getting out of depression may involve both patience and a preparedness to think that the brain is being overly pessimistic about the future.

One way to tackle this is to recognize that feeling overwhelmed can be a natural consequence of the situation we are in. However, this does not mean that nothing can work. It might be possible to break problems down into smaller bits. For example, when Dan had to do a project for his degree, he felt overwhelmed by it and was sure he was not up to it. But eventually he was able to challenge these thoughts with: 'Let's break the problem down. First, I'll talk to my adviser then get the relevant material and read as much as I can. Then I'll draw up a plan of what to include.' In a way, this is like mountain climbing: if you are frightened of heights, go one step at a time, and don't look down or up.

Sometimes we need to learn when to bow out gracefully. However, as a rule of thumb, if you give up too quickly, before trying out various plans to cope, and thus lack good evidence that nothing can be done, this might be because you have become overwhelmed.

Becoming Active

Predicting that things won't work out, that things will be too difficult or that nothing can help or work are reasons why we tend to do less, fail to put effort into things and become inactive. It is very important to challenge this view. Sometimes the key to success is to keep going even when things don't look promising. Suppose your inactivity is about carrying out some of the advice suggested in this book. Here are some challenges to this view.

Negative thought	Disputes and ways of coping
Nothing I do will work out.	Do I really have enough evidence to say this or is this just how I feel about it?
	I feel like this because I am depressed and therefore this is natural to feel like this.
	What have I got to lose by trying? If I put effort into this and it doesn't work out, I'll certainly be no worse off and might have gained something.
	Am I defeating myself before I start? If I try, at least I'll know I made the effort even if things don't work out.
	I can go one step at a time. If I break my problems down into smaller ones, they may not seem so overwhelming. I don't have to try to do too much at once.
	I will probably feel better if I try to do something rather than nothing.
	I can praise myself for effort.

The trick in overcoming inactivity is to try to start with something 'do-able'.

Emotional Reasoning

Strong feelings and emotions start us thinking in certain ways, and this can happen despite the fact that we know it is irrational. The problem is that, at times, we may not try to get our more rational minds to overrule our feelings. Given the strength of these we may take the view: 'I feel it, therefore it must be true.'

Feelings are very unreliable sources of truth. For example, at the times of the Crusades, many Europeans 'felt' that God wanted them to kill Muslims – and they did. Throughout the ages, humans have done some terrible things because their feelings dictated it. So, as a general rule, if you are depressed, don't trust your feelings – especially if they are highly critical and hostile to you. Here are some typical 'I feel it therefore it must be true' ideas.

Situation	*I feel it, therefore it must be true*
Going to a party	I feel frightened, therefore this situation is dangerous and threatening.
Feeling anxious	I feel as if I will have a heart attack, therefore I will.
Being accused of a minor fault	I feel guilty, therefore I am guilty and a bad person.
Losing your temper and shouting	I feel terrible when I get angry, therefore anger is terrible and I am bad and rejectable.
Wanting to cry	I feel that, if I start crying, the flood gates will open and I will never stop; therefore I must stop myself from crying.
Feeling self-conscious when I cry	I feel ashamed when I cry, therefore crying is shameful and a sign of weakness.
Making a mistake	I feel stupid, therefore I am stupid.

No matter how much you feel a failure or unlovable or stupid or any other thing, this does not make it true. The strength of your feelings does not reflect reality. So you can challenge and dispute these types of emotional reasoning with:

> *I may make mistakes or even behave stupidly, but this does not make me stupid. I am a mosaic of possibilities and potentials that can't be so easily judged, no matter what I feel at any one moment. After all, I could learn to be different. I may feel now that I will never get better, but again, this does not make it a fact. I may feel that I will never stop crying, but everyone stops in the end. Crying is a sign of hurt and the need to heal, not of weakness.*

In their right place, feelings are enormously valuable, and indeed, they give vitality to life. But when we use feelings to do the work of our rational minds, we are liable to get into trouble. The strength of our feelings is not a good guide to reality or accuracy. Perhaps you could give some thought to how your rational/compassionate self might dispute the thoughts and ideas in the table above. This, of course, does not mean that you cannot be intuitive, but make sure you get the evidence to back up your intuitions.

'I Must'

Feelings come into the picture in another way. As we become depressed, and sometimes before, we can believe that we *must* do certain things or *must* live in a certain way or *must* have certain things. For example, if you say, 'I would like to have a fortune, otherwise I will never be happy,' then you're in trouble. There is nothing new in this idea. For many centuries, Buddhists have suggested that the source of all suffering is derived from our wanting and attachments to things in the world, from our *cravings*.

We express our cravings in many ways and over many things. 'I *must* be loved all the time. I *must* never fail. I *must* prove that I am always in control. I *must*, I *must*, I *must* . . .' Nine times out of ten we don't realize that we are doing this to ourselves – but the strength of our feelings can be a guide. We can also '*must*' others like this: 'Others *must* always be nice to me. Others *must* never lie to me or let me down' and so on. Violence and frustration can be linked to the 'musts'. For example, some violent males believe that women *must* obey them and not strongly argue with them, and they *must* provide sex more or less whenever the man wants it. When we get into strong 'musts', we also get into strong tendencies to obey the dictates of our 'musts' – and, at times, force others to obey them.

Use the strength of your feelings to test whether there are some 'musts' around – and then challenge them. And, of course, our 'musts' are not either/or – in other words, the strength of the 'must' varies. Typical 'musts' are: 'I *must* be loved to be happy, 'I *must* achieve things to be loved,' 'Others *must* understand how I feel.' The key here is to try to turn your 'musts' into preferences – for example, 'I would *prefer* to be loved and in a close relationship, but I can still be happy if I am not,' or 'I would *very much like* others to understand how I feel, but if they don't, this would be disappointing but not the end of the world.'

If you find the rational approach a bit cold for you, try thinking about what the Buddha said: 'Our cravings are the source of our unhappiness.' By gaining control over our cravings, we are gaining control over our more primitive emotional minds. Whatever your own particular 'musts', try to identify them and turn them into preferences. Try to recognize that reducing the strength of your cravings can set you free, or at least freer. And remember that there is often an irony in our 'musts'. For example, at times we can be so needing of success and so fearful of failure that we may withdraw and not try at all. If you go to a party and feel that 'everyone *must* like you,' the chances are that you'll be so anxious that you won't enjoy it and even may not go. And if you do go, you may be so defensive that others won't have a chance to get to know you.

Disbelieving and Discounting the Positive in Personal Efforts

If we have been threatened or experienced a major setback, we may need a lot of reassurance before trying again. Now this makes good evolutionary sense. It is adaptive to be wary and cautious. We even have a saying for it: 'Once bitten, twice shy.'

The problem is that this same process can apply in depression in an unhelpful way. If we have experienced a failure or setback, we may think we need to have a major success before we can reassure ourselves that we are back on track. Small successes may not be enough to convince us. However, getting out of depression often depends on small steps, not giant leaps. Typical automatic thoughts that can undermine this step-by-step approach are:

- I used to do so much more when I was not depressed. Managing to do this one small thing today seems so insignificant.
- Other people could take things like this in their stride. Because it is such an effort for me, this proves that I am not making any headway.
- Anyone could do that.
- Small steps are all right for some people, but I want giant leaps and nothing else will do.

Now, remember what we have said about depression. In depression, your brain is working differently. Perhaps the levels of some of your brain chemicals have got a little on the low side. Perhaps you are exhausted. Therefore, you have to compare like with like.

Other people may accomplish more – and so might you if you were not depressed – but you are. So, given the way your brain is and the effort 'you have to make,' you are really doing a lot if you achieve one small step. Think about it this way. If you had broken your leg and were learning to walk again, being able to go a few paces might be real progress. Depressed people often wish that they could show their injuries to others, but unfortunately that is not possible. But this does not mean that there is nothing physically different in your brain and body when you are depressed than when you are not.

If you can do things when you find them difficult to do, surely that is worth even more praise than being able to do them when they are easy to accomplish. So we can learn to praise and appreciate our *efforts*, not just the results.

Also remember that, even if other people can do more than you, this does not mean you have to be the same. I know many good psychologists who accomplish far more than I do, and I can value them rather than think I have to be exactly like them or reach the same standards.

Dwelling on the Negative

Not only do we disbelieve the positive, but in depression, there is a tendency to notice and dwell and brood on the negative. It is as if we are wearing dark glasses. We see the flaws rather than the good in things. One way to challenge this is to say, 'Okay, I accept that I am very good at spotting flaws, but can I become equally good at seeing what is good in things – for example, in myself and other people?'

Put time aside to think about yourself and others and only look for what is good, helpful or useful. Another approach is to look at the alternatives and evidence for the idea that something is all bad – what can you come up with that challenges the 'all bad' view? Now this exercise should not involve only looking on the bright side and discounting genuine problems and difficulties. Rather it is designed to introduce more balance into your thinking, to get that part of your brain that controls positive feelings to do some work.

Disbelieving the Positive from Others

Another area where we disbelieve the positive is when others are approving of us. To quote Groucho Marx, 'I don't want to belong to any club that will accept me as a member.' Even being accepted is turned into a negative. Here are some other examples.

When Steve was paid a compliment at work by his boss, he thought, 'He's just saying that to get me to work harder. He's not satisfied with me.' When Ella was asked how she had been feeling when she returned to work after being ill, she concluded, 'They are just asking what's expected. They don't really care, but I guess *they'll* feel better if they ask.' When Peter passed a nice comment on how Maureen looked, she thought, 'He's just saying that to cheer me up. Maybe he wants sex.' Paul sent in a report at work, even though he knew there were one or two areas where it was weak. When he got approving feedback, he thought, 'Deceived them again. They obviously didn't read it very carefully. No one takes much notice of my work.'

Rather than allowing himself to keep on thinking so negatively, Paul was encouraged to ask his boss about his report, especially the shaky areas. He did not get the response he expected. His boss said, 'Yes, we knew those areas were unclear in your report, but then the whole area is unclear. In any case, some of the other things you said gave us some new ideas on how to approach the project.' So Paul got some evidence about the report rather than continuing to rely on his own feelings about it.

From an evolutionary point of view, the part of us that is on the lookout for deceptions can become overactive, and we become very sensitive to the possibility of being deceived. Moreover, fear of deception works both ways. On the one hand, we can think that others are deceiving *us* with their supportive words and on the other, we can think that, if we do get praise, we have deceived *them*. Because deceptions are really threats, when we become depressed we can become very sensitive to them. But again we can challenge these ideas. For example:

Even if people are mildly deceptive, does this matter? What harm can they do? I don't have to insist that people are always completely straight. And life being life, some people are more deceptive than others. But I can live with that.

Generally, if people offer you praise and you find yourself discounting or dismissing it, try to make note of that and work out why. Are they deceiving you or do you think you have deceived them? Do you think you don't deserve praise? Are you discounting the positive, and if you are, what use is that to you? Think of the advantages of accepting praise, rather than automatically dismissing it.

All-or-Nothing

All-or-nothing thinking (sometimes also called either/or, polarized or black-and-white thinking) is typical of the extreme forms of thought that can arise when we are threatened. We need quick answers, not indeterminacy. Mistakes, if we still lived in the wild, could be costly. Animals often need to jump to conclusions (e.g., whether to run from a sound in the bushes), and it is easier to jump to conclusions if the choices are clear – all or nothing. All-or-nothing thinking helps us to be certain and make quick decisions.

The problem here is that all-or-nothing thinking can lead us seriously astray. We do not take the time or effort to consider the evidence of alternatives thoroughly. Here are some typical all-or-nothing thoughts:

- My efforts are either a success or they are an abject failure.
- I am/other people are either all good or all bad.
- There is right and there is wrong, and nothing in between.
- If I'm not perfect, I'm a failure.
- You're either a real man or you're a wimp.
- If you're not with us, you're against us.
- If it doesn't go exactly as I planned or hoped, it is a fiasco.
- If you don't always show me that you love me, you don't love me at all.

All-or-nothing thinking is common for two reasons. First, we feel threatened by *uncertainty*. Indeed, some people can feel very threatened by this and must know for sure how to act and what is right, and they may try to create the certainty they need by all-or-nothing thinking. Sometimes we may think that people who 'know their own minds' and can be clear on key issues are strong, and we admire them and try to be like them. But watch out. Hitler knew his own mind and was a very good example of an all-or-nothing thinker. Some apparently strong people may actually be quite rigid. Indeed, I have found that some depressed people admire those they see as strong individuals, but when you really explore this with them, they discover that the people they are admiring and trying to be like are neither strong nor compassionate. They are rather shallow, rigid, all-or-nothing thinkers who are always ready to give their opinions.

There is nothing wrong with sitting on the fence for a while and seeing things as grey areas. Even though we may eventually have to come off the fence, at least we have given ourselves space to weigh up the evidence and let our rational minds do some work.

The other common reason why we go in for all-or-nothing thinking has to do with *frustration and disappointment* (*see* Chapter 15). Here is Anne again, who we met in the last chapter. During her dinner party, she was so focused on making her guests comfortable that she forgot the meal and it overcooked. She concluded: 'I messed up the whole evening. I can't even cook a simple meal. Everyone will now know how inadequate I am.' It was her disappointment/frustration and feelings of threat – of being seen to be no good – that led to her all-or-nothing thinking: 'The whole evening was messed up.' Again this is not that uncommon. How often have we thrown down our tools because we can't get something to go right?

But what was the evidence that the whole evening was messed up? I asked Anne some questions about this (Anne's responses are given in the brackets):

- Did people talk to each other? (Yes)
- Did they chat and laugh? (Yes)
- Was the atmosphere relaxed or tense? (Relaxed)
- Did people throw up after eating your food? (No)
- Did they say they enjoyed it? (Yes)

As Anne later reflected, the food *had* been a disappointment, but this failure had done no more than dent her pride a little. Maybe if she hadn't been so depressed and anxious, she might have seen the funny side of it and cracked a joke. And, if she were honest with herself (she said), her guests might not have realized that the food was overcooked, for only she had known what she had intended to achieve.

So getting out of all-or-nothing thinking and our tendency to make extreme judgments of good/bad or success/failure can be very important in recovering from depression. The state of depression itself can reduce our tolerance of frustration and push us into all-or-nothing thinking, so we have to be aware of this and be careful not to let it get the better of us.

Overgeneralization

If one thing goes wrong, we think that everything is going to go wrong. Our sense of failure can grow until we believe that everything we have ever done was a failure or faked. When we overgeneralize like this, we see one setback or defeat as a never-ending pattern of defeats. *Nothing* will work; it will *always* be this way.

- A student received a bad mark and concluded, 'I will never make it. My work is never good enough.'
- A friend had told Sue that she would come to her party, but then she forgot the date. Sue thought, 'This is typical of how people always treat me. No one ever cares.'
- Dan broke up with his girlfriend and thought, 'I will never be as happy again as I was with her. I will always be miserable without her.'

Let's explore some typical challenges/disputes to overgeneralization.

Negative thought	Disputes and ways of coping
Things will never work out for me.	'Never' and 'always' are big words. True, I feel really upset and frustrated now, but overgeneralizing is typical when I feel upset.
	I have thought like this before and things did work out – at least to a degree.

Let me focus on what I can do and the things that might go okay, rather than just blanking out everything.

Predicting the future is a chancy business. Maybe I can learn how to make things go better. I don't have to load the dice against myself.

If a friend had a setback, I would not speak to him/her like this. Maybe I can learn to speak to myself as I might to a friend.

Egocentric Thinking

In this situation, we have difficulty in believing that others have a different point of view to our own. The way we see things must be the way they see things – e.g. 'I think I'm a failure, thus so must they.'

But there is another way we can be egocentric in our thinking. This is when we insist that others obey the same rules for living and have the same values as we do. Janet was very keen on birthdays and always remembered them. But her husband Eddie did not think in these terms; he liked to give small presents as surprises, out of the blue. One year, he forgot to buy a present for Janet's birthday. She thought, 'He knows how important birthdays are to me. I would never have forgotten his, so how could he forget mine? If he loved me, he would not have forgotten.' But the fact was Eddie did not really know how important birthdays were to Janet because she had never told him. He was simply supposed to think the same way as Janet.

In therapy together, Eddie was surprised at how upset she had been and pointed out that he did bring small surprise presents, which showed that he was thinking about her. He also mentioned to her – for the first time – that she rarely gave gifts except at birthdays, and to his way of thinking, this meant that she only thought about giving him something or surprising him once a year! So people often have different views, and because of this, it is often unhelpful to assume that others think as we do – often they don't. All of us have different life experiences and personalities, and our views and values differ, too. These differences can be a source of growth or conflict. It is because we are all different that there is such a rich and varied range of human beings. Unfortunately, at times we may downgrade people if they don't think or behave like us. And on the bookstands today, you will find many books that address the fact that men and women tend to think differently about relationships and want different things out of them. This need not be a problem if we are upfront about our needs and wants and openly negotiate with our partners. It becomes a problem when we are not clear with them about our wants or we try to force other people to think as we do.

Key Points
- The way we think about things can lead us further into depression rather than out of it.
- When we are depressed, our brains change in such a way that we become very sensitive to various kinds of harm, threats and losses. Now it is (or was) adaptive for the brain to go for a 'better safe than sorry' type of thinking and to expect the worst when under threat. In these situations, control over our feelings is given more to the primitive emotional brain and less control is given to the rational brain.
- We should try to focus on our negative thoughts and recognize them for what they are.
- There are some typical types of thoughts that are encountered in depression. These include jumping to (negative) conclusions, 'I must', all-or-nothing thinking and overgeneralizing. All of these can be successfully challenged.

Exercises
- Review the different types of thinking outlined in this chapter. Identify which ones seem to apply to you.
- As you monitor your automatic thoughts, ask yourself which of

continued on next page

these depressing styles of thinking you might be using. The more practice you get at identifying and challenging them, the better.

- If you have written down your thoughts, try to spot which kind of depressive style each thought is an example of – for instance, is it an example of jumping to conclusions, or emotional reasoning, or all-or-nothing thinking?

- Use your rational/compassionate mind to remind you of which kind of thought you are using and how to challenge it. Do you have enough evidence? Are you trying to force a certainty when none exists? Are you disbelieving the positives?

- Try to check with yourself to see if these styles of thoughts are going through your mind. Identify them as they happen and try disputing them.

- Consider how you might help someone you like dispute, say, all-or-nothing thinking or jumping to conclusions. Learn to be gentle with yourself rather than harsh and critical, and see things in grey rather than insisting on black and white.

- Try to focus on what you can do rather than what you can't. Have the motto: 'The secret of success is the ability to fail.'

- Ask 'How am I looking after myself? Do my thoughts help me care for myself?' Slowly build on your insights.

8

Self-bullying and How to Challenge It

Thoughts and feelings about yourself as a person usually become very negative in depression. I say 'usually' because this is not always the case. For example, I recall a patient who became depressed when new people moved in next door, and played loud music into the early hours. She tried to get the authorities to stop them, but although they were very sympathetic, they were not much help. Slowly she slipped into depression, feeling her whole life was being ruined and there was nothing she could do. However, she did not think her depression was her fault or that she was in any way inadequate, worthless, weak or bad. Her depression was focused on a loss of control over a very difficult situation.

Sometimes depression can be triggered by conflicts and splits in families or other important relationships. The depressed person may feel very defeated and trapped by these relationships but not to blame for them. Sometimes depressed people feel bad about being depressed and the effects this is having on them and others around them, but they do not feel that they are bad or inadequate as people; they blame the depression.

Nevertheless, many depressed people have a very poor relationship with themselves, and certainly depression does nothing to improve what they feel about themselves. A poor relationship with yourself can predate a depression or develop with it. So in this chapter we will explore the typical styles of 'self-thinking' that depressed people engage in and consider how these thoughts can be challenged. All the styles discussed here can be seen as types of *self-bullying*. As you will see, we can bully ourselves in many different ways.

Self-Blaming

Blaming occurs when we try to seek the reasons for or causes of things – why did such and such a thing happen? When we are depressed, we often feel a great sense of responsibility for negative events and so blame ourselves. The reasons for this are complex. Sometimes we self-blame because as children we were taught to. Whenever things went wrong in the family, we tended to get the blame. Even young children who are sexually abused can be told that they are to blame for it – which, of course, is absurd. Sadly, adults in looking for someone to blame can simply pick on those least able to defend themselves.

Sylvia was a harsh self-blamer. Her mother had frequently blamed her for making her life a constant misery, and over time, this got through to Sylvia and she began to blame herself whenever other people close to her had difficulties. Yet when Sylvia looked at the evidence, she realized that her mother's life was unhappy for a number of reasons including a difficult marriage and money worries. However, Sylvia as a child could not see this wider perspective but had to believe what her mother told her.

When people are depressed, their self-blaming can be total. When bad things happen or conflicts arise, they may see them as completely their fault. This is called *personalization* – the tendency to assume responsibility for things that are either not our fault or only partly so. However, most life-events are a combination of various circumstances. When we are depressed, it is often helpful to stand back and think of as many reasons as possible about why something happened the way it did. We can learn to consider alternative explanations rather than just blame ourselves.

Sheila's husband had an affair for which she blamed herself. Her thinking was: 'If I had been more attentive, he would not have had an affair. If I had been more sexually alluring, he would not have had an affair. If I had been more interesting as a person and less focused on the children, he would not have had an affair.' All her thoughts were focused on herself. However, she could have had alternative thoughts. For example, she could have thought, 'He could have taken more responsibility for the children, then I wouldn't have felt so overloaded. He could have spent more time

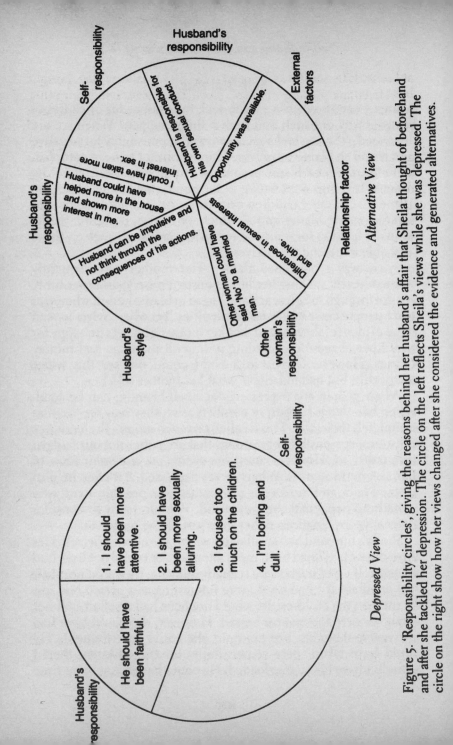

Figure 5: 'Responsibility circles', giving the reasons behind her husband's affair that Sheila thought of beforehand and after she tackled her depression. The circle on the left reflects Sheila's views while she was depressed. The circle on the right show how her views changed after she considered the evidence and generated alternatives.

at home. If he had been more attentive in his lovemaking, I might have felt more sexually inclined. Even if he felt attracted to another woman, he did not have to act on it. The other woman could have realized he was married and not encouraged him.'

One can then write down these various alternatives side by side and rate them in terms of *percentage of truth*. Or one might draw a circle and for each reason allocate a slice of the circle. The size of each slice represents the percentage of truth. In Figure 5 on page 106 you can see how this worked for Sheila. The two circles represent a depressed view and a more balanced view. Note how some situations often have many causes. Sheila's more balanced, 'alternative view' circle seemed more true to her once she had considered it.

The same basic principle can apply when we blame others. We may simply blame them without considering the complexity of the issue, and we may label them as bad, weak and so forth.

Self-Blame and Control

One reason we might self-blame is that, paradoxically, it might offer hope. For example, if a certain event is our fault, we have a chance of changing things in the future. We have (potential) control over it and so don't have to face the possibility that, maybe, we actually don't have much control. In depression, it is sometimes important to exert more control over our lives, but it is also important to know our limits and what we cannot control. Sheila had to face the fact that she could not totally control her husband's sexual conduct. It was his responsibility, not hers. We have to be careful that, in self-blaming we are not trying to give ourselves more control (and power) than we actually have (or had).

Avoiding Conflict

Another reason for self-blame is that it may be more comfortable to blame ourselves than to blame others. It may be that self-blame keeps the peace and stops us from having to challenge others. If, when we were children, our parents told us that they hit us because we were bad in some way, we might have accepted their view and rarely argued. This attitude can be carried on into adulthood. The other person always seems blameless, beyond rebuke.

Sometimes we recognize that we are not totally blameless in something, but when it comes to arguing our case, the part that is our responsibility gets blown out of proportion. We become overfocused on it and feel that we have not got a leg to stand on. However, most things in life have many causes, and the idea here is to try to avoid all-or-nothing thinking. By all means, accept your share of responsibility – none of us is an angel – but don't overdo it. Healing comes from forgiving yourself and others.

Expecting Punishment

Sometimes when bad things happen, depressed people feel that they are being punished for being bad in some way. It is as if we believe that good things will only happen if we are good and only bad things will happen if we are bad, so if bad things do happen, this must be because we have been or simply are bad. When Kate lost a child to sudden infant death syndrome, she felt that God was punishing her for having had an abortion some years earlier. The sense of being punished can be quite strong in depression, and quite often, if this is explored, it turns out to relate to a person's own guilt or shame about something in the past. For instance, Richard's parents had given him strong messages that masturbation was bad. But when he began doing it when he was twelve, he enjoyed it – but also felt terribly guilty. For many years, he carried the belief that he was bad for having enjoyed masturbating and sooner or later he was going to be punished for it. When bad things happened to him, he would think that these were 'part of his punishment'.

To come to terms with these feelings we usually have to admit to the things we feel guilty about and then learn how to forgive ourselves for them. It can be difficult to come to terms with the fact that the principles of 'justice' and 'punishment' are human creations. There is no justice in those who starve to death from droughts in Africa. Good and bad things can happen to people whether or not they behave well or badly.

Self-Criticism

Related to self-blame is self-criticism. At times, we can blame ourselves for things but also accept that this was unfortunate and that we can forgive (i.e. be compassionate with) ourselves. However, when we are depressed, we often give much more power to the internal (self-critical) bully who can have a fine time commenting on and criticizing everything we do.

Some people believe that self-criticism is the only way to make them do things. For example, a person might say, 'If I didn't kick myself, I'd never do anything.' They use their self-bullying part to drive them on – sometimes in rather sadistic-masochistic ways. Such a person may believe that threats and punishments are the best ways to get things done. In some cases, this view goes back to childhood. Parents may have said things like, 'If I didn't always get on at you, you wouldn't do anything' or 'Punishment is the only thing that works with you.' They may also have been poor at paying attention to and praising good conduct and rather more attentive of and quick to punish bad conduct. As a result, the child becomes good at self-criticism and self-punishment but poor at self-rewarding and valuing.

In depression, however, self-criticism can get out of hand. The internal bully/critic becomes so forceful that we can feel totally beaten down by it. Then, when we are disappointed about things or find out our conduct has fallen short of our ideal in some way, we can become angry and frustrated and launch savage attacks on ourselves.

It–Me

Self-criticism can lead to an 'it–me problem': 'I only accept "me" if I do "it" well.' The 'it' can be anything you happen to judge as important. For example, if you are a student, the 'it' may be passing exams. You might say to yourself: 'I'll only accept myself if I pass my exams and I'll hate myself if I don't.' Or the 'it' might be coping with housework or a job: 'I'm only a good and worthwhile *person* if I do these *things* well.' Success leads to self-acceptance, but failure leads to self-dislike and self-attacking.

This kind of thinking means: 'I am only as good as my last performance.' But how much does success or failure actually change us? Do you (as a person) really become good if you succeed and become bad (as a person) if you fail? Whether we succeed or fail, we have not gained or lost any brain cells; we have not grown an extra arm; our hair, eyes and taste in music have not changed. The essence of our being has not changed. Of course, we may lose things that have importance to us if we fail. We may feel terribly disappointed or grieve for what is lost and what we can't have. But the point is that these will be more difficult to cope with if our disappointment becomes an attack on ourselves and we label ourselves rather than our actions as 'failures'.

So it can be helpful to learn that succeeding and failing may feel good and bad; we can be disappointed by failing, but this does not make us good and bad *people*. If we place too much emphasis on our actions rather than on feeling good about our inner selves, we are at risk of becoming *addicted* to a need always to succeed. We may only feel good if we do succeed. Every failure hurts us so badly because we think that it turns us totally bad inside.

These are not new concepts. In Buddhist and other spiritual traditions, there has long been the idea that we suffer because we become too attached to external successes or failures. They say, 'Be in the world but not of the world.' These approaches can help us recognize that, if we devalue ourselves rather than become disappointed in our actions, we are digging away at the very foundations of our being. Or consider it this way. Your inner being, yourself, is like the inside of a house. Failures and disappointments are like storms that can swirl around it. If a storm blows up, it is preferable to close the doors and windows and protect the inner house rather than throwing open all the windows and doors and letting the storm rip through it.

The key challenge to this problem is to separate *self*-rating and judgments from *behavior* rating and judgments. It may be true that your *behavior* falls short of what you would like, but this does not change the complexity and essence of you as a *person*. We can be disappointed in our behavior or at what happens to us, but as human beings, we do not have to rate ourselves in such all-or-nothing terms as 'good' or 'bad', 'worthwhile' or 'worthless'. If we do that, we are giving away our humanity and turning ourselves into objects with a market value – we literally dehumanize ourselves. We are saying, 'I can be treated like a car, soap powder or some other "thing".' 'If I perform well, I deserve to be valued. If I don't perform well, I am worthless junk.' But we are not things or objects. We are living, feeling, highly complex beings, and to judge ourselves as if we are just objects carries great risks.

Self-Attack

Recent research has suggested that depression is much more likely if a person's weak/bad, hopeless sense of self is triggered than if self-critical thoughts alone are activated. It seems that, rather than the self-criticism itself, it is the person's response to self-criticism that is associated with depression. When self-criticism becomes hostile and activates basic beliefs and self-labels (e.g. of being weak, bad, inadequate, hopeless, etc.), then depression really takes root.

We all have a tendency to be self-critical. However, when we become angry, frustrated and aggressive with ourselves and start bullying and labelling ourselves as worthless, bad or weak, we are more likely to slip deeper into depression. In a way, we become enemies to ourselves; we lose our capacity for inner compassion. It is as if the self becomes trapped in certain ways of feeling and then (because of emotional reasoning) over-identifies with these feelings. We think our feelings are true reflections of ourselves. For example, 'I *feel* stupid/worthless, therefore I *am* stupid/worthless.'

The main challenges here are to all-or-nothing thinking and emotional reasoning:

- To sum up a person (e.g. myself) in simple terms of good/bad, worthwhile/worthless is all-or-nothing thinking. It is preferable for me to think that there are some things I can do okay and some things I don't do as well as I would like.
- Because I feel stupid and worthless does not make it true.
- The idea of worth can be applied to objects such as cars or soap powder but not to people.
- I don't have to treat myself as an object, whose only value is what I achieve or do.
- If I say 'worthless' is just one of a number of possible feelings that I, as a human being, can have about myself, I can put these negative feelings in perspective.

- If I over-identify with the feelings of worthlessness, I am more likely to get depressed.

Self-Hatred

At the extreme, some depressions involve not just self-criticism and self-attack, but also self-hatred. This is not just a sense of disappointment in the self; the self is treated like a hated enemy. Whereas self-criticism often comes from disappointment and a desire to do better, self-hatred is not focused on the need to do better. It is focused on a desire to destroy and get rid of.

Sometimes with self-hatred are feelings of *self-disgust*. Now, disgust is an interesting feeling and usually involves the desire to get rid of or expel the thing we are disgusted by. In self-hatred, part of us may judge ourselves to be disgusting, bad or evil. When we have these feelings, there may be a strong desire to attack ourselves in quite a savage way – not just because we are disappointed and feel let down, but because we really have come to hate parts of ourselves.

Kate would become overpowered by feelings of anxiety and worthlessness. When things did not work out right, or she got into conflicts with others, she'd feel intense rage. But even while she was having these feelings, she was also having thoughts and feelings of intense hatred towards herself. Her internal bully was really sadistic. She had thoughts like: 'You are a pathetic creature. A whining, useless piece of shit.' Frequently the labels people use when they hate themselves are those that invite feelings of disgust (e.g. 'shit'). Kate had been sexually abused, and at times she hated her genitals and wanted to 'take a knife to them.' In extreme cases, self-hatred can lead to serious self-harming.

Sonia had not been sexually abused but hated the shape of her face and was constantly seeking out plastic surgeons. It is not uncommon for self-hatred to be directed at the body, although this is not always so. It is also often related to shame.

It is important to try to work out what you actually feel about yourself, and see if your bullying, self-critical side has become more than critical and has turned to self-dislike or self-hatred. Even though you may be disappointed in yourself and the state you are in, can you still maintain a reasonably friendly relationship with your inner self? If your internal bully is getting out of hand, you may want to try the following challenges. Using your compassionate mind, and in as warm and friendly a way as you can muster, say:

- My self-hatred is highly destructive.
- Am I a person who values hatred?
- If I don't value hatred and can see how destructive it is, maybe I can learn to get more control over this part of myself.
- What value does my self-hatred serve?
- I know perfectly well that, if I cared for someone, I would not treat them with hatred.
- Am I engaging in all-or-nothing thinking here? Am I discounting my positives?
- Am I as bad as Hitler? No? Then maybe I need to get my hatred into perspective.
- Maybe I need to be tougher with this internal bully and not let it get away with what I am allowing at the moment.
- After all, my self-hating or self-disliking does me no good. It just beats me down.
- Maybe I have learned to hate myself because of the way others have treated me. If I attack myself, I am only repeating what they did to me.

The tough part in all this is that you will need to be absolutely honest with yourself and decide whether or not you want hatred to live in you. Only when you decide that you do not, can you train yourself to become its master rather than allowing it to master you. However, if you are secretly on the side of self-hatred and think it reasonable and acceptable to hate yourself, this will be very difficult to do, and it will be hard to open yourself to compassion and healing. For some people, this is a most soul-searching journey. But as one patient said to me:

> *The hard part was realizing that, whatever had happened in the past and whatever rage and hatred I carried from those years, the key turning point had to be my decision that I had had enough of my hatred. Only then could I start to take the steps to find the way out.*

And, of course, it is not just with depression that coming to terms with and conquering hatred can be helpful. Many of our problems of living together in the world today could be helped if we worked on this. We all have the potential to hate — there is nothing abnormal about you if you feel it. The primary question is: how much life will we give it?

Hatred often comes from hurt — we hate what hurts us or causes us pain. So rather than focus on hatred, it is useful to focus on what the pain and hurt is about. Also, of course, if you discover that there are elements of self-hatred in your depression, don't turn this insight into another attack. Say instead:

> *I am glad I have discovered my hatred. I can now set about learning to be compassionate and test the rationality of my self-hatred. Maybe I am engaging in all-or-nothing thinking or emotional reasoning. When I feel hatred I can recognize it as a symptom of hurt.*

Social Comparisons

Some of our negative self-attacking thoughts arise when we look at others and compare ourselves disparagingly with them. In fact, humans are constantly comparing themselves with others: 'Is mine bigger than yours?' and so on. Even animals use this 'social comparison' to work out which individuals to challenge and which to avoid, who they can beat and who they are likely to be beaten by. Our brains are set up to socially compare and it can be very difficult to avoid doing it.

Social comparison provides us with much important information. It can be used to make decisions such as 'Am I like others or not like them?', 'Am I one of them or not?', 'Am I an insider or an outsider?', 'Am I better [brighter, stronger, more attractive, more competent] than others, less so, or about the same?' Even a failure can feel better if his or her social comparison turns out to be positive. Imagine that you fail at an important task – e.g. an exam or driving test. You feel down about your failure. Then you phone your friends and find out that they failed, too. The chances are that you will feel some relief. You will know that it was not just you.

When we are depressed, we tend to compare ourselves with others in negative ways. And for these comparisons, we pick individuals who are indeed (we think) much better than us in some way. In other words, we don't compare ourselves with Mr or Ms Average but with someone we think is doing really well. Jane, a mother of two who devoted herself to their care, had a number of friends who went out to work even though they, too, had children. Jane thought, 'I'm not as competent as them because I don't go out to work, and I have to struggle just to keep the home going.' When I asked her if she had other friends with children who did not have outside employment, she agreed that most of her friends didn't. However, it was not them she compared herself with but the few who did have jobs.

Diane felt really depressed after the birth of her child. She thought that her reaction was different from that of all her friends and therefore there was something wrong with her to feel this way. As a result, she never told anyone but suffered in silence. Then there was Bill, who was a keen tennis player. He was average for his club, but because he would compare himself with the top players, he constantly felt inferior if his performance did not match theirs.

Depressed people tend to discount comparisons with those who would give them good feelings about their abilities and only compare themselves with those who would tend to leave them feeling bad about their performance. In other words, they tend to choose the wrong targets for comparison. Instead of thinking that they are better than XYZ, they focus on how far short they are from ABC. Now ideally we would not socially compare at all, but set our own standards and live by our own internal feelings. But research suggests this can be difficult, especially for people who have low self-esteem. So if you do compare yourself with others, it is useful to ensure that you don't make these comparisons in ways that leave you feeling depressed and inferior.

Social comparison is rife in relationships between brothers and sisters and other family members. If you have children, you will know that they are always trying to work out if you (as the parent) prefer one of their brothers or sisters. How often have you heard: 'But you let Ken or Sue stay up and watch television – why can't you let me?' 'You said it was all right for Ken or Sue to go and see their friends – why can't you let me go?' Sometimes depressed people have many unresolved problems about these early relationships. They may feel that they have always lived in the shadow of a sibling – were less bright, less attractive and so forth. Jim went to university and did well, but his brother Tom was a more practical person and not cut out for the academic life. However, instead of being happy with himself, Tom constantly compared himself with Jim and felt a failure. He would say, 'Why couldn't I have been the bright one?'

These kinds of problems relate to envy, which can be very destructive if it gets turned against oneself. For example, you might envy those who win prizes or make a lot of money, but if you start to tell yourself that you failed and feel cheated unless you get those thing, too, you will run into trouble. In the example above, Tom was very focused on an idea that life had been unfair to him.

Social comparison is one reason why people who seem to have quite prestigious positions in society can become depressed. Some time ago, I worked with a doctor who had done quite well during his training yet, when be became qualified, found the work stressful. He thought that he was doing much worse than his colleagues. Compared with them, he did not feel confident or on a par. So again, the targets of our social comparisons – those with whom we choose to compare ourselves – are important.

Although it can be very difficult if not impossible to avoid making social comparisons, there are some things that we can do to challenge the negative thoughts that arise from them.

- Choose a target to compare yourself with who is most like you. In other words, avoid comparing yourself with those who are clearly a lot better in certain ways.
- When non-depressed people compare themselves with others and find that they don't do so well, they usually discount the comparisons. Depressed people, however, do not discount such comparisons but dwell on them. So if a comparison turns out badly, consider the reasons and evidence why this comparison may not be an appropriate one for you.

- If certain comparisons are making you unhappy, write out the advantages and disadvantages of making such comparisons. If a comparison benefits you, avoid looking down on others. But if it just leaves you feeling bad and frustrated (and you look down on yourself), there are more disadvantages than advantages.
- If you do compare and feel down, avoid self-attacking. Try to remember that, in all things, there are those who are better at doing certain things or have more, but this does not make you a failure or inadequate because you can't do these things or don't have as much.
- Try to think of your life as your own unique journey, with its own unique ups and downs and challenges. Although you might want to live the life of someone else, this is not possible. Focus on you as yourself rather than you as compared with others.
- Focus on what you can do rather than on what others seem to do better. Don't disqualify the positives in your own performance.
- If you are depressed, try to avoid labelling yourself as inadequate because you think others don't get depressed. Sadly many people do get depressed and anxious.

The Inner Bully

All these negative, self-directed thoughts are forms of bullying, so I shall refer to them as the 'inner bully'. The inner bully observes the self and passes judgments ranging from mild criticism to hatred. Where it comes from is unclear, but often it arises from early childhood (see also page 236). If you ask people who their inner bully most sounds like, it is sometimes one or both of their parents. It tends to spring to life in situations of frustration and disappointment with ourselves – when we don't do certain things or fail to reach certain standards.

As I have already pointed out, some people think that, if they did not bully themselves and goad themselves into action, they would never get anything done. But we can see that, if the inner bully gets too much out of control, it can do great internal damage. Consider Anne and the overcooked meal again. When she did not cook the food well enough, she told herself that she had messed up the whole evening and that she was a failure. But note how destructive her thoughts are. Suppose you said such things to a friend. Would you say, 'You've messed up the whole evening with your poor cooking. You're a failure'? Your friend would be very upset if you did – and would probably never invite you back. But this is the kind of thing depressed people say to themselves constantly.

The inner bully (or internal critic) sets up a self-defeating spiral:

Figure 6

So the bully – your internal self-attacks – actually causes many of the problems (e.g. doing less) that it attacks you for. It's as if, after I knock you down, I then hit you because you have gone down. It is very important to see this spiral for we shall meet it many more times on the journey ahead.

When faced with an inner bully, it is always worth saying something like:

Look, I'm not nearly as lazy/bad/inadequate as I think I am. To be frank, it is my bully hitting me so hard that makes me depressed. This causes most of my problems. I kick myself when I'm down. If I'm really as keen on success as I say I am, the best way to treat myself is with kindness and support when things are not going well. If I feel confident, I am likely to do far more than if I am full of fear, anger and disappointment.

The next thing is to plan out actions so that you can learn to praise your success rather than attack your disappointments. Suppose your inner bully is berating you because you have not worked hard enough on something. You can say:

I am depressed right now, so it's natural not to have my normal drive. Even though I can't do everything I used to, I can still do some things. I can praise myself for what I do rather than attacking myself for what I don't do. There is no way I'm going to bully myself out of depression. All I do is what I am able to do. I can go step by step. By praising my steps, no matter how small they may seem to be, I am moving forward.

And if you fancy a bit of rebellion, you might say to your chores: 'To hell with it. They can wait. I'm going to do something that I want to today!'

Key Points
- We often self-attack ourselves without really realizing what we are doing. Our feelings and moods seem to carry us along into certain styles of thinking and evaluating ourselves.
- If we are to climb out of depression, we may have to take a good look at ourselves and decide if our self-criticism, anger and self-hatred are justified or useful – and what we can do to heal them.
- The hard part can be helping ourselves to focus on the need for inner healing. Once we have, we can then start to focus on what we need to do to be healed. Often the first step is to sort out our relationships with ourselves.

Exercises
- Review the styles of self-bullying thinking covered by this chapter.
- Try to consider which of these styles (if any) apply to you in general. Get to know the typical ways you bully yourself.
- If something happens and you feel bad about yourself, ask yourself: 'What am I saying about myself? What does this mean about me?' Write down these thoughts.
- Consider in what ways you might be using: all-or-nothing thinking, emotional reasoning, disbelieving positives.
- Using your 'thought form' focus on the D column (pages 280–

continued on next page

continued from previous page

283). Use your rational/compassionate mind to generate alternative views about yourself. Look through the examples given in this and other chapters to dispute your negative self-directed thoughts.

- Consider how you might help someone you like stop self-attacking and bullying themselves, and then apply this to yourself. Learn to be gentle with yourself. Imagine a really caring person advising you. What would he or she say? Look at the evidence and think of alternatives. Ask yourself: How am I looking after myself with these thoughts/feelings? Do my thoughts help me to care for or look after myself?' In this way slowly build up your insights.

9

Calling Ourselves Names: How Negative Labels Affect Us

The last chapter focused on thoughts and feelings against the self. Here we consider other types of self-evaluations: how we come to experience ourselves and label that experience. These labels are not necessarily hostile to ourselves but can still play a major role in depression.

Self-Labelling

Most of us have had the experience of feeling bad, inadequate and useless at times. These feelings usually arise when we are disappointed by our actions, have failed at something or have been criticized by others. As we grow up, our parents, teachers, siblings and peers label us in various ways and occasionally call us things that are hurtful. We may be told that we are a nuisance, bad, unlovable, stupid. Or perhaps overprotective parents say that we are not able to make our own decisions or cannot cope by ourselves. Over time, we develop various ways of thinking about ourselves as being certain kinds of people – that is, we come to label and describe ourselves in various ways.

For example, suppose you wrote a letter to a pen friend – how would you describe yourself? Now supposing you were writing for a job – how would you describe yourself? If you were writing to a dating agency, how would you describe yourself? And finally, if you were writing to a priest or someone similar to confess something and seek forgiveness, how would you then describe yourself? If you wrote each of those letters, the chances are that each one would say different things about you.

This is because we as humans are very complex and have many

1

different qualities. But when we become depressed, the richness, variety and vitality of our potential selves drains away and we start thinking of ourselves in rather simple terms, or labels. The labels might be triggered by life-events. For instance, you might be rejected by someone you love and then label yourself as unlovable. Or you might fail at some important task and then label yourself as a failure. Negative *labels* are often sparked off by negative *feelings*, which in turn may be strong echoes from the past.

Suppose you were rejected by a lover who you were very keen on, and you started to think that you were unlovable. If you are becoming depressed, this is what might happen. When you go into work the next day, the rejection is on your mind. You go down to see a colleague, but she/he is too busy to chat to you and seems to have her/his own problems. Now you start to think, 'Maybe my friend is not so keen on me after all. Actually, maybe we aren't as close as I thought.' Can you see what is happening here? This internal feeling and label of unlovability is now being used to judge other relationships and situations. So the point is that internal labels – the way you think and feel about yourself as a person – can influence many of your perceptions.

Self-labelling is essentially a form of name-calling. In depression, we come to experience ourselves as if that label (e.g. weak, inadequate, worthless, bad) sums up the whole truth about us. Our whole self becomes identified with the label.

The judgments, labels and feelings that we have about ourselves when we are depressed tend to be the same the world over. Whether we live in China, the United States or Europe, depression often speaks with the same voice. The following are some of the words depressed people typically use to describe themselves:

bad	inadequate	outsider	unlovable
empty	incompetent	rejectable	useless
failure	inferior	small	victim
fake	loser	ugly	weak
hopeless	nuisance	unattractive	worthless

To challenge self-labels requires us, first, to recognize that we are thinking (and experiencing) ourselves in single-word descriptions. We can try to stand back from the depression and see that it tends to come up with these harsh judgments over and over again. However, we can train our minds to realize that these are only one of many possible sets of judgments. There are others, such as: honest, hardworking, carer, helper, lover, old, young, lover of rock music, gardener. Our depressed negative judgments, which seem so certain and 'all or nothing', can also be examined for their accuracy and challenged. Although depression tends to push us towards certain types of extreme judgments, it is helpful to think that these are only parts of ourselves. Like a piano, we can have and play different notes, and we are far more complex than our depression would have us believe.

Challenges to self-labels can include the following:

- As a human being, I am a complex person. I am the product of many millions of years of evolution, with an immensely complex genetic code and billions of brain cells in my head. I am also the product of many years of development, with a personal history. I can operate in many different states of mind and in different roles. Therefore to judge my whole self, my being and my essence, in single negative terms is taking all-or-nothing thinking to the grossest of extremes.

- When I am depressed, it is natural and understandable that I tend to feel bad and inadequate but this does not make *me* bad or inadequate. To believe it did would be a form of emotional reasoning. I might feel worthless but this does not make it true.

- Although I tend to focus on negative labels when I am depressed, I can try to balance out these with other ideas about myself. For example, I can also tell myself that I am honest, hardworking and caring – at least sometimes. I can consider alternative labels and inner experiences.

- I can check to see if my thinking has become rather one-sided. Am I discounting the positives in my life, relying too much on my mood to tell me how things really are, overgeneralizing and thinking in extreme ways?

- How do I see myself when I'm not depressed? Okay, maybe not as good a person as I might like, but certainly not as I do now.

- Although depression likes simplistic answers to complex problems and tends to see things in black and white, good and bad, I don't have to accept this view but can try challenging it.

Having explored the issue of self-labelling and how, at times, we can use very simplistic and crude labels to judge ourselves, we can now consider some typical labels and how to challenge them.

The Empty Self

In some depressions, people can see themselves as empty. Depression tends to knock out many of our positive emotions, and it is not uncommon to find that people lose feelings of affection for those around them. Hence they feel emotionally dead, drained and exhausted. As one patient told me, 'I am just an empty shell.'

An important challenge may be to recognize that this can be a natural symptom of depression. It can knock out your capacity to feel. Thus, it is not you, as a person, who cannot feel, but rather you are *in a mental state of not feeling*. As soon as your mood lifts, you will feel again. Try not to attack yourself for your loss of feelings, even though it can be desperately sad and disappointing. Indeed, if you focus on the sadness of it, rather than the badness, you might find that you want to cry, and crying might be the first glimmerings of a return of feelings.

In some depressions, the experience of emptiness is not linked to negative things about the person but the absence of positive things. Paula explained this feeling to me: 'I've never felt bad about myself really. I think I'm not a bad person on the whole, but I just feel that I'm a "wallpaper person".' She felt neither lovable nor unlovable; she just didn't feel anything strongly about herself one way or another. She revealed a history of emotional neglect by her parents. They had not been unkind to her in an aggressive way but were simply not interested in her. With no one in her life who she felt valued her, she had been left with feelings of emptiness and drifting through life. When Paula looked at the advantages and disadvantages of this idea of 'being a wallpaper person', she discovered that, although it gave her a feeling of emptiness, it was also serving a useful purpose: it protected her from taking any risks. She had a motto: 'Nothing ventured, nothing lost.'

Beginning to work towards overcoming this feeling of emptiness often requires a number of things.

- A preparedness to take risks and learn how to cope with failure, disappointment and possible rejection.
- A willingness to explore the possibility that emptiness may, in some way, be protecting you from other fears (e.g. of failure, and taking risks).
- A recognition that emptiness is a form of emotional reasoning – e.g. 'I feel empty therefore I am,' which, of course, does not make it true.

To start to challenge the idea of inner emptiness, let's be clear that you do have preferences, desires, wants and wishes. The pattern of your preferences make you a unique person. Now, if you do have preferences, wishes and wants, you can't be empty or just wallpaper. For a start, you probably want to feel different from how you do now. So that must mean that you desire to achieve a certain state of mind – i.e. non-depressed.

Let's begin by looking at your preferences. What kinds of films do you prefer and what kinds of films do you tend to avoid? What kind of music do you like and what leaves you cold? What kind of food do you like and what makes you feel sick? Would you prefer to eat a piping-hot baked potato or a raw snake or a cockroach? So you *do* have preferences! What kinds of people do you like and feel comfortable with? Which season do you like best? What kinds of clothes do you prefer? If you say that you have no preferences, try wearing a salmon pink top with fluorescent green trousers that don't fit!

People who feel empty need to awaken something inside themselves. It is as if that 'thing' is asleep. Think about what would happen if it did wake up and you started working on and developing your preferences. Since this means not only thinking about your preferences but also acting on them, this might lead to some anxiety. If so, try to write down your anxious thoughts and challenge them – see if your fears are exaggerated. How could you take steps to overcome your anxieties?

Okay, so you admit that, however mild they might be, you do have preferences. Therefore, you are not completely empty: your situation is not all-or-nothing. But then you might say, 'Yes, but I don't have any qualities that another person might find attractive.'

If this is what you think, then your feelings of emptiness may possibly be more related to *loneliness*. Or it may be that it is a problem of confidence. Have you shared your preferences with others? If not, what stops you? What would it take to turn to someone you know and say, 'I'd like to do this or that. Would you?' If you find that you have thoughts of 'But they may not want to, or they might think that I was being silly or too demanding,' the problem is less one of emptiness and more one of confidence.

It may also be that you are being unrealistic. Do you want to be attractive to some people or to everyone you meet? Are you too focused on social comparison (*see* pp. 114–17)? Do you believe that, because your parents didn't seem that interested in you, nobody will ever be?

The challenges for this kind of emptiness might include:

- Telling myself I'm empty is a form of emotional reasoning.
- I can learn to focus on my preferences and start to share these with others.
- Emptiness is not a black-and-white issue, not all-or-nothing.
- I may be discounting the positives in my life and saying that some things about myself don't count. If so, what would they be?
- I might be self-labelling here and not appreciating that all human beings are highly complex.
- Maybe it is not so much that I am empty but that I am lonely and I have difficulties in reaching out to others.
- Maybe it is a problem with confidence. If I felt more confident in expressing myself, would I feel empty?
- Am I attacking myself by saying that nobody could be interested in me without giving them much of a chance? If so, how could I give them a chance?

The Nuisance

Nearly all of us humans want the approval of others. This often means that we want to be seen as having things (e.g. talents and abilities) to offer others. And it may be easier to care for others than to be cared for. One problem that can arise is that, when we have needs that can only be met by sharing our difficulties with other people, we feel that we are being a nuisance and may not deserve to be cared for. People can be riddled with guilt and shame about needing help. In their early life, their needs may not have been taken seriously. One patient of mine – whose motto was: 'A problem shared is a problem doubled' was constantly monitoring the possibility that she was a burden to others. This led to guilt and feeling worse, which, of course, increased her need to be cared for and loved.

The fear of being a nuisance is a sad one. It often means that these people have difficulty in being fully open about their needs and asking others for help. Instead, they tend to 'beat about the bush' when it comes to their own needs and feelings, and send conflicting messages to others. Sometimes patients come to therapy but feel awkward, and instead of getting down to the business of trying to sort out what they feel and why, they constantly worry about burdening me. I try to explore this fear of being a nuisance quite early on. Sometimes it relates to shame, sometimes to a fear that I won't be able to cope with their needs because these are too great and complex. At other times it relates to trust: they think that, while I will be nice to them on the surface, secretly I will be thinking that they are time-wasters, that I will deceive them about my true feelings.

Some challenges to these thoughts might include:

- All humans have a need for help from time to time.
- Am I labelling and criticizing myself for having these needs rather than facing up to them and understanding what they are?
- What does my compassionate/rational mind say about that?
- What is the evidence that others won't help me if I ask them?
- Am I predicting a rejection before it comes?
- Am I choosing to ask people for help who I know in advance are not very caring or would have difficulty understanding my feelings?
- Am I saying that all my needs must be met before I can be helped and therefore am thinking in all-or-nothing terms? Are some of my needs more important than others? Can I work on a few specific problems or needs at a time?

- Can I break my needs down into smaller needs, rather than feeling overwhelmed by such large ones?
- Can I learn to be more assertive and clear about my specific needs? Would that help me?

There is another aspect that can be useful to consider. Sometimes we know that we are in need of healing or help and that we have to reach out to others, but we don't know what for or what exactly our needs are. That takes some thought. But if you do become clearer on these issues, consider: 'What will you do to help yourself if you do find someone who can meet some of your needs?' This is quite an important question. Of course, you might feel happier with some of your needs having been met, but how will this change you? How will you use these met needs for personal growth?

Sharon was afraid to ask her husband to spend more time with her and to be more affectionate. She thought that this would interfere with his work and that she was simply being a nuisance to him. However, as she explored these needs and considered how she would be different if they were satisfied, she realized that she actually needed his support and approval to boost her own self-confidence and then she would be more able to go and look for work. By thinking what she would do if some of her needs were met – that is, how this would change her – she recognized two things: first, that there were things she could do for herself to help boost her own confidence (e.g. not criticizing herself and learning to be more assertive); and second, she recognized that she could be clearer with her husband about the fact that she wanted him to help her gain confidence to go looking for work.

Let me make one final point about being open about our needs in our close relationships. Sharon also realized that seeking more affection from her husband might not be a burden but would actually strengthen the relationship, and this was something she could test. On reflection, she saw that her husband may well benefit from talking more about his feelings and needs, too. She was able to see that her needs could be joint needs. When she spoke to her husband about this, at first he did not really understand. But she stuck to her guns, and later he, too, came to see that he had been so focused on work that he had become lonely in himself and felt their relationship was drifting. Moreover, he admitted that he knew that Sharon had felt down but was not sure what to do because she only spoke about her feelings in a general way, not the problems that lay behind her feelings – how she was bored and lonely in the house and she wanted to get out and find a job. Also, in order not to burden *her* when she felt down, he had stopped sharing his own problems with her.

So sometimes our needs may seem very personal to us and we may feel that we are being a burden to others, but sometimes we are actually feeling things about the quality of our relationships. If we worry too much about burdening our nearest and dearest, we will all end up not sharing our problems – everyone keeps things to themselves and the emotional quality of the relationship suffers.

Fakery

Related to emptiness but different from it is the feeling that one is a fake. Now from an evolutionary point of view, deception and fakery have been very important behaviors for both animals and humans. Quite a lot of animal behavior depends on fakery and bluff, often preventing serious conflict. It is also important to note that children have to learn how to lie. The ability to lie and fake things is actually an important social skill. Sometimes it is better to be slightly less straight or at least diplomatic with people rather than risk hurting their feelings. Those who insist on being 100 percent honest, believing that genuineness is the most important human quality, can actually be real pains. By being honest, they usually mean having the right to be as critical as they want; they don't think about the other person's feelings, but only their own need to be honest. However, the moment someone is as direct with them, they get really upset. At times, we do need to cover our true thoughts and feelings – too much honesty is not always helpful.

The psychoanalyst Carl Jung argued that we all have a 'persona', or mask, that we wear to make ourselves acceptable to others. We simply would not be able to cope with raw feelings all the time. We need to obey certain social rules and be reasonably polite. However, as in most things, a well-functioning persona is a question of balance (not all-or-nothing). If we back off too much from being honest with people and feel that they are taking advantage of us, we can feel intense inner resentment.

When we become depressed, however, we can feel as if everything we have ever done has been a pretence or a fake, or simply the result of luck. Depressed people begin to devalue their previous or current successes. The reasons for this vary. Sometimes these individuals are perfectionists and think less of things that they feel are not up to standard. They know that there are flaws in their actions or achievements but become overly focused on them. They think that they were pretending to be more competent, more good or better in some way than they now feel is reasonable. When one patient – who held an exalted position in the academic world and had won a prestigious prize – became depressed, he felt that he had fooled everyone and that all his writings were false – of little value.

We may also start to worry about whether the feelings we had for others in the past were genuine or were we just fooling ourselves? However, depression is the worst possible time to start making these kinds of decisions. This is because depression reduces capacity for positive feelings, and we often become less affectionate. In addition, feeling that we are deceiving others can lead to guilt, which we then try to cover up.

When Brenda became depressed, she became preoccupied with having fooled Nick into marrying her and that she was now faking love for him. When she came to see me, we had a conversation that, boiled down to its essentials, went something like this:

PAUL. When you got married, did you think that you were faking your love for Nick?

BRENDA. No, I wouldn't put it like that. I was, to be honest, more unsure about him and more worried than I let on, but we got on okay and I thought it would work.

PAUL. Marriage *can* be a scary time. So maybe you had mixed feelings and were unsure of what to make of those feelings.

BRENDA. Yeah, I guess so. It was a big step to get married and I was worried about whether I was making the right decision.

PAUL. Do you think that being understandably worried about making the right decision means that you were being deceptive?

BRENDA. I'm not sure.

PAUL. Okay, well, let's put it this way. If you are being deceptive with Nick, is it possible that this is because you are confused in your mind and not sure what you really feel about him?

BRENDA. Oh, yes, all my feelings seem confused right now.

PAUL. Okay, well, let's see this problem as one of confusion rather than one of deliberate deception. Sure, right now you may not feel a lot of love for Nick, but we aren't sure why that is. Maybe there are things you are resentful about, or maybe there are other reasons, but if we work through these, step by step, we might get a clearer picture of what you feel. The problem is, if you just attack yourself for feeling that you are deceiving Nick, then you will feel guilty and find it more difficult to sort out your feelings.

This gradually made sense to Brenda. It turned out that, because she had not been passionately in love with Nick from the start, she felt in her heart that she had deceived him and this made her feel terribly guilty. To overcome her guilt, she would do things in the relationship that she did not want to do (e.g. sex, going out), but she also felt resentful for giving in. She felt rather used by Nick. Slowly Brenda began to see that her main feelings were actually anger and resentment. Once she stopped feeling guilty for having deceived Nick and faking love, she could move on to sort out the genuine problems in the relationship. To do this, she also had to recognize that love is complex and not at all like the movies make out. Brenda discounted the positive in her life by only focusing on her negative feelings and the times she felt confused about her feelings for Nick rather than on the times she enjoyed being with him.

Sometimes people feel that they have no choice but to fake things. For instance, they may feel that they have to fake love in order to hold together a relationship or a family or, as in the following example, a career. Mike faked a liking for his boss who, he thought, could sack him if he did not make a good impression. But he came to hate himself for being (as he saw it) weak. However, he could have looked at it differently. He could have said, 'I understand that I need to hold on to this job and I don't have that much power to do this other than creating a good impression and getting on with my boss. Actually, I am a very skilled social operator.' This is not to say that it's okay to fake – that's a personal decision. Rather we need to be honest about it, understand the reasons for it and avoid attacking ourselves for it. If we want to reduce the degree to which we fake things with others, we need to learn how to be more self-confident, compassionate with ourselves and others and assertive. That will be hard to do if we are attacking and running ourselves down.

The fear of being a fake is not only associated with guilt (as it was for Brenda) but carries the fear of being found out. Some people live in constant fear that, because they are living a pretend life, they will be found out, ridiculed and shunned.

Some challenges of fakery might be:

- It may be true that I may have been lucky in some things, but this cannot account for everything I have achieved. I must have some talent even if it is not as great as I would like.
- Sometimes I fake things because I am confused and/or frightened. It would be better to work on this confusion and fear rather than simply attack myself for the fakery and pretence.
- Faking or not faking is rarely all-or-nothing. There are degrees of faking.
- If I say, 'Everything I have done is a fake,' this is an over-generalization.
- If, since I feel like a fake, I believe I *am* a fake, this is emotional reasoning. I need to focus on the evidence for and against.
- Feeling like a fake is often a symptom of depression. My depression may not be giving me an accurate view of things or myself.
- If faking is upsetting me, it would be better for me to understand my reasons for it. I might then be in a better position to change. If I attack myself for faking, I will feel much worse and need to fake more, not less. Let's try to be compassionate here and see what lies behind these feelings.

Fakery and deception are more commonly experienced in depression than is often recognized. And the question of fakery and deception often goes to the heart of many social dilemmas. We can feel intensely guilty when we know that we are not being fully honest and genuine. Or we can feel very vulnerable when we are not confident of our behaviour or performance and think others might spot the flaws and regard us as fakes. The problem is that, in many situations, there is often no one *genuine* feeling but many. If you have a row with your partner today, this does not mean that all the other good times you had together were fake. If you are depressed, this does not mean that the other times when you felt good or achieved things were a pretence. It means that you can feel different things at different times and when in different states of mind.

Key Points

- We often experience ourselves as if we could be summed up in single words (weak, empty, inadequate, unlovable, fake, etc).
- The labels may vary from person to person, but most of them imply a negative rather than positive judgment of ourselves.
- When negative feelings and labels about ourselves become central to the way we experience ourselves, they can influence much of what we feel and think.
- It is helpful to try to challenge these labels.

Exercises

- Look at the labels that appeared on page 122 and see if you think that any of these apply to you. If not, maybe there are others that might apply. Examine whether you tend to sum yourself up in single words.
- Think about when you first started to think of yourself in this way. Is it the depression speaking or was it others who told you these things (labelled you)? If it is the depression, don't believe it. If it is others, think about what was happening at the time. How did it benefit them to label you in this way? Did it stop them having to blame themselves? Were you simply an easy target? If so, tell yourself: 'The time has come to give up the labels that others have given me. I wish to become my own person.' Allow

continued on next page

---

continued from previous page

yourself to think of giving up these labels – you don't need or want them. What effort would that take? What would the advantages and disadvantages be? What would stop you doing this?

- In the original 'thought form', on pages 280–3, are four columns. Here you can use two, which represent the B and D columns on the original form. Begin to use your compassionate/rational mind to challenge these single labels. For example:

Label says	*Compassionate/rational mind says*
I am a failure	This label comes from feeling depressed, and when I am depressed, I tend to think in a lot of negative ways.
	For example, I tend to discount the positives in my life and indulge in emotional reasoning.
	Sure, right now I feel bad – but let's not turn that bad feeling into an attack on the whole of me.
	What evidence is there against this label? Am I being all-or-nothing here?
	If I was helping a friend in a similar situation, what would I say to him or her?
	What would someone who cared for me say? How might they help me look at my other qualities? What could I do to stop myself from saying, 'Their views don't count'?
	Am I comparing myself disparagingly with others?

Try to work out other challenges that might help you. Be aware that you might tend to undermine your challenges. Ask yourself: 'What have I got to lose by going with these challenges for a while and seeing if they help?'

10

Further Methods to Challenge Negative Thoughts

The last few chapters focused on various ideas on how to identify and challenge depressing thoughts and feelings: monitoring your thoughts; developing clarity by writing them down; learning to spot depressive thinking styles (e.g. overgeneralization, all-or-nothing thinking, self-attacking); challenging these thoughts by considering the evidence for and against; and looking for alternatives. This chapter explores some other options for challenging depressive thoughts and feelings. I would suggest that you try some of the exercises in the previous chapters first (so that you have some experience of identifying your thoughts and challenging them) before you try the ideas here.

Using Flash Cards

Flash cards can be used as reminders of the sorts of useful things that you tell yourself when you are feeling depressed. To make a flash card, get a blank postcard or a similarly sized piece of paper. On one side, write down one of your most typical negative thoughts; then, on the other side, write down some key challenges to this. Repeat this exercise for all the negative thoughts you usually have.

For example, suppose that you have the constant thought: 'I will never get better.' On a day when you don't feel quite so bad, write out this thought on one side of a card. Now, on the other side, write down what you imagine you might say to a friend or how you imagine someone who cares for you might speak to you. Remember, try to consider these ideas not with a cold mind but with as much warmth and friendliness as you can muster – as if someone who cares about you is encouraging you to make your journey out of depression. Here are some ideas:

- It is natural and normal to feel like this because I am depressed.
- This is typical of my depression – it always looks on the dark side.
- Because I feel like this it does not make it true or a fact. The evidence is that people do recover from depression.
- Although I (understandably) want to feel really well right away, I might be trying to achieve too much. Maybe I could aim for just a little improvement and work with that, step by step.
- Focusing on the idea 'I will never get better' will make me feel worse. It would therefore be preferable to focus on what I can do rather than what I can't.
- It would be a good idea to distract myself from dwelling on these thoughts by listening to music or the radio, by taking myself out for a walk or by doing some gardening.
- If I learn to go step by step, I might learn to get more control over my depression. Let's really give it a go and see how far we can get.

When you look at these ideas, how do they seem? Running through your mind are there ways of discounting them – as is typical in depression? Are you thinking 'yes but', or 'this might be okay for others but not me'? If you are having these thoughts, remember – this is the depression speaking. What have you got to lose by trying? How might you challenge these dismissive thoughts?

Let's try another typical negative thought that involves self-labelling: 'I am a bad, weak or inadequate person for being depressed. I never thought it would happen to me.' Your flash card might list some of the following:

- There is nothing bad, weak or abnormal about me because I am depressed. Up to one in five people could have times when they feel like me – at least to a degree.
- Many people in high places (film stars and politicians) have suffered from depression. Depression can't be about weakness if all these people can get depressed, too.
- There is a lot of evidence against depression being about weakness or badness. Winston Churchill got depressed and he was hardly a weak person.

- I would not speak to friends like this. I would try to understand and encourage them. Labelling them (and me) bad or weak does no good at all. It is just another form of bullying.
- When I get depressed, I focus on all my bad points. I need to focus on what I have done and can do.
- I'm better off not dwelling on depressing ideas. I can try to distract myself right now.

You can carry your flash cards with you (in a pocket or handbag) and take them out to give you a boost and help you focus on controlling negative thoughts. Some people have also found that pinning them up in particular places around the house can be beneficial. For example, a woman I know who wanted to lose weight and had trouble controlling her snacking put a card on her refrigerator. It read:

So you feel like a snack right now? But think about this. Do you really need it? Would you feel better if you resisted the urge? Have a cup of tea instead. Hold on and you will be pleased with yourself tomorrow.

By reading this every time she was tempted to snack, she gained just that little bit of extra control.

Preparing Yourself for Stressful Situations

If you know that you have something stressful coming up, you can prepare for it in advance. You can use flash cards as reminders for coping. For example, suppose you are going to have people over for a meal. One response might be: 'Oh God, it's too much. I'll never cope.' You could write down some key coping thoughts before the event:

- Maybe it won't be as bad as I think. Let's get the evidence.
- I can break down what I have to do into small steps. Each small step might be 'do-able'.
- I can try to avoid filling my head with 'can't do' thoughts even though I don't feel like doing it.
- I can develop a plan of action. I can rehearse the relaxation skills while I'm doing it, keep a check on my body and try to control any tension. Concentrate on what I'm doing. If I start to criticize

myself, I'll say, 'Look, I'm doing okay, not great maybe but okay.'

- When the guests arrive, I can give them drinks and ask them about themselves. People like to be asked things about themselves; the focus does not have to be on me.
- If I feel tense during the meal, I can work on my relaxation. I can get up, go to the kitchen, or go outside for some air. I am not trapped here. I am free to go where I want – it's my house.
- I can try imagining it going off reasonably well rather than only imagining it going badly. The aim is to show myself that I can cope and this is all I want to do right now. I will avoid all-or-nothing thinking (i.e. it has to be great or it's a failure).
- Each step of the way, I will focus on doing okay and try to avoid telling myself negative things. I can do my best to keep my inner helper with me and praise myself for any small success.

The aim of this kind of work is to help you to prepare for things that you might find difficult. The more you try focusing on coping, the easier it may get.

If Emotions Could Speak

Some depressed people say that they do not have clear thoughts going through their minds, only feelings. I remember once driving to work feeling rather down. At first, I could not focus on anything in particular, so I used the technique of 'If my feelings could speak, what would they say?' I tried to get my 'down' feeling to tell me what was wrong. As I followed this idea, I found that I could begin to identify what my 'down' feeling was about. It said, rather out of the blue. 'Your life is going nowhere. You're getting old now and your chances have gone.' As I followed this thought, I recognized that it had been triggered by playing cricket. Through my thirties, I had been too involved with work to play the game, which I had enjoyed in my youth, but had taken it up again in my mid-forties. Although I'd been a reasonable player when at university, I was not now. Compared to the younger players, I was a lumbering oldie with a poor eye for the ball. I suddenly realized that I was grieving for a lost youth! When we allow our feelings to speak freely, they can take us to some strange places.

So if you can't identify thoughts but you can identify feelings, say to yourself, 'If my feelings could speak, what would they say?' Speak out loud the things that come into your mind; let the ideas flow. As you allow your thoughts to flow, be aware of them but avoid trying to direct them anywhere. Just see what comes up, what passes through your mind when you focus on the feelings. Be prepared to draw a blank sometimes or for thoughts not to make much sense. The idea here is to allow yourself to go on your own journey of guided discovery.

Joe felt angry but said he did not have any particular thoughts. I invited him to sit back in his chair, close his eyes, focus on that part of his body that seemed to hold his anger and just let thoughts go through his mind. I said: 'Okay, Joe, feel the anger in your body, go into it. Now, if your anger could speak, what would it say?' Joe found his mind coming up: 'Why do people treat me so badly?' and 'Life is such a shit.'

This was the beginning point for more work. It became possible to focus on precisely what it was that, for Joe, made life a shit. Because of experiences in the past, he felt that he was missing out on things. We were able to explore how, when he felt angry, there was often a background thought that he was missing out. He was then able to see how this thought made his life more painful, thus increasing rather than reducing his tendency to miss out on things and feel depressed. He worked out how he could challenge these ideas with more helpful ones. He came up with:

- I can learn to live from day to day rather than constantly looking back in anger.
- My anger is understandable but not helpful. Anyway, what is gone is gone.
- I can be sad about that but don't have to walk around feeling hard done by all the time as this makes it more difficult to live the kind of life I want *now*.
- In reality, there are some good things in my life, such as my marriage, which I am not making the best of.

He realized that he had been so eaten up with anger about the past that he could not move forward to enjoy life. He also had the idea that he had to hang on to his anger and should remain a living testament of how bad things had been.

Speaking with Different Parts of Ourselves

In the book so far, we have talked about having depressing thoughts, anxious thoughts, angry thoughts, rational thoughts, compassionate thoughts and so on. Sometimes, it is helpful to think of these thoughts as if they represent different parts of ourselves, and use an approach that allows us to name these various 'parts' or types of thoughts. Self-critical thoughts can be called the 'internal bully', self-supportive thoughts can be named the 'inner helper' and so forth. If we give space to these inner selves (types of thoughts), it allows us to observe and listen to the different types of conversations going on inside us. The point is that we are not one-dimensional beings, and in many situations, we can have a mixture of thoughts and feelings.

Sometimes it is useful to imagine that you are an outside observer or, if you prefer, a mediator – someone who is going to invite various parts of yourself to have their say. Here is one way you might do this. Get three chairs. Sit in one of them with the other two facing you. When you are in the chair that you are sitting in, you are the observer or mediator. In one of the chairs facing you, imagine the internal bully. Then, ask yourself, 'What does my bully [self-critical thoughts] say about this or about me?' Then write down all the things that come to mind. When you have done this, go over it, perhaps reading it aloud. Say, 'Okay, I want to check that I have understood the bully's point of view. You, bully, are saying that [your name] is a no-good person because he/she did not work hard enough on _____ , or failed at _____ ' – whatever self-critical thoughts you are having about yourself.

Now focus on the other chair, from which you can imagine your rational and compassionate self (your inner helper) will have a say. The inner helper might say:

> Well it's easy for the bully. Anyone can knock things down and criticize. The bully might think it's tough and strong, but real

strength comes from supporting people when times are hard – not in lashing out at them. Bullying is not helpful. [Your name] needs support and encouragement. The evidence is that the bully is going in for a lot of all-or-nothing thinking [overgeneralizing, discounting the positives, self-labelling and so forth].

Let the rational/compassionate mind (represented by the inner helper) focus on the evidence, and *give examples* of how the bully is indulging in all-or-nothing thinking, etc.

The idea here is to help you externalize and clarify your various inner thoughts, to bring them out into the open. By carrying out this exercise, you will be allowing yourself some space to get to know your self-criticisms and the degree to which they might be affecting you without you realizing it. This will help you gain some clarity on what is going through your mind. It also allows you to try listening to your inner helper.

We can't hold many thoughts in our heads at once. So this process – of allowing the various parts of yourself (the various thoughts that are in your mind) to have their say in a controlled way – can help to make clear which thoughts and evaluations are most important to you. You can try it with different types of thought: anxious thoughts, angry thoughts, sad thoughts, etc.

As you ask the questions and listen to what is said (thought), you as the mediator want to bring some harmony to your inner world. You want to bring some inner peace. So you will always be on the side of the inner helper. You might also gain more insight into your inner self-critical part so that it won't get away with the things that it has done (e.g. all-or-nothing thinking). Again the idea is simply to help you become more aware of your negative thoughts and to try challenging them.

Something else you might find helpful is a 'playful' style, e.g. playing each part as if you were trying to win an Oscar. Now this is not at all easy when we are depressed, but this does not mean we cannot try to be playful and take our inner thoughts less seriously. Another thing you might ask yourself is, 'Does the bully remind me of anyone? If so, who?' Then consider what you would really like to say to that person or persons. I mean, *really* like to say. Look around you – you are alone with just three chairs. You can say whatever you like – absolutely anything.

If you find that you are having a hard time getting your compassionate mind to deal with the inner bully, remember some of the things I've written in this book and try saying them. Put some feeling into this. Remember that the compassionate/rational mind can help to control bullies.

If it is still difficult to bring your self-critical bully under control and you find the exercise makes you feel worse in an unhelpful way, then this method may not be for you. Instead stick with writing things down.

Writing About Yourself

Sometimes it is useful to try shifting perspectives on how we see ourselves. One way of doing this is to write a short letter about yourself, from the point of view of someone close to you who cares about you. Such a letter might include:

- I have known [your name] for about twenty years. To me, he/she has been _____ .
- I find him/her _____ .
- I think he/she struggles with _____ .
- I like him/her because _____ .
- His/her strengths are _____ .
- It would help him/her if he/she could _____ .
- I think he/she needs to _____ .

Write whatever comes into your mind, although on the whole, I would avoid focusing on negative things – something that, when you are depressed, comes all too easy. This exercise is designed to help you develop the habit of getting other perspectives on yourself. If you like, show what you have written to someone you are close to and trust and see what he or she thinks.

Changing Negative Images

When we are depressed, we often feel as if we are in a deep hole or pit and our internal images are very dark and harsh. Because this internal world can blacken our lives, it is sometimes helpful to work with these images directly. If you feel in a deep hole, imagine a ladder coming down to you and that you are climbing out, rung by rung. It would be nice to jump out in one go, but that's only possible for a superman or superwoman and I have yet to meet one of those. Each time you succeed at something, that's one more rung up.

If your inner image is dark, try imagining getting some light in by installing some windows, or build a door and get out. Try not to accept the image passively but start to change it so that it becomes more healing.

Carol had thought about getting out of a difficult relationship and coping on her own, but her internal image was always of living in some dark, cold place that nobody ever visited and which she never left. Carol thought that some of her dark images might have had their origins in being left in a cot in a dark room as a child. By focusing on one of these images and using active imagination (i.e. moving *into* the image), it became clear just how dark this image of being out of the relationship actually was. Then it became possible to explore and change the image. She imagined what she could do in this place to change it, how she would like her own place to look, how she might decorate it, what pictures she might put on the walls, what flowers she might buy, what friends she might invite around, and so on.

The key thing about images is that, once you have a sense of them, you can work on how you would like them to change. Avoid simply bringing the image to mind and then feeling worse because you are not working to change it. It is changing the image that is important.

Sometimes people enjoy painting. Now when we are depressed we tend to paint dark pictures, but it can be helpful to try to paint healing ones. Think about the kinds of images that are healing. These may be of a country scene or of water – a seascape, for instance. Again the key idea is to acknowledge the dark images but also to introduce light and healing.

To Do or Not to Do?

The main reason for doing things is that they should help you. The primary idea is to avoid only doing things because you feel you *have* to do them – this often leads to exhaustion. Sometimes, in depression, we really do need to do less, not more.

Betty told herself that she had to do things because her therapist had said that this would make her feel better. So she was really doing them because she had been told to, not because she saw the value in doing them. Before embarking on an activity when you are depressed, keep in mind the following questions:

- If I do this, will I feel better for doing it?
- Am I doing enough positive things for myself?
- Am I only doing this because I have to, or have been told to?
- Do I give myself enough praise when I succeed?

Changing Values

We learn some of our values and attitudes because important people in our lives have told us that some values are good and/or punished us if we did not conform to them. Our attitudes towards sex, religion or expressing anger are often learned in this way. Sometimes we adopt values by copying others, even those in society in general. For example, there is concern today that thinness is so highly valued as a female trait that many young women are getting caught in over-restrictive diets that can spiral into anorexia. We take certain of these values into ourselves (i.e. internalize them) and they become *our* values and the ways that we judge *ourselves*.

Getting out of depression sometimes means that we have to re-examine our values and our attitudes. We may find this enormously difficult and painful because we may lose our sense of who we are and have to accept new risk. And to make matters worse, we may feel a great sense of disloyalty in changing our values from the ones our parents have given us. Sometimes we cling to values that are quite harmful to us because, in the back of our minds, we still hope to succeed with them and make our parents (or others) proud of us.

Sam had a high need to achieve and do well because his father had told him that only achievement counts in the world. Sam knew that his achievement style and intense self-criticisms were doing him no good, and he also worked out that the voice of his inner critic sounded very much like his father. And yet despite this insight, he could not let go of the idea 'If I don't achieve anything, I am worthless.' For him to give up these values required him to give up the idea that he would, one day, get it right and prove himself. That had always been his hope, and to abandon that seemed like letting his father down and leaving himself with nothing in life to aim for. It took a long time for him to see that, while achieving things was nice and gave him a buzz, it was not helpful to base his whole self-worth on it; that putting all his eggs in one basket was a severe restriction on his sense of worth; and that his father had been wrong to imply that Sam was nothing without achievement.

To help you explore this, write down two columns. In the first, write down the values that you think that you have learned from others. In the second, list the values you would like to impart to someone you love – e.g. a son or daughter. Here is an example.

Possible attitudes/values I have learned from others in my life	*Attitudes I would like to impart to someone else (e.g. a child or friend) to help them be happy*
Women should not enjoy sex.	Sex can be fun and enjoyed. Everyone has the right to a satisfying sexual life.
You should not express anger.	It is important to be able to express your true feelings and not hide them. Anger can be turned into assertiveness.
Other people's needs are more important than your own.	Everybody's needs are important. If you only attend to other's, you will become out of touch with your own needs and become just a servant. Eventually you will get depressed and be less able to care for anyone.

| Being depressed is a sign of weakness. | Depression is a painful state of mind that needs to be understood. Throughout history, many millions have been depressed. |

Far from being weak or no good, depressed people are often following their values to the letter, bending in every conceivable way to try to make them work. If such people fail at this, they don't re-examine their values but attack themselves vigorously. In fact, it is the strength of their efforts to maintain their values that can, at times, drive them into depression. The main problem here is that, although they may try to 'fight' the depression, do all the things they believe they *should* do and stick rigidly to their (learned) values and judgments, they end up enduring their depression but not actually challenging it. They think that, with just a little more effort, they will win through. But challenging depression may mean exploring values and attitudes that are no longer useful. Working hard to get well may mean working hard to change some of our attitudes – not just following them more vigorously.

Life Scripts

Another way to think about attitudes and values is to tackle them in the form of 'life scripts' or as typical roles we easily slip into. These offer an identity. For example, think for a moment about what kind of person you are. Try completing this sentence: 'I am the kind of person who _____.' You may have many endings, not just one.

What did you come up with? Did you have things like 'I am the kind of person who cares for others/is a hard worker/should never show anger'? Or 'I am the kind of person who always loses out/gives in/gets left behind/fails at the last hurdle'? Or 'I am the kind of person who waits to be chosen rather than actively chooses/does not show off'? The point about life scripts is that they are like parts in a play. At times, it can seem as if we are performing a part written by someone else. We might even blame fate. But over the next few days ponder on how you might answer this question and see if any new ideas come to your mind. See if one of your life scripts – i.e.

a role – seems to repeat. If so, write these repetitions down and think about where this script might have come from. *Gently* consider what you would have to do to change it, how might you act in different ways if you had different values. To begin with, just *play* with a few ideas.

Another life script you might try is: 'I am the kind of person who is or does not _____ .' Here you might note: 'I am the kind of person who is not selfish/deliberately hurtful to others for fun/cheats on others.' Or 'I am the kind of person who does not enjoy sex/put my needs first' and so on. To form an identity often means discovering both things we think we are and things we think we are not.

If you identify a life script – a style of living that makes you 'you' – think about how you might wish to change it. What would you need to do? Can you go some way towards being more as you would like to be?

Key Points

- You can make flash cards with negative thoughts and alternatives to act as reminders.
- Allow your emotions to speak. Give them a voice and then explore their inner meaning.
- Use chairs to enable yourself to express out loud the various types of thoughts that might be going through your mind.
- Consider some of the images that you have in your mind when depressed and try to introduce more soothing and healing images.
- Consider some of your basic life values and attitudes and decide if they are useful to you. For those that aren't, try changing them by thinking about the values you might want to impart to someone else. Those values are more likely to be your own, genuine values and attitudes.
- All of us live out various roles or 'life scripts'. These can be changed if we give ourselves the space to consider what they might be and how we might tackle them step by step.

PART III

Special Problems Associated with Depression

In this section, we will apply some of the ideas discussed in Part II to specific problems in depression, some of which may apply to you and some may not. I have written this section so that the chapters make more sense if you work through them in the order given. If you don't understand certain sections, skip them and come back to them later. Some chapters cover the same ground and same issues but from different points of view.

11

Approval, Subordination and Bullying

Approval

We begin Part III with the issue of approval because a desire to be approved of, recognized, wanted, appreciated, valued and respected is often at the heart of many of our personal conflicts and worries when depressed. When we explore other problem areas, such as shame, anger, disappointment and perfectionism, we will find that the issue of 'approval from others' is often in the background, if not in the foreground.

Some people may become vulnerable to depression because they have an excessive need for approval, sometimes called 'approval addiction'. A person may believe that approval is always good and necessary and disapproval a disaster. Some individuals have a need to impress others and be seen as special. Others feel completely downcast if they are criticized. Yet others feel unlovable or abandoned if they don't get constant approval. Sometimes, the loss of approval affects us badly because we take what others say about us to be the whole truth. If others say that we are unlovable, useless or silly, we feel that this is true (even if their judgments are rather extreme and ignore the positive aspects of ourselves). Or we may overgeneralize, concluding that if one person thinks badly about us, then others will too.

Approval, Shame and Acceptance
For some people, an excessive need for approval comes from a need to make up for feelings of intense inadequacy and shame – i.e. there is a belief that 'If others approve of me, I can't be so bad/inferior.' However, before exploring ways in which we can become less

sensitive to the need for, and loss of, approval, it is important to recognize that the need for approval is very much part of human nature. Think, for a moment, what our world would be like if no one cared what others thought of them, if no one worried about gaining approval.

Much of our competitive conduct is related to gaining approval – whether it be passing an exam, winning a sports competition or beauty contest or even having friends say nice things about our cooking. We often do these things to court other people's approval, to feel valued. We would like them to see us as able and competent, in order to raise our status. We also have a need to belong to groups and to form relationships and so avoid being seen as inferior or rejected altogether. Indeed, people will do all kinds of crazy things to win the approval of others, be this of friends, parents or even God. And the fashion business would have a hard time if we were not concerned with gaining the approval of peers by following the latest fashion. So by obtaining approval, we raise our own status and feel accepted in our groups and relationships.

Keith, an ex-soldier, said that getting drunk and being seen as tough was a way of gaining approval from other men. To be regarded as weak would result in not being accepted and shamed. He had suffered terrible hangovers rather than risk being seen as 'not one of the guys.'

Debby grew up in a very wealthy family where associating with certain kinds of people or having left-wing political views was very disapproved of and seen as shaming. In therapy, she struggled to find her own values and develop a way of living that suited her rather than follow the lifestyle of her parents and social group. Debby was often in conflict with what she felt she 'ought to do' and what she 'wanted to do.' The approval of her parents mattered a great deal to her, and her hardest task was breaking free of the fear of possible family condemnation and finding her own values. There have been many accounts of the agony that people have felt when they have wanted to marry out of their class or religion – and thus risk the disapproval of others close to them. So, following family traditions, or adopting totally the values of the group we are in, can play an important role in our approval-seeking behavior. Nearly all humans have a basic fear of disapproval, especially when it comes from those we value or look up to, or on whom we feel, in some way, dependent. If we do not value the person, his or her approval matters rather less, unless he or she has some power over us – for instance, as a boss might.

Don't criticize yourself if you recognize that you are an approval seeker – frankly, most humans are. The problems come if you are too dependent on it, feel overwhelmed by the loss of approval, and become self-critical without it. You need to try to keep the desire for approval in balance – not all-or-nothing (e.g. I must be totally approved of, or I don't give a damn).

Approval and Self-Judgments

Unfortunately, our need for approval can become a trap when we pursue it to an excessive degree. When this happens, it is not just fear of rejection or not fitting in that causes us problems but our whole sense of ourselves can be affected. We take the approval or disapproval of others to be judgments on our whole selves. We may become very self-critical if we do things that do not meet with approval or are criticized. Coping with disapproval is easier if you come from a loving background because then you are more likely to have developed a basic sense of being 'okay as a person.' But even if your background was not such a good one, there are many ways of learning how to cope with disapproval and reduce an excessive need for approval.

In general, it is helpful to recognize that it is not a good idea to put too much faith in other people's judgments of you. This does not mean that specific criticisms are never valid, but global labels (e.g. 'weak', 'stupid') and put-downs say more about them than you. Even our nearest and dearest can be disapproving some of the time or fail to notice things about us that we would like them to give special attention to. This can lead to disappointments but not serious problems unless we start to attack ourselves or those we love.

For example, Liz had a new hair style and hurried home to show Carl. He had liked her old hair style and was unsure about the new one, so he was cagey about whether he liked it or not. Liz felt deflated and started to think, 'I thought he'd really like it but he doesn't. Maybe I made a mistake. Perhaps others won't like it. Why can't I do anything right?' Liz started to feel inadequate and angry with Carl. Note how Liz's disappointment turned into:

- *All-or-nothing thinking*: 'he doesn't like it,' rather than 'he's unsure' or 'he likes it a little' or 'he may come to like it when he's used to it.'
- *Overgeneralization*: 'others won't like it,' instead of 'I like it and the people in the shop said it looked good. Just because Carl is unsure doesn't mean that everyone won't like it.'
- *Self-criticism and self-attack*: 'why can't I do anything right?' instead of 'a hair style is a hair style and not evidence that I do things right or wrong.'

Liz had developed various fantasies that the new hair style would really impress Carl, and it was a disappointment when this did not happen. If this sort of thing tends to happen to you, consider some of the pointers for coping outlined in chapters 12 and 15, on shame and frustration.

Some people have feelings of inner emptiness if they do not constantly gain the approval of others. Wants, wishes and what were once thought to be good ideas seem to evaporate the moment another person does not go along with them or seems to disapprove. If this is the case for you, think about the possibility that you can start to find your own *self* by exploring your own *preferences*. Search inwards rather than outwards. Review the section on the empty self in Chapter 9. Ask yourself: What things can I value that do not depend on other people's approval? Even if someone disagrees, this is not 'all-or-nothing' – e.g. they are right and I am wrong.

Mind Reading

When we become depressed, we can need so much reassurance that we become extremely sensitive to the possibility that others do not like or approve of us – they might be deceiving us – and we can engage in what is called 'mind reading'. In this situation, rather small cues of disapproval are seen as major put-downs or rejections. A friend hurries past in the street and does not seem to want to talk to you. If you are depressed, you might think 'My friend does not really like me and wants to avoid me,' rather than 'He/she seems rushed and hassled today.' So if you are unhappy with someone's attitude towards you (perhaps because they were critical or ignored you), it is important for you to reflect on the evidence. Ask yourself:

• Did the critical remark or look really represent a major put-down?
• How would I have felt about it if I was not depressed?
• Am I mind reading and thinking that the person thinks more negatively about me than they actually do?
• Am I assuming that a small disruption in the relationship is a sign of a major breakdown in it?
• Am I thinking in all-or-nothing terms or overgeneralizing? For example, am I saying, 'If someone cares about me, they must never ignore or criticize me.'
• What will I think about this event in a week's or month's time – am I likely even to remember it?
• Am I expecting others never to have a bad day and be grumpy and irritable?

The Subordinate Self

The Subordinate Approval Trap

The subordinate approval trap often begins when you feel low in self-worth but you work out that you can feel better about yourself if others approve of you. So you set out on a life's task of winning approval – which, on the face of it, may sound like a good idea. But the way you seek to gain approval might involve various unhelpful things. For example, you might try to be what the other person wants you to be. You might avoid owning up to your own needs. You might hide your anger. You might be overly accommodating, hoping that the other person will appreciate this. Sadly, what can happen is that other people may get used to you simply fitting in, and the odd nod of disapproval can have you hurrying back to please them. So you end up feeling like a doormat and worthless. However, you know how to deal with feeling worthless – you try to win other people's approval – and so around and around we go.

Figure 7

Getting out of this circle requires that you are aware that you are in it, and that it is, to a degree, you who are setting yourself up for it. Next you need to challenge the idea that you are worthless. Remember that this is a self-label and is more likely to be kept in place by your inner bully up to its old mischief. Perhaps you might go back a few chapters and recall how to challenge your inner bully. Remind yourself that 'worthless' is a label and unhelpful. Try not to discount the positive aspects of your life. Focus on what you can do rather than what you can't. What would your friends say about you? Remind yourself of some of the disadvantages of constantly seeking approval and some of the advantages of learning how to accept disapproval without attacking yourself.

Approval feels good but you can't base your self-esteem on it. Try to praise yourself more and avoid disbelieving it when you do. Treat yourself as you would treat a friend. Remind yourself that you do not have to be anyone's servant. Try being assertive about your own needs (*see* Chapter 14).

One of the major problems with an excessive need for approval is that it can lead to a subordinate sense of self. It is as if we can't do much on our own initiative but must always get permission. We feel that we have to ensure that whatever we want to do is approved by others. This kind of subordination increases our vulnerability to depression.

The Puppet

A puppet, as we all know, is a toy that moves when the strings are pulled by a puppeteer. Pull the strings up and down and the puppet dances; let the strings go slack and the puppet flops. At times, if we become too dependent on approval, we are in effect making ourselves into puppet people: if other people approve of us, we feel good, but if they disapprove, we flop.

Of course, approval may matter a lot when it helps us get a job or get on in a relationship. However, a serious difficulty arises when we make negative judgments about ourselves if we don't get the approval we want. If you are wondering if you have puppet tendencies, think of a recent event that upset you which involved either disapproval or criticism. Now write down your thoughts and check if the disapproval sparked off any negative thoughts in you. If it did, consider what the rational/compassionate mind would say.

Here's an example: You put what you thought was a good idea to others at work but they are not impressed and said that it was poorly thought out. Your negative thoughts might include:

- Oh no! They must think I'm not very bright.
- This is terrible. I've damaged my reputation.
- I should have thought it through more.
- I am stupid to have opened myself up to such criticism.
- Why do I always put my big foot in it?

You might challenge these negative thoughts with the following alternatives:

- Well, it's disappointing that my idea did not catch on, but reputations are not damaged in single incidents like this. Maybe I'm upset because my pride's been hurt a little. I can live with that.
- Other people get criticized, too – not just me.
- Nothing risked, nothing gained.
- If I can learn to cope with this type of criticism rather than telling myself how bad it is or how stupid I am, I'm going to be better able to cope in the future and will increase my confidence.
- My self-esteem doesn't need to depend on what others think about my suggestions unless I tell myself it does.

- Even if I fail, this does not make me a stupid person. And in any case, failure is rarely all-or-nothing. There are parts of my idea that are still good – I just need to work on them more.
- I am letting my disappointment mask all the positive aspects of my self.

Pleasing Others

It may also help if you consider whether you work too hard to please others in order to win their approval. If so, you may end up as a subordinate with a loss of a sense of your own identity (*see below*). One of the big disadvantages of being overly dependent on others' approval is that you may do things that you don't really want to do – and then later feel resentful. So one advantage of learning how to avoid being too upset by a lack of approval is that it helps you become more independent. This does not mean that we become selfish and do not care for others, or selfishly follow our own course regardless of other people's feelings, or turn others into servants to fulfil our own needs. Rather, it means that we can be pleased with approval but not devastated without it.

Research suggests that, in mild depression, there is an increased tendency to try to please others, but as depression worsens, people actually give up trying. No one is entirely sure why this is. It may be because of build-up of resentment; it may be because these people no longer believe in their ability to be pleased; it may be because they are simply too exhausted.

A Loss of Identity

Similar to the need for approval is the need to feel appreciated and not taken for granted or exploited. The latter need can involve trying to get other people to see us as valued individuals and not just subordinate to them – we want to be valued as people in our own right, with some status and control over our own destiny. The development of such a personal identity is helped by living in a way that others seem to value or give some credit to. The problem comes when, in situations and relationships, we feel that we have become highly subordinate because of having to 'please the other.' We don't feel valued for ourselves but only as servants to others.

The most extreme example of this is in various forms of abuse (especially sexual). The abused person may feel that they have no real identity of their own but only that given by the abuser.

When we feel ourselves to be subordinate to others, that we are being used by them in a way we do not like, all kinds of changes happen in us. Beth and Martin had a good sex life. Martin was always keen, and at first Beth took this to mean that he really fancied her and she was a 'turn-on' to him. That made her feel good. However, gradually she came to think that, in other areas of their life together, he did not seem so caring. Eventually she had the thought, 'I am just a body to him.' This thought, of being used by Martin and being highly subordinate to his sexual needs, had a dramatic effect on her. She lost all interest in sex, became resentful of Martin and wanted to escape. Moreover, she felt that he had gradually taken over her identity and that she had lost any of her own. Men can have similar feelings but these usually focus on money-making – e.g. men are more likely to think: 'My wife only stays with me because I'm a soft touch, a good pay packet.' Whatever the source of feeling exploited and only a servant to the other, the result is often resentment and a belief in a loss of identity.

However, Beth's thoughts got out of perspective as she became more depressed. Slowly she was able to change her thinking:

- It remains true that Martin fancies me and I don't need to discount that aspect of our relationship.
- I can talk to Martin and tell him that I'm unhappy with other areas of my life.
- I can take more control in my marriage. If I feel exploited, maybe it's because I'm not asserting my own needs enough.
- Martin is not really an unkind man, but he is rather thoughtless at times. I need to help him be more attentive.
- Maybe it's my resentment and unexpressed anger that are also causing problems here.

It had been Beth's feeling used and unappreciated that had sparked off her negative feelings, but she had not had an opportunity to focus on them, challenge their extreme nature and take more control in her marriage. When she did this, she saw that there were problems in the marriage but she felt more able to try to sort them out. And perhaps she had rather allowed Martin to be inattentive for too long. What Beth also realized was that she and Martin needed to engage in more mutually enjoyable activities, not just sex.

A loss of identity can occur when we are in conflict about whether to live for ourselves or for others. Such conflicts can become all-or-nothing issues rather than faced as difficulties in balancing the various needs of each person in a relationship. Nell gave up her job to have children and support her husband, but she gradually found this less and less fulfilling. Over the years, it had become accepted that her husband Eric should do all he could to advance his career, and in the early days, this had seemed like a good idea. But when he was offered a good promotion that involved relocation, Nell became depressed. What had happened?

Nell felt that she had lost her identity, she didn't know who she was any longer and she wanted to run away. She did not want to move to another city but, on the other hand, felt she was being selfish and holding Eric back. Although she had for many years voluntarily subordinated herself to his career, and at first had valued this, she gradually had come to think of herself as merely his satellite, spinning around him, and simply fitting in with his plans. Slowly her subordination had become less and less voluntary. However, she felt it was wrong to assert her own needs, and she was very frightened of doing or saying things that might be strongly disapproved of. Even her own parents said that she should do what she could to support Eric and she worried about what they thought of her. As she became less satisfied with her position in the family, she found it difficult to change it because she thought she was being selfish and 'ought' to be a dutiful housewife. She thought that doing things that might interfere with her husband's progress would make her unlovable. But relocating and leaving her friends was a step too far. As for Eric, he was stunned by Nell's depression for he had simply come to expect her to follow and support him. He had not learned anything different. In fact, Nell's depression was a kind of rebellion.

The first thing Nell had to do to help herself was to recognize the complex feelings and deep conflicts she was experiencing. I then recommended that she watch the film *Shirley Valentine* – in which a housewife goes on holiday to Greece with a woman friend, leaving her husband behind, and then decides to stay on – and to consider her depression as a kind of rebellion – not as a weakness or personal failure (as she did at first) but something that was forcing her to stop and take stock of where she was and where she was going. An important idea was to see the depression as making her face certain things, and this, although painful, could be an impetus for change. When she gave up blaming herself for being depressed and telling herself that she was selfish for not wanting to move house, her depression lessened. We then did some of the exercises for the empty self (*see* pp. 125–6).

Sometimes people feel that they have to accept a subordinate position because they have lost confidence in other areas of their lives. This was certainly true for Nell, so the next thing was to explore with her her loss of confidence. She wanted to go back to work but felt that she was not up to it. Underneath this loss of confidence was a lot of self-attacking – for example, thoughts of 'I'm out of touch with work,' 'I'm not good enough,' 'I won't be able to cope,' 'I might do things wrong and make a fool of myself,' 'Everyone is more competent than me.' Nell had also become envious of her husband's success and his independent lifestyle, but again, instead of seeing this as understandable, she told herself that she was bad and selfish for feeling envious.

Confidence is really related to practice. Think of driving a car. The more you do it, the more confident you will be, but if you rarely drive, you won't have the chance to become confident. It is the same for social situations. Women who have given up work to look after children can sometimes feel very afraid at the thought of returning to work later in life, and this can simply be a matter of being out of practice. If this happens to you, think of whether you lack confidence due to a lack of practice. Avoid the tendency to criticize yourself. Work towards building your confidence step by step. Get the evidence rather than assume that you wouldn't be able to cope. If you give up too quickly, it may be because you are self-attacking.

Nell was also beset with various problems that are not unusual in depression, including intense conflicts of whether to live for herself or for others (partner, children etc.). She was also receiving many signals from her social environment that indicated that she was considered selfish to want to 'do her own thing.' Now if you have these kinds of conflict, avoid developing all-or-nothing thinking – for example, 'I either do exactly what the other wants of me or I do my own thing.' It is a difficult balance to maintain but it is useful if both the needs of self and others are to be catered for. As Nell became more confident she was able to work out some of the issues about moving with Martin. She felt that her voice was being heard.

These conflicts are not untypical of people who feel highly subordinate in relationships. Sometimes the need to please others, gain approval and feel appreciated and valued has led them further and further down a road of being subordinate and self-sacrificing to others. Slowly, the thought comes that they are nothing other than what the other person wants them to be. Feelings of being unappreciated and used can be powerful in depression.

Conflicts Over How to Live

It will take time, but you may slowly be able to take more control of your life. If you can come to terms with a possible loss of approval, this is going to place you in a better position than before your depression: others will not be able to frighten you with their possible disapproval.

At times, people feel inhibited about saying what they really feel because they are worried about what others will think of them. They may worry about being seen as selfish and thus unlovable or inadequate. Kim was married to a wealthy businessman, and before she came to see me, she had been given drugs and told that her depression was biological. She herself could not understand her depression – after all, she had as much money as anyone could want and her husband was not unkind and did not beat her. She thought she should be happy, but instead felt weak for being depressed.

Within a few sessions, Kim began to talk about how she had come to feel like a painted doll. She had to appear with her husband at important functions and often felt 'on show'. Her husband was often away on business trips, and when he returned home tired, she felt that he used her to relax. She began to express her own needs – she wanted to go to university and wear dirty jeans – but she also thought that her needs were selfish and stupid for a woman in her position and would court serious disapproval. She believed that, because her husband could provide her with any material thing, she was being ungrateful and selfish for wanting to live differently. She said: 'Many people would be delighted to have what I have.' She also had many self-critical and self-doubting thoughts about going to university: for instance, 'I'm too old now,' 'I wouldn't fit in,' 'Others will think I'm odd,' 'I'm not bright enough,' 'I'll fail.' Of course, she did not try to discover the evidence for any of these beliefs – and the depression was taken as proof that she would not be able to cope.

When Kim began to help herself to get out of her depression, she started to:

- Learn to take her own needs seriously.
- Change the self-labels of 'ingratitude' and 'guilt' to 'need to develop'.
- Avoid discounting the positives in her current life (e.g. 'Nobody is interested in me for myself,' 'I'm only a doll for my husband').
- See her depression as a signal that her life needed to change, rather than as a sign of weakness.
- Understand how her thoughts were driving her further into, rather than out of, depression.
- Talk more frankly with her husband.
- Find out whether she could cope with university.
- Avoid attacking herself (especially in social situations).

Some people who feel highly subordinate to others can also feel so inferior that they think they don't have the power to change. Once they can give up seeing themselves as inferior and inadequate, they open the door to change.

Subordinate to a Way of Life

In a way, Kim felt as much subordinate to a way of life as to any particular person. Sometimes, it is making money that causes problems, or maintaining a certain lifestyle. A family may have become so dependent on the money that a couple make that their lives revolve around money-making and intimacy falls away. Both partners feel trapped by the demands to 'keep going.' But the evidence is very clear on this: after a certain point, money does not add to happiness. If relationships are totally subordinated to the need to make money, there is often a reduction in intimacy and happiness.

There is increasing concern about these problems in our society today. The fear of losing a job can lead to working long hours. However, even in these situations it is important to try to do what you can to work yourself out of feeling trapped. It can help to share your dilemma with others and try to devise ways to get free of the trap, at least to some degree. Are there some positive activities that could be done that would help? Has the relationship become too split into 'the one who cares for the children' and 'the one who works'? And, most important, is the trap partly due to one person having lost confidence in him/herself? Does he or she see his/her own needs as selfish or impossible?

Sadly, at times people find themselves in situations where there seems little opportunity to develop personally. They feel powerless. They may live in poverty and feel overwhelmed by the needs of looking after children or just coping day to day. Sometimes there are very few positive activities in the person's life and this can be one place to start to change (*see* Chapter 4). However, the important thing is to see the depression as something that has been activated in you and not as a personal weakness.

Approval and Relationships

We have various kinds of relationships, some intimate, others friendly/social and still others that occur in the workplace. When we feel highly subordinate, we think that we need approval and appreciation from others whom we see as more able or powerful than us. However, we may not think that we should also give approval and show appreciation to these people. So, for example, a boss might learn how to praise his/her workers, but the workers are rarely taught how to praise the boss (they are more likely to be taught how to complain). It is surprising how many of us think that approval has to travel *down* through a hierarchy, not up.

This is because we think that those above us don't need approval – they are so much more powerful than we are that our approval does not matter to them. We can be so busy trying to gain their approval and do things to please them that we forget how to show appreciation of what they do give us. For example, Lynne had a great need to be approved of. When I asked her how she showed that she valued her husband Rob, she said, 'By doing things for him, keeping the house clean.' My response was: 'Well, his approval of you makes you feel good, but what do you say to him about how you value him?' Lynne went blank, then said, 'But Rob doesn't need my approval. He's all right. Life's easy for him. I'm the one who is depressed.'

When they were together, Lynne and Rob tended to blame each other for what they were not doing for each other:

LYNNE. You never spend enough time with me.
ROB. But you're always so tired.
LYNNE. That's right – blame me. You always do.
ROB. But it's true. You're never happy.

Around and around we went. Neither Rob nor Lynne could focus on how to offer approval to the other. Instead, they continually focused on the negative and thus there was little to build on. They rarely said things like 'You look nice today' or 'It was really helpful when you did that' or 'I thought you handled that well' or 'You were really kind to think of that.' Lynne tried to earn approval but was not able to give it. It was painful for her to come to see that, in placing herself in a subordinate position, she felt that others should attend and approve of her (and she'd work hard to get this approval) but she did not need to show approval of others. She saw them as more able than her and believed that her approval of them did not matter.

Depression can make us very self-focused in this regard. Sometimes depressed people are resentful of their partners, and giving approval and showing appreciation is the last thing they want to do. It can be useful, therefore, to consider how we can praise those around us – not just do things for them, but show an interest in them and recognize that all humans feel good if they feel appreciated and not taken for granted.

Parent–child relationships can also be like this. Even as adults we might seek the approval of parents but not take an interest in them as people in their own right. Lynne wanted recognition from her mother but rarely praised her.

Relationships are like flowers, they cannot grow unless they are nurtured and fed. And feeding a relationship means that approval has to go both ways. At times, trying to look after children, holding down a job and so forth can make it all too easy for relationships to be taken for granted – the only time a couple may spend together is at the end of the day when each is exhausted. So try to plan activities which are mutually rewarding and enjoyable. Spend time together on positive things and show each other appreciation for sharing those things. Build on the positives rather than be separated by the negatives.

Nonverbal Communication

As I have suggested, humans have a basic need to feel approved of by others. This begins almost from the first days of life. For example, babies are very sensitive to the faces of their parents. If babies are happy and smile at their mothers and they smile back, the positive feelings between them grow. But if mothers present a blank or angry face, the babies become distressed. When mothers and babies are on the same wave-length and approving of each other, we say that they are 'in tune' or are 'mirroring' each other. Throughout childhood, approval signals from parents help us to feel loved and wanted, and later in life they help to make relationships gel and friendships to build. Approval nearly always feels good (unless we are discounting it in some way). It gives us the feeling that we are accepted and wanted and that our efforts are valued (*see* Chapter 3).

The nonverbal communication of some depressed people is very unfriendly. They look grumpy and fed up most of the time and rarely think about how this will affect others. Yet when others become distant, they feel worse. Unless one is very depressed, it is often helpful to try to send friendly nonverbal messages – to smile and be considerate of others. You may protest, 'But aren't you just suggesting that I cover up my feelings, put on an act?' The answer is yes and no. Yes, to the extent that you need to be aware that a constantly grumpy appearance is not a good basis for developing positive relationships – a depressed attitude can push others away. Moreover, if you try to smile and be friendly, this can affect your mood positively. However, the answer is also, to the extent that, if there are problems that you need to sort out, then they need sorting out – don't hide what you feel. But being grumpy and making no effort to be friendly actually sorts out very little – it can lead to brooding resentment in both you and others.

Being Bullied

It is one thing to be criticized and to learn how to cope with that, but it is another to be on the receiving end of bullying. There is now much evidence that being on the receiving end of a lot of criticisms and put-downs (called high expressed emotion) is associated with mental ill-health. These criticisms and put-downs can be verbal, nonverbal or even physical attacks. Indeed, in adult life, approval is not only signalled by the words people use but by the types of attention they give, the smiles, facial expressions and nods. Sometimes, we find ourselves living in a world where approval signals are hard to come by but put-downs are rather common.

As we have seen, the need for approval begins early in life and is conveyed in the facial expressions of child and parent. But even as adults, the sense of being approved of or criticized can be conveyed by nonverbal communication. A smile or a frown can say a lot, and a hug can do much to reassure us. A depressed person may say: 'My husband/wife doesn't need to say anything. I can just tell by the way he/she looks at me that he/she disapproves of me.' Now again there is nothing abnormal about this. In both humans and animals, nonverbal communication can be powerful. If you were going to train as an actor, your talent would be judged not just by your ability to remember lines but by how you say them and your nonverbal expressions and other body language.

Many depressed people become very sensitive to nonverbal communication. Seeking reassurance and sensitive to not getting it, they can become easily upset by how people respond to them nonverbally. Depression makes us very aware of the judgments of others, and nonverbal signals are taken as cues to how others are judging us. We can feel put-down and bullied because we exaggerate the degree of threat in a particular interaction with someone.

Although it is quite common in depression to overestimate the degree and implications of criticism, it can also be the case that put-downs are not exaggerated. The problem then becomes whether anything can be done to change the situation or whether it is best to try to get out of the relationship.

Bullying and Intimate Relationships

When someone is able to make us feel bad 'by a look', in effect they are exerting a certain power over us, so it important to recognize this sensitivity to nonverbal communication and learn how to handle it. If you are living with someone who is depressed, it might help you to realize that your nonverbal attitude can be important. Remember that we often convey warmth (or a lack of it) not just by what we say but by how we say it. I would like to explore a rather extreme example.

Mark rarely said positive things to Jill and acted as if he was disappointed in her. In therapy, he would rarely look at her but instead scanned the room as though uninterested in what was going on. Even when he did say some positive things to Jill, it was said in such a hostile and dismissive way that you could understand why she never believed him. The problem here was not just Jill's depression but Mark's difficulty in conveying warmth. Many of his communications bristled with hostility and coldness; he saw depression as a weakness and was angry at Jill's loss of sexual interest. She came to dread Mark's moodiness and how he would look at her.

Sadly both Jill and Mark had become locked into a rather hostile and disapproving style. She experienced him as a disapproving dominant male, and her life was spent trying to elicit his approval and get some warmth from him. When she failed, she blamed herself and became more depressed, with a strong desire to escape the relationship – for which she also felt guilty and frightened. She held the view that she should make her relationship work regardless of the cost or how difficult it was. She prided herself on not being a quitter. But sadly only if she subordinated herself to Mark's every need could she elicit approval from him. Moreover, she came to believe that all men were like this.

These kinds of problems often require marital therapy. However, if you blame yourself for such problems or are ashamed of them, this might stop you from seeking help. If you feel frightened and are not sure where the next put-down is coming from (be this in a close relationship or at work), it is possible that you are caught up in a bullying relationship. The degree of your fear can be a clue here – although consider whether you would be fearful if you weren't depressed, because sometimes we become fearful of others because of depression. I have certainly come across many couples who fight a lot, feel resentful and so forth, but they are not necessarily frightened of each other. So fear may be a key.

The first thing is to be honest with yourself and consider if a frank exploration of your relationship and its difficulties would be of benefit. Sometimes it is the bullying partner who feels ashamed about examining feelings of closeness and how to convey affection. Mark, for example, came from a rather cold and affectionless family and felt uncomfortable with closeness. He acted towards Jill in the same way that his father had acted towards him and his mother. As Jill came to recognize this, she gave up blaming herself for his cold attitude, and although this did not, of itself, cure her depression, it was a step on the way. She learned that trying to earn approval from a person who found it virtually impossible to give was, sadly, a wasted effort. Eventually the relationship ended.

So the lesson of all this is: Don't blame yourself for another person's cold attitude towards you. If you do you are giving too much power away to the other person. Research has shown that a woman still living with an abusive partner will often blame herself for the abuse inflicted on her, but will come to see it as not her fault if she moves away. So try using the 'responsibility circle' (Figure 5, p. 106) and see how many things you can think of that might be causing the problem. What are the alternatives for the other person's cold attitude?

Another thing you can try is to openly discuss these issues with your partner. It may be that the relationship has drifted to such an extent that you have forgotten how to value each other and are taking each other for granted. Try to put aside a special time when you can be close and talk about things. Review your relationship together. See if you can pinpoint where it went wrong and what was happening at that time. Try to be honest with each other. If you are, you may say some unpleasant things to each other, but try to share these in the spirit of reconciliation. Remind yourself that the reason for having this discussion is to improve closeness – not just to get your own back. And you may need to examine closely whether you are guilty of all-or-nothing thinking: 'I must stay in a relationship, come what may.'

Finally, sometimes it is necessary to recognize that a relationship is abusive and that it will be extremely hard to get out of your depression unless you also get out of the relationship.

Bullying at Work

A key theme so far has been that, although we can be very sensitive to the opinion of others, we must be careful not to swallow their views of us hook, line and sinker. There is increasing concern today at the amount of bullying that goes on in families and schools and at work. To be on the receiving end of a bully's attacks can be pretty depressing. As a society, we need to learn how to be more accepting of others and less unkind. As individuals, we also have to learn how to protect ourselves as best as we are able from the effects of bullying.

You can sometimes spot a bully because you will not be the only one who experiences his or her attacks. So it can be useful to get the views of others – get the evidence that it is not just you. For example, in the case of Jill and Mark, many of their mutual friends saw Mark as a 'difficult' person. When Jill thought about this evidence, it helped her to give up blaming herself.

Colin became depressed when a bullying boss came to work at his company. The boss would attack and criticize his work, and gradually Colin lost confidence in his own abilities. He began to help himself when he changed his thinking:

- Just because the bully says I'm no good does not make it true.
- I've done good work in the past, and my colleagues think my work is good.
- The boss is using all-or-nothing thinking and disregarding the positive aspects of my work.
- Other people have the same problems with him that I do.
- Maybe I want his approval too much and feel enraged when I don't get it.

Another set of Colin's beliefs had increased his depression: 'I should be able to cope with this. I'm letting him get to me. If I were a real man, I'd put him in his place. I shouldn't let him get away with it. I'm weak.' Thus, his (in)ability to stand up to the bully was taken as evidence of his lack of manliness and weakness.

Disapproval and criticism by others can be used to judge ourselves. Once Colin gave up seeing his problems with the boss as a test of his manliness, he was able to work out other ways to deal with it. In this case, he accepted his limitations and sought a transfer to another department. I agreed with him that, in an ideal world, the bully would be brought to account – but Colin was taking too much personal responsibility for sorting out his boss and he simply did not have the power or support to do it. Colin understandably remained angry about this, but his depression subsided when he gave up seeing himself as weak. Sometimes the best response to a bully is to get away, if this is possible, and/or get others to support you. Don't turn it into some kind of individual test.

In sexual harassment, however, specific individuals may be picked on. Others may not experience the bully in the same way. If this happens to you, again try to obtain support from others and to be as assertive as possible. Raise the issue as openly and frankly as you can at work. Don't be stopped from raising the issue with thoughts of 'it's only me'.

Key Points
- If we become too focused on gaining approval, we can become like puppets and subordinate to the needs of others.
- We can get caught up in a subordinate approval trap, in which the only way we see to gain approval is to become more subordinate and pleasing to others – to sacrifice our own needs and wishes.
- We can become subordinate to the lifestyles of others, or even to a lifestyle we may, at one time, have chosen. This can lead us to feeling that we have lost our own identities.
- When we lose a sense of our own identities we are actually saying that we have lost control of where our life is going. This

continued on next page

---

continued from previous page

is often associated with confusion and a loss of confidence. The best approach is to take your own needs and preferences seriously and avoid attacking yourself, which undermines confidence.

- Just as you need approval and signs of acceptance, so may others around you. It is important that you don't discount this aspect.
- Sometimes we accept the judgments of a bully as true reflections of ourselves, and/or we think we ought to be able to put the bully in their place – and we are weak if we can't. However, sometimes the best response is to seek help from others and/or get away.

Exercises

Use the 'thought form' to work through these exercises. Write down your negative/depressing thoughts, try to identify the kinds of thinking styles you might be using (e.g. all-or-nothing thinking, discounting the positives, self-blaming, etc.) and then look for the evidence against these ways of thinking. Use the rational/compassionate mind to consider and suggest alternatives.

- First, consider how you deal with approval. Do you discount it in some way? If so, the next time someone says something nice to you, try accepting it without 'reading between the lines.' Monitor your thoughts if you discount praise, and challenge those thoughts.
- Consider what goes through your mind when something that you did that you thought was good is hardly noticed by others. Are you making more of this than you need to? Check yourself for self-attacking thoughts (e.g. 'If I were more powerful, good or did this even better, they'd notice'). Try the alternative thoughts of: 'Well, I would like them to notice, but if they don't, this does not mean it's no good. I can still value something even

continued on next page

if others don't. In fact, it may be my ability to hang on to what I value, even if others may not see much in it, that makes me a unique person.'

- If you feel that you must please others, write down your thoughts about what would happen if you don't. Are you afraid of their reactions? Are you putting yourself down and labelling yourself as, say, selfish? If so, work out some alternatives. For example, 'If I don't want to be a satellite to someone else, I need to try to put forward my own views. What thoughts stop me?' How could you think in a different way that takes both yours and the other person's views into account?

- If you are on the receiving end of bullying, check to see if you are blaming yourself. If so, how could you give this up? Are you taking the bullying as a judgment on yourself in some way? If so, how would a compassionate friend speak to you?

12

Confronting Shame

Of all the emotions that are likely to reduce our ability to be helped, to reach out to others and to treat ourselves with compassion, shame is the most important and destructive. Indeed, people can feel ashamed about being depressed, so they try to hide it from others. If you can recognize your inner shame and work to reduce it, you will do much to heal yourself.

The word 'shame' comes from the Indo–European word *skam*, meaning to hide. Adam and Eve ate of the apple of the tree of knowledge, became self-aware and realized their nakedness. At that moment, they developed a capacity for shame and the need for fig leaves – or so the story goes. Part of their shame was fear that, having transgressed against God's instructions, they would be punished. In general, shame – like embarrassment, pride, prestige, status and integrity – is related to how we think others see and judge us. The potential for shame is universal, but sometimes this can get completely out of hand.

The Feelings of Shame

The emotions and feelings of shame are varied and include feeling inferior, self-conscious, angry, inhibited and very frightened. The most powerful experiences of shame often arise from feeling that there is something both different and inferior/flawed or bad about ourselves. We may believe that, if others discover these flaws in us, they will ridicule, scorn, be angry and/or reject us. So shame is an extreme form of the fear of a loss of approval.

We can feel paralyzed by shame and acutely aware of being scrutinized and judged by others. Shame not only leads us to feel inferior, weak or bad in some way but also threatens us with the loss of valued relationships – if our shame is revealed, people won't want to help us, be our friends, love or respect us. A typical shame-based view is: 'If you really got to know me, you would not like me.' A major feeling in shame can be aloneness. We can feel isolated, disconnected and inwardly cut off from the love or friendship of others. Shame gives us the feeling that we are separated (different) for others, an outsider.

The Focus for Shame

According to the psychologist Gershen Kaufman, there are at least three areas in which shame can cause us much pain. We can feel shame about our *bodies*, shame about our *competencies and abilities* and shame in our *relationships*. There is an additional one that is especially common in depression: shame of *what we feel*. Let's briefly look at each of these.

Shame of the Body
Some people don't go to see their doctors because of shame. There are all kinds of conditions that people regard as shaming: piles (hemorrhoids), impotence, bowel diseases, problems with the waterworks, bulimia (where people vomit after eating binges). Shame, perhaps more than any other emotion, stops us from being honest with ourselves and seeking help, and there is general agreement that doctors could be more sensitive to this. Sadly, people who have various disfigurements can feel shame, especially if others laugh at them, reject them or appear disgusted by the way they look.

People who have been sexually abused often have an acute sense of body shame. They can feel that their bodies have become dirty, contaminated and damaged. In extreme cases, these individuals may come to 'hate' their own bodies. Talking about the experiences and feelings of abuse can, in itself, produce strong feelings of shame, and for this reason people may hold back from discussing them. However, healing this shame requires coming to terms with one's body and reclaiming it as one's own.

Concern with the way we look is, of course, a driving force

behind fashion. However, some people feel so awkward and ashamed of their bodies that they will do almost anything to themselves to try to avoid these feelings. Men might spend hours at a gym body building, and women might put great effort into dieting to make themselves thinner. Make-up and plastic surgery may also be used to avoid feelings of body shame.

However, it is one thing to be mildly dissatisfied with one's body, but body shame often involves strong self-condemnation and anxiety at being seen by others. Valerie could not bear to look in a mirror. When she did, she would think, 'You look awful. Why are you so ugly?' This feeling of body shame was linked to an underlying belief that she was not lovable because of the way she looked. She also discounted any positive comments her husband made (e.g. 'He's just saying that to make me feel better').

Shame About Our Competencies and Abilities

Although Melanie would have liked to have played tennis, she had poor eye–hand coordination. When she tried to play at school, she would dread it because every time she hit the ball out of the court (which she often did), she suffered an acute feeling of shame. This kind of shame relates to how we think others judge us when they see us performing physically or mentally.

Pete would become very angry with himself when he was unable to make things work. When things around the house broke down, he took it as a personal criticism of his abilities and manhood. When his car wouldn't start, he would think that, if he were a proper man, he would be able to understand mechanical things and would be able to fix his car. He hated taking it to the garage and showing his incompetency to the garage staff, and so always asked his wife to take it.

In my own case, my poor English has often been a source of mild shame. Dyslexic children also often experience much shame and feelings of being defective and inferior.

The main point here is that, when we try to do things and fail, this can be a source of shame. It is made worse when we rate ourselves as good–bad and attack ourselves for failing. As a rule, it is easier to cope with mild shame if we don't attack ourselves. The next time you feel embarrassed at a failure, check to see if you are self-attacking and try to bring your rational/compassionate mind into play.

Shame in Relationships
You can sometimes tell that someone has a relationship shame problem because he or she usually respond badly to criticism and conflicts. Shame-prone people are liable to become angry, sulk or give in quickly. Some like to be in control in relationships and beyond criticism. Such people have difficulty owning up to their own vulnerabilities for fear that, if others become aware of them, they would be marked down as weak and inadequate.

There is also increasing concern in our society that some people (especially, but not only, men) are very prone to shame when it comes to expressing feelings of affection in relationships. Some feel awkward when confronted with gentleness, touching and hugging. It is as if there is an invisible wall around them. In situations of close intimacy, their bodies stiffen or they back away. Men may hide their shame by clinging to the idea that 'grown men don't do that sort of thing' or that to be tender is 'to be soft and unmanly.' This can cause problems in how they act, as intimate friends, lovers and fathers. For example, children often seek out physical affection, and it can be very hurtful to them if their fathers push them away when they try to get close.

Shame of What We Feel
We sometimes try to conceal our true feelings for fear of the consequences. We can be ashamed of feeling anxious, tearful or depressed. We can also be ashamed of feeling angry – as if by having these feelings there is something wrong, flawed and/or unlovable in us. For many years, Alec suffered from panic attacks. He dreaded going to meetings in case the signs of his anxiety showed, and he was so ashamed that he did not even tell his wife. Eventually he broke down, became depressed and could not go to work. Then the story of his long suffering came out. From a young age, his father had told him that real men don't get anxious; they are tough and fearless. When Alec had been anxious about going to school, his father had been dismissive and forced him to go – shaming him in the process. By the time he was a teenager, Alec had learned never

to speak of or show his inner anxieties.

Susan, who was married, met another man to whom she felt very sexually attracted. She flirted with him and would have liked the relationship to become sexual, but she felt deeply ashamed about her feelings and that she was a very bad person for wanting such things. As she came to understand that such (sexual) feelings are natural and to explore what it was about the relationship that so attracted her, she discovered a desire for closeness that she could not get from her husband. This, of course, raised the question of what she could do about that, but it helped stop her being ashamed of her feelings and allowed her to accept that she like other human beings wanted closeness – and good sex.

Jenny's mother had told her that sex is dirty – just something that men enjoy because they are more primitive and superficial than women. When Jenny later had sex, she could sometimes push these thoughts aside, but afterwards she was left with the feeling of being dirty and of having betrayed her mother's values. When she monitored her thoughts during the day, she noticed that, when she had sexual thoughts and feelings, she would also think: 'These are bad thoughts. A good woman doesn't have these feelings – therefore I'm dirty, and if my mother knew what was going through my mind, she would be disgusted and disappointed with me.' Jenny then distracted herself from her sexual feelings and turned them off. However, when she was clear that she was having these kinds of thoughts (and she had to really focus to 'catch' them going through her mind), she was able to say to herself:

This is my sexual life and it does not belong to my mother for her to control. If I feel sexual, this is because I feel sexual and it has nothing to do with being dirty. My sexual feelings also give me energy and are life-enhancing. I don't need to act out my mother's sexual hang-ups in my own life.

Andrew was ashamed of his homosexual desires. Brought up in a strict religious way, he thought that they were a sin against God and that he was a bad, worthless human being for having them. With some struggle, he began to explore the possibility that there were alternative ways to think about and explore his sexuality – without being ashamed of it.

Gary was ashamed of his anger and rage. When he became angry, he felt terrible, unlovable. He said that he just wanted to act like a decent human being, and more than anything, he felt that his anger made him a horrible person. Indeed, the bully in him often told him that he was horrible, ungrateful, selfish and self-centred. As a result, he could not explore all the things that hurt him and the reasons behind all his anger. Instead, he simply tried to keep a lid on his anger rather than acknowledge its source and heal it.

At times, Patricia felt very tearful, but she would not allow herself to cry – she was too ashamed. Leo hid the extent of his drinking out of shame. Zoë was too ashamed to talk about the fact that her husband was abusing her. Amanda could not go far from her house just in case, needing to use the bathroom, there was none available and she would wet herself . . . And so we can see that shame can operate in many areas of our lives. It can be a huge block to healing and coming to accept ourselves. We may feel ashamed at revealing our pain and difficulties – so we hide them.

Deeply shaming experiences are not easy to forget. They can weave themselves right into the fabric of our being. Shame can lie within us, ready to pounce. And when we feel shame, we often ruminate on it, going over and over it in our minds.

The Origins of Shame

If shame is so powerful, where does it come from? Well, one answer is that we all have the internal capacity to feel shame – that is, it is part of our evolved minds. In effect, shame alerts us to all those situations that could be detrimental to us – such as being rendered inferior and subordinate, rejected and ostracized. These have always been serious threats to animals and humans, and over millions of years we have evolved, within our brains, the capacity to be alert to them and take defensive actions. Shame operates on the 'better safe than sorry' rule (*see* Chapter 3). In other words, the brain makes the decision: 'It is better to conceal this [aspect of ourselves] or change it rather than risk rejection.'

There are a number of other theories about the origins of shame. According to one view, evolution has equipped children to enter the world as social beings who need positive things from others.

Our entry into the world is marked by an enormous need for relating, care, joyfully shared interactions and recognition. The treatment we receive at the hands of those who care for us will have a major effect on whether we move forward with confidence (the result of the many positive experiences encountered while growing up) or with a sense of shame, of being flawed, not good enough, lacking value or worth. Research has shown that the way the caregiver and infant interact has a major effect on the infant's nervous system, emotions and sense of self.

Shame can arise from at least three different types of reactions to the treatment we received from our parents or others who have cared for us in our early lives: thwarted efforts to be recognized as good and able, pressure to conform, and direct attacks and puts-downs.

Failure to be Recognized as Good and Able

Consider the following scenario. Three-year-old Tracy sits quietly, drawing. Suddenly she jumps up, rushes to her mother and proudly holds up her drawing. The mother responds by kneeling down and saying, 'Wow – that's wonderful! Did you do that?' Tracy nods proudly. 'What a clever girl!' In this encounter, Tracy not only experiences her mother as proud of her, she also has emotions *in herself about herself* – she feels good about herself. Tracy gets positive attention. However, suppose that, when Tracy went to her mother with her drawing, her mother responded with, 'Oh God, not another of those drawings. Look, I'm busy right now. Can't you go off and play?' Clearly, this time the way that Tracy experienced her mother, the interaction between them and the feelings in herself about herself were quite different. Tracy would be unlikely to have had good feelings in herself and may have had a sense of disappointment and probably shame. Her head would have gone down and she would have slipped away. Thus, a lack of recognition and dismissal of ourselves, when we try to display something attractive to others, can be shaming. Experiences like this happen in even the most loving of homes and the child learns to cope, but if they are common and arise against a background of insecurity and low parental warmth, they can, over time, be quite damaging.

One of my patients who read this section said that it brought back memories of herself as a child, when she would be sent to her room to play and 'just keep out of the way.' Throughout her life, she had never felt deeply wanted and had developed a sense of being in the way and a nuisance.

When people fail to win approval or praise, they can often feel shame. Remember Anne who felt her dinner party had been ruined because she had overcooked the meal? Her experience was one of shame – an intense anger with herself and wanting to hide.

Donna's parents were very ambitious. They wanted the best for her and for her to do her best. If she came second or third in class, they would immediately ask who came first and indicate that coming second or third was okay but not really good enough; with a bit more effort, she could come top. Donna came to believe that nothing, other than coming top, was good enough to win the approval from her parents that she so desired. Anything less always felt like a disappointment for them and herself. Well, you can guess what this all led to – an underlying belief that, unless she did everything perfectly, she was flawed and had let herself and others down. Thus, failures were always deeply shaming, and Donna was rarely able to focus on what she had achieved but only thought about how far short she had fallen.

Pressure to Conform

We all have a very strong desire to conform and be accepted. We want to feel that we belong somewhere. We follow fashion and express the same values as others so that we can signal that we are one of the group. We are highly motivated to try to be valued by others rather than devalued. Men, for example, may try to conform to cultural stereotypes of being tough, competitive, strong and independent and by not showing feelings (which could be taken as a sign of weakness). Women may feel ashamed if they can't reach the standards set by others of their set. They are not supposed to be hypersexual or aggressively competitive. They are supposed to be sexually coy, caring, attractive, non-aggressive, sensitive and loving. All around us are values and standards we are supposed to conform to if we don't want to be shamed.

We may even try to avoid shame by going along with others, showing that we are the right stuff – even if, in the centre of our beings we know that our action is immoral. Keith, the ex-soldier, told me that getting into fights was often more to do with avoiding the shame of not fighting than with any real enjoyment or desire to fight, yet no one wanted to 'break ranks' and point this out. Conforming to cultural values to avoid shame is a powerful social constraint. To risk exposure to shame is to risk not being accepted and not belonging.

Direct Attacks

We also know, of course, that children and adults can be shamed directly by being told that they are stupid, bad, don't fit in or are unwanted and by being physically attacked. Indeed, some people will deliberately use the threat of and the human built-in aversion to shame to control others. So shame not only arises because approval and admiration of a performance are withheld; direct verbal and physical attacks can shame, too.

The Shaming Loop

As we enter depression, we can get caught up in various 'circles' of negative thinking and behaviour. Shame, too, can lead to different forms of self-perpetuating difficulties. This is particularly true with teenagers, adolescence being a time when the approval of peers and the potential for shame can have major effects. Many children are prone to being teased, but sadly some more than others. At times, this can lead to what I call a 'shaming loop' (see Figure 8).

Coming to terms with teasing can be important for adolescents, and might lead a person to do all kinds of things to ensure that he or she is not rejected. One way is to find other friends, or learn to ignore the teasing. Simon, however, told me that he stole from local shops to give things to 'friends' so that he would be accepted and win some status/prestige from them. Sadly, through much of his life he had felt that he had to give 'tokens' to others before they would accept him.

So it is not always the case that feeling inferior leads to social withdrawal – but it can do. This is more likely to be the case when people label and attack themselves. When such thoughts do lead to social withdrawal, then such individuals are also more likely to be rejected because they signal their feelings of inferiority to others.

Figure 8   The 'shaming loop'.

Now, unfortunately, adolescents particularly, but also adults, do not find withdrawn behaviour attractive. So the very thing that these people were hoping to avoid – being seen as inferior and being rejected – can happen because of the way they behave. However, if you stop being self-critical and labelling yourself as inferior, and learn to expect criticism from time to time, you are less likely to become withdrawn and thus less likely to be ignored or rejected. One cannot avoid criticism, but one can learn not to be knocked out by it.

Avoiding Shame

If shame is so powerful, how do people cope with it? One way is to avoid it by avoiding being seen as inferior, weak and/or vulnerable. While the methods below may work in the short term, problems can arise if they are adopted for a long time.

Compensation

This involves efforts to prove to yourself that you are good and able, and to avoid at all costs being placed in an inferior position. Sometimes we engage in vigorous competition with others to prove our own worth to ourselves and others. It is as if we are constantly in a struggle to make up for something or prove something. Of course, we are trying to prove that we are not inferior, bad or inadequate and thus can be accepted rather than rejected.

Concealment

This occurs when individuals hide or avoid that which is potentially shameful. Body shame (including shame of disease) may lead to various forms of body concealment. In the case of shameful feelings, we may hide what we feel. Other people are always seen as potential shamers who should not be allowed to peer too closely at our bodies or into our minds. When we try to deal with shame in this way, much of our lives can be taken up with hiding – even hiding things from ourselves. We can repress memories because they are too painful and shameful to know and feel.

Laughter may be used to distract from shame. We may make jokes at times we feel shame to divert others' attention from it. Joking, when used to stop us from taking ourselves too seriously, can be very useful, but laughter employed to avoid shame often feels very hollow underneath.

Concealment can at times produce another form of shaming loop. For example, Janine would become defensive and irritated if the members of her therapy group began to touch on issues that caused her shame. This made the other group members irritated in turn. They felt she was not being honest or facing up to her problems. This actually caused Janine to feel even more shame and she closed down even further. So her way of trying to hide her shame actually produced more shaming responses from others.

Violence/Attack

'If you shame me, I'll hit/hurt you.' This is retaliatory shaming or humiliation. Violence, especially between men, often arises as a shame avoidance strategy – a form of face-saving.

Ray had been caught stealing at school. When his father found out, he gave him a 'good thrashing'. What happened here is that Ray's father felt shamed by his son's conduct, believing that his son had disgraced him and the family. Not able to recognize or deal with his own shame, the father had simply acted out his rage on his son. This, of course, compounded Ray's shame and anger. Had Ray's father not felt so ashamed of his son, but instead had been concerned to help him, he might have been able to sit down and explore what this stealing was about.

Natalie and Jon had a disagreement in public, and Natalie contradicted Jon. When they got home, he threatened her, saying in a very menacing way, 'Never show me up in public again or else!'

Now usually shame and counter-shaming interactions do not reach the stage of violence. None the less, they can involve a good deal of blame and counter-blame. Each person attempts to avoid being placed in the bad or wrong position. Let's recall the inter-action between Lynne and her husband Rob from the last chapter.

LYNNE. You never spend enough time with me.
ROB. But you're always so tired.
LYNNE. That's right – blame me. You always do.
ROB. But it's true. You're never happy.

This blaming and counter-blaming is a form of 'shame passing'. It is as if someone has to agree that he or she was wrong. The moment we shift to a more positive way of resolving the conflict, the shame cycle might be broken. For example, Lynne could have said, 'I really enjoy the time we spend together – how could we organize our time to do it more often?' Rob could have said, 'Well, I can understand how you would be upset by that.' They would avoid 'all or nothing' blaming and could try to work on the positive aspects of their relationship and try to resolve their problems.

Projection

Projection is used in two ways. In the first type, you may simply project on to others your own opinions of yourself. So if you think that your performance is not very good and label yourself as a failure, you believe that others will think the same. You assume that you are not very lovable so you take it as read that others will think so, too. You feel that crying is a sign of weakness, so you think everyone else does, too.

A more defensive kind of projection involves things about yourself that you are fearful of or have come to dislike. You hide these from yourself, but see them in others. So it is the other person who is seen as the weak, shameful one – not you. Condemning homosexual desire, for example, may be a way of avoiding acknowledging such feelings in oneself (which are feared), seeing them only in others who may then be attacked. Sometimes bullies hate the feelings of vulnerability in themselves and so they attack others in whom they see them. Some bullies label others in the same way that they would label themselves if they could ever reveal their own vulnerability or hurt. Such people project those aspects that they see as inferior in themselves. Racist and sexist jokes can be a result of this.

If people criticize or attack you, it is possible that they see something in you that they don't like in themselves. For example, Sandra often cried about feeling alone. Her husband Jeff would become quite angry at this, which Sandra took as a criticism of her crying. But it turned out that, as a child, Jeff had himself been criticized for crying. Not only did he view Sandra's crying as a criticism of himself (he thought it meant she was not happy living with him) but he also hated the feelings of vulnerability that might lead to himself crying. Thus, Sandra's crying reminded him of things he was ashamed of in himself.

So if people put you down or try to shame you about something (e.g. for crying or failing or needing affection), ask yourself: How do *they* cope with these things? How do *they* cope with crying or failing? If you reflect on this and recognize that they don't allow themselves to cry or they become quite angry when they fail, or they have problems with affection, then it is wise to consider that perhaps they are criticizing you because they can't cope with these things themselves. Whatever you do, don't get caught up in the idea that they are right and you are wrong.

Shame, Humiliation and Revenge

Humiliation is both similar to and different from shame. Both involve painful feelings, of being put down, harmed or rejected. We believe that the other person (e.g. parent, partner, boss) is sending signals that we are unacceptable, inadequate or bad in some way. In shame, we take this as evidence that there is, in truth, something bad about us, but in humiliation, we may not feel this. To use an extreme example, in torture people may be humiliated but do not feel shamed, because they do not see themselves as bad.

So much depends on whether we *blame ourselves* for the insults/ hurts or *blame others*. Of course, this may not be a clear-cut issue, for we can blame both ourselves and others. And we can feel that, as a result of others' bad actions towards us, we have been turned bad. For example, those who have been abused might feel humiliated (and terrified) by the abuse and blame their abusers. But they may also feel that, as a consequence of the abuse, they have been damaged and rendered inferior.

Feelings of humiliation, where we feel unfairly criticized or injured, can ignite powerful desires for revenge. Indeed, you can tell the extent to which you feel humiliated by the thoughts about the injustice done to you that you may have and the strength of your desire for revenge. For some people, their fantasies of revenge are frightening and hidden. In such cases, acknowledgment of anger is a first step. For others, the anger and desire for revenge are constantly present, and they need to discover ways to work through the humiliation and let it go.

It is quite important to consider whether your humiliation is the result of a serious and genuine injury or whether you have a sensitivity that makes you fly into rages if you are criticized. Quite often this needs psychological help to work out. As I have said before, self-help books are no substitute for professional help, although they may give you the insight and courage to seek it. As with many things in life, wisdom is in recognizing what we can do for ourselves and what we need help with.

You may be vulnerable to feelings of humiliation now because of things that happened to you in the past. However, sitting on a lot of desires for revenge is not helpful to you. This is not to say that there might not have been things done to you that have been very harmful. Rather it is to say that, left unworked through, these feelings can lead to a lot of mistrust of others and a tendency to want constantly to get your own back. This is actually a terribly lonely position. You can take the first steps to change by acknowledging your pain and hurt and deciding to seek help. You may also need to grieve for past hurts and losses.

Now it is one thing to have a desire for revenge on someone we do not care about but what happens if it is someone you do want to have a close relationship with? Ted's father knocked him about as a child and yet Ted also loved his father and wanted to be close to him. In therapy, Ted found it extremely difficult to recognize the feelings of humiliation that his father had inflicted on him and his own desire for revenge. But until he did recognize this, he was not able to move on to forgiving both himself and his father.

Shame and Guilt

At this point, it is useful to say a couple of things about shame and guilt. Shame, as we have said, involves being seen as inferior, worthless or bad in some way. It often invades the very sense of ourselves. Guilt, however, is focused on other people. We see that we have harmed or hurt them and our feelings are about wanting to repair that hurt. In shame, we hide and conceal things; in guilt, we reach out to repair.

Now shame and guilt often run together. For example, Betty had hit her children, for which she felt guilty. However, she was unable to reach out to them and repair their relationship because she felt too ashamed about what she had done. Instead of just focusing on her particular behavior and understanding the reasons why she had acted in that way at that time, she felt that her action made her a bad mother and even a bad person. It was this shame, which she had locked away, that stopped her from looking at the issues and trying to make her behavior more as she would like it to be.

In most situations if we behave badly – and we all do from time to time – it is useful to focus on that action and ask ourselves questions about it. Use the compassionate/rational mind to consider if this could have been avoided and think about the circumstances of the action. If we start to attack ourselves and feel internally completely bad, this will paralyze our ability to work through these problems, change, grow, adapt and try to put things right.

Shame and Responsibility

If you feel ashamed because you believe that you are responsible for something bad that has happened, use the 'responsibility circle' (*see* p. 106) to try to discover all those other factors that were impinging on you at the time. Even very distressing occurrences such as being abused when you were young turn out not to be your fault. For example, the abuser was older than you, might have had poor impulse control, might have threatened you; there may have been no one to turn to who would help or listen; you may have been confused or only trying to do your best to win love.

If you *have* hurt others, acknowledge this honestly without putting yourself down. The chances are that you did not harm others for the fun of it. You were probably hurt or stressed, and you may have been trying to cope with a difficult situation alone. Maybe you were confused and simply didn't know what to do or did not realize that your behavior was hurtful. Perhaps you wanted revenge because of past hurts.

Sometimes we simply have to accept and digest our responsibility and learn to forgive ourselves and others, and not expect that we can go through life without (at times) hurting others. In an ideal world, we would all be loving to each other all the time, but sadly we do not live in an ideal world. The more you are able to acknowledge honestly your power to hurt and the reasons for it, the easier it will be to come to terms with it and change.

Healing Shame

Self-Consciousness

One of the main difficulties of shame and the thing that can really paralyze us is self-consciousness. We become acutely aware of ourselves and how we exist in the world 'for others'. Our attention is focused in on ourselves. Indeed, in shame it can be as if we are outside ourselves looking in. We become aware that our faces have turned red, or that our voices are shaking, or that we are not saying anything interesting. In shame, there is a monitoring of our actions and appearances and a highly negative evaluation. We might think: 'Oh no, I'm not doing this well. Others will think I'm stupid. I'm making a fool of myself. I'm foolish.'

Ruth hated driving, not because she felt she did it badly, but because she was always acutely aware of other drivers. She was worried about what they would think if she made a mistake, did not drive fast enough or did not seem confident. She constantly monitored her own driving and looked at the other cars in her mirrors.

People with body shame have a constant sense of their body as they think it must appear to others. Intense self-consciousness can make it difficult to show off, initiate things or get close to others. As a result, some people wait for others to initiate things, or feel that they need permission before they can do things. For example, if you initiate something, like going out or having sex, you may constantly monitor the responses of others to make sure that they are enjoying it and that they don't think you made a bad decision. You may become so focused on these concerns that you lose the enjoyment of the activity itself.

This self-monitoring of your own behaviour and appearance, and the negative judgments that go with it, can be highly disruptive. To overcome this, it is first necessary to notice how you monitor yourself. Try to catch yourself when you are doing it and see how often you give yourself put-down messages. Then learn to recognize and challenge your internal bully.

Challenging Your Internal Bully

Personal shame that depresses people nearly always involves the internal bully, which gives you thoughts and feelings of being inadequate, useless, bad, weak and so forth. The internal bully lives in the state of depression; it feeds off it. Just as in some science fiction movies, where an alien or evil entity feeds off fear and the heroes/heroines realize that once they are not afraid the evil entity can't survive, so it is with the internal bully. Once you stop listening to its messages and bring your rational and compassionate mind to bear on it, it tends to shrivel.

Let's look at some bullying and shaming messages and ways to challenge them:

Inner bully says	Rational/compassionate mind says
You failed at this task, therefore you are a failure, useless.	Failing is a disappointment, of course, but this is all-or-nothing thinking. One failure does not make me, a human being, a failure.
	That's the trouble with you, bully. You're always so simple in your accusations and, dare I say, boringly repetitive.
	If you are so keen on success, how come you put me down so much that you take away all my energy to try?
	The best way to help people if they are struggling is to encourage them and give them a boost. As I see it, you are just into shaming and blaming – that's not helpful.
	I'm going to face my limitations and what I feel ashamed about. If I listen to you, I'll just want to run away and then I won't learn anything, grow or mature.
	So I failed. Big deal. Who hasn't failed in life? I'm disappointed and upset about this, but learning to fail and then recover is the real mark of health, not simply beating myself up over it.
Crying is a sign of weakness.	Crying is a sign of pain and hurt – not weakness.
	Maybe it is our ability to cry that makes us human.
	When we lose the ability to cry, we may lose the ability to feel and to heal.
	Even if others see crying as a weakness, this does not make it true. Maybe they also have a shame problem about it.

> After all, if we were not meant to cry, why
> do we have the physical capacity for it?
>
> Crying is often about feeling sad or lonely,
> and this is an important message to listen
> to. The more I can acknowledge my tears,
> the more in touch with my feelings I may
> become.

Direct Engagement

Coming to terms with shame involves accepting it, facing it and
working through it. In many cases, recovery from shame is more
likely if people explore it. Confronting and healing shame, rather
than avoiding or compensating for it, may be a source of personal
growth.

To accept our shame, we have to give up seeing ourselves in
terms of 'all-or-nothing' negative labels, such as 'inferior' or 'inadequate'. Rather we need to be specific about what it is we are not
happy with and then try to change that or come to terms with it. If
we stick with negative labels, we stay in hiding and withdraw. Then
our chances of recovery are reduced.

Relating with Others

In overcoming shame, we have to learn to relate to other people in
a different way. We have to come out of hiding. It may be that you
want to seek out professional help. The main issues here are how
you feel with your helper and whether he or she can understand
and work with shame. However, it is also possible that there are
people close to you who would be helpful if you allowed them to
be. At times we can block ourselves from connecting with others
because we cannot face revealing what we feel ashamed about.
However, just because you think something is bad does not mean
others will.

Since shame is usually about hurt, sometimes it is possible to tell
others what has hurt us and explain our feelings. It is important that
we don't discount their efforts to help with ideas of 'They can't/
won't understand.' Try to think: 'Maybe they won't understand but
do I have the evidence for that?' Of course, if you do have evidence

that the other person is rejecting and critical, then he/she may not be a good person to confide in, but try not to assume it before you know better.

If people try to be helpful, respect their efforts rather than discounting them. Avoid thinking in all-or-nothing terms – e.g. they must understand completely or it's pointless. Maybe a little understanding is helpful. Maybe it's part of a step-by-step approach. Try to avoid attacking others if they do not understand in the way you would wish, as this will just put them on the defensive.

Coming out of shame is often a slow opening-up process. We gradually learn to reach out to others, and become more compassionate with ourselves and others. Once you make the decision to come out of hiding, numerous possibilities become open to you.

Key Points
- We all have the potential for shame.
- Shame can be focused on many things – our bodies, our actions, our feelings. The origin of these feelings may be recent or in the past.
- Shame grows in us when we label ourselves as bad, inferior, inadequate, etc.
- Commonly it is when we want to feel good about ourselves, loved, wanted and valued but seem unable to elicit this from others that we feel shame.
- Feelings of shame often come from our internal bully, and it is not a good idea for anyone to be controlled by a bully.
- Shame can be a paralyzing experience, and we may spend a good deal of our lives trying to conceal it or make up for what we think is shameful.
- Recovery comes from gradually acknowledging what we feel ashamed of and learning to treat it with compassion, and recognizing that many depressive styles operate in shame (e.g. discounting the positives, all-or-nothing thinking, overgeneralizing, self-labelling and even self-hatred).

Exercises

- Complete the following sentences:

  I feel ashamed about myself because _____ .

  I feel ashamed of myself when I do/fail to do _____ .

  I feel ashamed of myself when I feel, think or fantasize about _____ .

  I feel ashamed of myself because in the past I _____ .

  Now that you have outlined some of the things you feel ashamed about, you can start to use your rational/compassionate mind to face these honestly and heal them. To do this, review pp. 189–93.

- Write down some alternatives to the thoughts of shame you might have. For example: I am not a bad/inferior/worthless person because _____ .

- Try using healing imagery. Imagine yourself when you feel ashamed: what is (or was) happening to you? Now imagine that someone who cares about you has come to help you. What do you need from them? Ask for it. Imagine what they say to you – maybe they put an arm around you. Let their compassion flow to you. Decide how you will change to overcome your shame. Next imagine how you would act if you were less shame-prone and think about the steps to take to make this come true.

- Try to change the way you behave. For example, if you feel you must always wear make-up before going out, try going out without it. Check on your thoughts and challenge them. Remind yourself that this exercise is designed to lower your fear of what others might think about you.

  Leave your house untidy if people come to visit. Try to develop a more informal approach with others you know. In other words, focus more on the friendliness rather than on appearances.

  Take the first steps to initiate positive activities with other people. Decide if you are a person who waits to be chosen or are a chooser. Try to exert more control over positive choices, not just vetoes.

13

Coping with Anger

Strong feelings of anger are common in depression. Freud believed that unexpressed anger actually causes depression, as if anger can be turned inwards. However, we now know that, in some depressions, feelings of anger actually increase; people become more angry and short-tempered with others, not less. Nevertheless, Freud was correct to draw attention to the fact that sometimes anger and disappointment are directed at the self, and that people can be very fearful of their anger.

Anger is often related to feeling frustrated, blocked, thwarted, ignored or criticized. Something or someone is not as we want it or him/her to be. In evolutionary terms, anger gives us the energy to overcome the blocks to our goals, or to fight harder (counter-attack) in a conflict situation. Thus, anger can be a natural response. Anger can also be used to threaten others and coerce them to do as one wants. Various forms of retaliation (revenge) fit this function. Of course, we can work to overcome obstacles to our goals without feeling angry, and we can also coerce and threaten people without necessarily feeling anger – but in depression, efforts to coerce others often involve anger.

This emotion can also be experienced as powerless or impotent anger – that is, we feel unable to do anything about what we feel angry about. This may be because we think that nothing we do will work, or that anger is bad and makes us unlovable, or that we have no right to feel angry. All such thoughts can lead to a feeling of powerlessness. When we feel this way, we also feel *subordinate* to others, that other people have far more power than we do. Although depressed behavior can have a powerful effect on others, depressed people rarely see themselves as powerful.

Anger depends on certain kinds of thinking. If someone harms you accidentally, you are likely to feel less angry than if you think he or she did it on purpose. The problem here is that, even though someone may not have harmed you on purpose, you still have to deal with the feelings of being harmed. For example, when we are bereaved, we obviously know that the person did not intend to die, but the death can still generate much anger: 'How could he/she leave me like this?' Indeed, intense anger in grief is not an uncommon experience. Sometimes this can be directed at others – for example, at doctors who were unable to save the person.

Like frustration, we can be angry with things outside us in the world (e.g. other people) or we can be angry (and a bully) with ourselves. To put this another way, we can blame ourselves for our difficulties (or states of mind) or blame other people. The same is true in how we express anger. It can be directed outwards (e.g. at other people) or inwards (e.g. at ourselves). We can even become angry with ourselves for feeling angry.

What Triggers anger?

A common theme that ignites anger is a perception of some kind of threat, damage or block to things we personally value. Examples of some of these are damage or threats to:

- our sense of self (be this physical or self-esteem)
- our possessions
- our plans and goals
- our way of life

Commonly, we might see others as transgressing against us in some way, doing things we feel they should not do. But not all anger is related to transgressions. The most important source of anger is a threatening situation. These threats are usually associated with a sense of damage, of being harmed/thwarted, and can show up in various ways.

Frustration related Frustrative anger occurs when things in the world don't go as we want them to – e.g. the car won't start in the morning. The damage in this case is to our goal to get to work on time. Stress and depression can lower our tolerance for frustration and thus our susceptibility to feel anger. When stressed, we may feel generally more vulnerable to things that can damage or block us, and there are also some basic self-beliefs that can affect our tolerance for frustration – for instance, 'This shouldn't happen to me' 'This is going to seriously interfere with or block me in what I want to do.'

Injury related We can feel anger when others pose a threat to us and/or injure us in some way. Physical or verbal attacks can lead to feelings of anger. Anger is likely to be greater if we think the injury was deliberate, or the result of carelessness, than if we think it was unintentional or unavoidable. The anger that we feel towards an intentional injury can be revenge, and the impulse is to harm (counter-attack) the other verbally or physically.

Exploitation A very common theme in anger is exploitation. This is when we think someone is taking advantage of us, using us or taking us for granted. As we have seen, most of us have a desire to feel appreciated and for relationships to be equitable. Be it in child–parent relationships, between friends and lovers, or even between countries, perceptions of being exploited or taken advantage of can lead to anger and its consequences.

Lack of attention Anger can arise when others don't give us the attention we want. They may ignore us or dismiss our point of view. For example, Emma wants Chris to spend more time with her and help around the house, but he says that he's too busy. Or maybe Chris says he will help but does not keep his promise. Emma feels angry with Chris. However, with this kind of anger, we rarely want to harm the other person, but rather behave (e.g. scream and shout) so that he or she does not ignore us. We want to renegotiate our relationship, not necessarily destroy it.

Envy and jealousy This kind of anger arises when we think that someone is getting more of something than we have. Linda thought that she would win the beauty contest but didn't, and she felt envious anger towards the winner. In envy, we want what someone else has, be this material possessions, a position in society, a popular personality, intelligence and so on. In jealousy, we think that someone we value might prefer to be with a person other than ourselves – for example, a married woman shows an interest in another man and her husband has pangs of jealousy. This type of jealous anger (if expressed) acts as a threat to the woman, suggesting serious consequences if she were to defect or cheat on her husband. Sexual jealousy is more likely when a partner sees the other as a possession.

Lack of social conformity This anger relates to the feeling that others should do as they are told. Parents become angry with children who disobey them. A religious person becomes angry if the members of his church do not obey the rules. We may become angry with our government over how they spend our money. The basic belief here is: 'Others should conform to and obey the rules of conduct that I believe are important.' The anger occurs because, in some way, we see the other person's conduct as potentially damaging to our own interests or way of life.

Compassionate anger This is when we feel anger by seeing harm come to someone else – for instance, when we see people starving and feel angry that this has been allowed to happen. The anger fuels the desire for us or others to do something.

There are two aspects common to all these situations: first, things are not as we want them to be; and second, we place a high value on the things that we are angry about. If they become less important to us, then clearly we are less prone to be angry about them. For example, if it does not matter to Emma if Chris helps with the housework, she is unlikely to feel angry if he does not help out. If you would be relieved if your partner found someone else and thus made it easy to end your relationship, you are unlikely to feel strong jealousy. In helping ourselves with our anger, it is possible that we may discover that we are overvaluing something, drawing conclusions about a situation that may not be warranted or seeing more potential damage in a situation than there is.

The Shades of Anger
Anger itself is not 'all-or-nothing', 'black or white' – it is more shades of pink. For example, imagine a line that starts off white and

gradually becomes pinker until the other end is red. At the white end, there is no feeling at all, nothing matters. At the other end, one is enraged. The trick is to be somewhere along this line where you can keep control, but not in the white area or the red area. Anger is like a car that we need to learn how to drive. You don't want to drive everywhere at 100 miles per hour, but neither do you want to leave the car locked in the garage because you are frightened of it.

Sometimes depressed people do not know how to drive their anger. They continually lock it up and enter only as far as the vaguely pink area – at least as far as expressing their anger goes. That's fine if you are confident in doing that and don't need to show your anger. But it is not so good if you do need to reveal it and feel weak and inferior if you back down too quickly. If you feel that your anger tends to get out of control, you can learn other strategies – how to apply the brakes when you need to by, for example, breaking off encounters that are becoming too heated (too much in the red zone). Instead, you could give yourself space to calm down. Learn to control your anger rather than allowing it to control you.

Anger is often defensive in the sense that we are defending ourselves against a block to something or from criticism or being ignored or dismissed. As we have seen, when we behave defensively we often go for 'better safe than sorry' thinking and our emotions are triggered quickly. This is why many psychologists think that beneath the veneer of an angry person is a very vulnerable one – not someone who is confident or strong. Confident people rarely need to get angry as they are less easily threatened and more assertive. It is because anger implies that we have felt something as a threat or block that it can be so 'hot' and difficult to control. In working with our anger, we need to discover why we feel threatened and then work with our feelings of vulnerability.

Why Anger Expands

Why can anger feel so powerful? Why does it hit the red zone? It is not uncommon to find that what triggers it can be quite trivial. We might suddenly find that we are seething with anger over rather small events. It appears as if our anger has expanded. In some depressions, there are 'anger attacks', when people find themselves enraged for reasons they can't put their finger on. Some researchers believe that, in some cases, anger attacks are to do with the depression itself (and the biological changes associated with it). It has also been noted that some patients on certain antidepressant drugs can experience increases in anger. If you find that you have become far more irritable and angry since starting an antidepressant, go back to your family doctor, who may recommend a change in medication.

But there are also psychological reasons for 'blowing up' over a trivial event. Let's think about the example of Emma and Chris given above. Suppose Emma says to herself, 'If Chris really cared about me, he would help with the housework.' Clearly the anger is not just about the housework but about the fact that Chris's lack of help is being taken as a lack of caring. Emma may also feel taken for granted. Thus, what seems like a trivial event actually has a much larger meaning.

When you think about the things that make you angry, it is useful to ask yourself some questions:

• What is it about this situation that I really value and feel could be damaged?
• Let's suppose I cannot change the situation. What does this say about my future?
• What am I saying about me if this [the source of the anger] happens? Am I drawing negative conclusions about myself?
• What am I saying about the other person? What motives am I reading into his or her action?

Another question that can be very useful is to ask is : 'In what way does this situation hurt me?'

In depression, as a rule, it can be helpful to focus on the feelings of hurt rather than on the anger. If we focus on the anger, we could miss the fact that it relates to feeling vulnerable or damaged in some way. Indeed, by being angry we can sometimes block out deep fears of being abandoned, ignored and hurt. Behind anger in depression is commonly a lot of hurt, a need to grieve for past hurts and problems of shame. If the person can work through the grief, both the anger and depression may subside.

If we focus on our hurts rather than on our anger, we might gain more insight into our anger. In Emma's case, she saw that she believed that Chris's lack of help had the extra meaning of 'not being cared for', which led to the idea that maybe he did not value her or thought she was worth caring for, which led to the idea that maybe he was right. When Emma explored this, she realized that caring was not 'all-or-nothing' and that there were in fact many other instances (evidence) that showed that Chris did care.

So our anger can expand when we overestimate the damage that can be done to us. Here's another example. Derek was working on a project that required help from others. However, they did not finish their own work on time and he became furious. His thoughts were: 'If I don't get this project in on time, that will be a very bad mark against me.' He had a fear of being seen as inadequate by his boss. 'They are making me look incompetent to my boss. This could affect my chances of promotion. Therefore, these people, by not doing their work on time, are shaming me and ruining my whole future.'

When Derek focused on his own fear of shame, he began to see that he often got angry with anyone who might 'show him up.' This led him to consider why the approval of those (mostly men) in authority mattered so much to him. This in turn revealed the poor relationship he had had with his father and his belief that 'I must please those in authority, otherwise they will be angry and ignore/ discount me.' These thoughts ignited many of the feelings and fears he had as a child. So his anger was powerful because of the meanings he put on the situations that triggered it. Later, Derek was also able to see that his belief that 'his whole future would be ruined' led to a high degree of anger.

Derek learned to deal with his anger by making a number of flash cards:

- When I feel anger, I need to slow down and monitor my thoughts.
- If I don't slow down and monitor my thoughts, I am likely to see many events as a re-run of my childhood.
- When I get angry, I often overestimate the damage that can be done to me.
- What is the evidence that this situation is damaging? How can I cope with it without getting angry?

- I don't have to feel ashamed by every block or setback.

Having the flash cards gave Derek just that extra bit of space to avoid letting his anger run away with him. It helped him to take his foot off the accelerator.

Robert became enraged when he went to a hotel and found that he had been put in the wrong room and the young assistant did not seem to care. He ended up telling her that he did not think the hotel should employ people like her. When he got to his room, he felt ashamed and depressed about his over-reaction, sat on his bed and burst into tears. What had happened here? Later in therapy he was able to work out his thoughts as the following:

- Why can't people get things right?
- This assistant obviously sees me as a fool and a soft touch.
- If I were manly, I would sort this out without any difficulties. People should respect me and not treat me this way.
- I must be seen as a weak, useless bastard.
- But that's not fair – I'll show her that I'm somebody to be reckoned with.

In just a few seconds the problem had grown out of all proportion and had become a question of respect, manhood and being seen as a soft touch. The assistant's attitude had triggered Robert's underlying fear of being someone not worthy of respect and his sense of inferiority – all of which he defended with rage.

But later, while still sitting on the bed, he recognized that he had behaved aggressively to the assistant. He then thought:

- I'm losing control.
- What's happened to me? I used to be caring of others.
- Maybe I'm just a selfish person who has to have his own way.
- I am unlovable and bad for being like this. I hate myself for being like this.

So we can see how Robert's anger expanded because he had overestimated the damage to his self-esteem and had believed that this was a test of his manhood. In fact, it is not that uncommon to find that depressed people can have rages and then feel intensely unlovable and hate themselves for it (i.e. anger with themselves for being angry). Consider the man who became enraged with another driver while driving with his family. His children were frightened and started to cry so he screamed at them, too. Later, he felt ashamed and guilty. He thought that he had ruined their day and was a horrible man to 'go off like that.' At 3 a.m., feeling alone and unlovable, he started to think that they would be better off without him and contemplated suicide. His anger was a sign that he was not coping and was feeling very vulnerable underneath the rage. Anything that blocked his desires was taken as a personal put-down and fuelled an underlying sense of inferiority and weakness.

So understanding the values you place on the things that make you angry is a first step. Then consider the ways that you feel hurt and vulnerable. If you sometimes feel that you lose control, try to avoid globally attacking yourself and instead look for alternatives. The following are the ones that Robert eventually came up with for himself:

- Okay, I did go off the deep end and that is disappointing.
- However, I know that I'm not always or even usually like this.
- I need to recognize that I'm under stress right now and that my life is not easy, so my frustration tolerance is low.
- I need to learn to back off when my feelings are hitting the red zone. However, a low frustration tolerance does not make me a bad person – even if some of my actions are undesirable.
- I will help myself if I learn to be more assertive rather than aggressive. If I label myself as bad, I will only feel much worse, and when I feel bad and ashamed of myself, my frustration tolerance level goes down further.
- I can forgive myself for this, apologize to the hotel assistant if I need to and move on. Hating myself is failing to treat myself with compassion and recognize the stress I'm under. If I treat myself better, I'm more likely to treat others better.

You may have noted that the anger in the various examples outlined above could also be seen as 'shame anger'. The anger acts as a defensive measure against being put down, feeling small, discounted or rejected. Indeed, in situations when you feel anger, it is always worth thinking that shame may be part of your feelings. You can get into shame/anger spirals where you are angry at being shamed and ashamed of being angry. The first step to get out of this is to avoid attacking yourself.

Shoulds and Oughts

One reason why we can feel anger is when we are using 'shoulds' and 'oughts'. Robert, in the example above, had thought: 'Others should not behave this way.' Unfortunately, we can't write the rules for how others will behave. If we are not careful, we can get stuck and simply go over and over in our minds what another person should or shouldn't do. At times, these 'shoulds' are related to other thoughts, such as 'If X loved/respected me, he/she would/wouldn't . . .' You can change these ideas by telling yourself:

- I would prefer that others did not do this.
- However, I cannot write the rules for their conduct.
- Each person is free to behave in their own way.
- If I don't like the way they are behaving towards me, I can learn to be assertive and put my point of view.
- I do not have to personalize every conflict situation and see it as a personal attack on my worth, selfhood, manhood or whatever.

Who is to Blame?

A boy runs into the busy street. When the danger has passed, the boy's mother screams at him and smacks him. The mother is blaming her son for putting their relationship under threat and for the panic she had felt, as well as ensuring that the boy will remember this event—a lesson not to be forgotten. Later the mother may blame herself for having been so aggressive towards her child.

Blaming others is often a first response in anger. But in depression people frequently feel bad about themselves for getting angry. How can you treat yourself kindly if you have become so angry? Again, we need help from the compassionate/rational mind. It may help us with such thoughts as:

- It is indeed upsetting to become very angry.
- It may mean that underneath I am feeling very vulnerable.
- However, my anger doesn't make me completely unlovable as a

person – that would be overgeneralizing, thinking in all-or-nothing terms and self-labelling.

- It is this particular action at this particular time that was rather harsh.
- Remember the times that I've been caring and not angry and how it's possible to do positive things for myself and others.

Sometimes, if we have been angry (especially with children), we feel so guilty that we think we have to make it up to them and start to allow them to do things that we would normally not allow – because of guilt. However, this can backfire because the children, being children, might start to take advantage of the situation, which can trigger our anger again. So, if necessary, apologize for your action and then try to work on gaining more control over it rather than acting out of guilt.

Hatred

Sometimes, because we believe that we have been very hurt or damaged, anger turns to hate. Then the desire is to harm others and this can be frightening. Bella came to hate her mother because of a very physically and emotionally abusive past. She felt that her mother had 'an evil tongue.' She had fantasies about stuffing a pillow in her mother's mouth and watching her choke to death. However, she was desperate to be loved, and she took her hatred and murderous thoughts as evidence that she herself was evil. Her thoughts were:

- Hatred is bad.
- I should not feel like this.
- It is abnormal; others don't feel like this.
- I must be bad/evil for feeling hate this strongly.
- I can't reveal to others the depth of my feelings because they will think that I am evil, too.
- I hate myself for hating.

Her doctor, who had been treating her with drugs, had no idea of this inner life. This is not surprising, for such hate–anger is often not revealed if there is strong fear or shame associated with it. Bella was able to begin to challenge these thoughts and ideas:

We all have the capacity for hatred – it is not itself abnormal. Indeed, sadly, history shows the consequences of hatred, so there have been many who have felt like me. I am not abnormal. To call my hatred 'evil' is all-or-nothing thinking and self-labelling, and leaves out the hurt I have felt because of what happened to me. I did not wake up one day and think that it would be a good idea to hate my mother. These feelings have come from a lot of painful experiences, and it is understandable for me to hate someone who has hurt me so much. However, I do need to learn how to work with my hatred and come to terms with it. I need to learn how not to hate myself for hating. This is because my hatred hurts me and holds me back in my efforts to get well.

Avoid Brooding

If we think about what anger is designed to do, and recognize that one of its functions is to help us to fight harder, we can see the danger of brooding on angry thoughts. These turn on our fight/flight system, when stress hormones and other chemicals are pumped around our bodies, which become tense and alert. But if no 'fight' or 'flight' happens, these chemicals can get up to mischief.

Allen was asked to take early retirement, and a new manager started to undo all the changes that he had introduced in his section. He had various arguments with his boss, but all to no avail. Allen became depressed and had serious sleep difficulties. I asked him to monitor his thoughts when he woke in the middle of the night. These turned out to be: 'The bastard. After all the years that I have worked there and this is how they treat me. There must be some way I can stop them. I can't just roll over and let this happen.' When these thoughts began to run through his mind, he became quite agitated and would pace about the house, going over and over them. If his wife tried to calm him down, he would snap at her and then feel guilty. Then he would say to himself, 'They're even breaking up my relationship with my wife.'

My discussion with him went something like this: 'When you have these thoughts, they activate your primitive fight/flight system and that's designed to hype you up to fight or to run away. However, you've done what you can and there seems to be no way that fighting can help you now – especially at three in the morning. So you're left in a hyped-up state that has nowhere to go except in pacing about and snapping at your wife. You've recognized that, in reality, there is not much you can do.' Allen reluctantly agreed. 'So we have to find a way for you not to activate your fight/flight system because it drives you into depression.'

As Allen came to understand the processes that he was activating in himself, he was ready to start to explore alternatives. So we wrote out some flash cards for him to read if he woke early:

- I am disappointed with this situation, but I have to face the fact that I have done my best and this is the way of the future.
- I have given the company many good years, and it has not been too bad really. I can be proud of that.
- Perhaps the time has come to let go and think about the next phase of my life.
- All these thoughts of fighting and getting my own back only hypes me up and to no real purpose.

We also examined the advantages and disadvantages of taking early retirement, including the fact that he would have more free time and that it would probably be better for his health. Once Allen gave up fighting an unwinnable battle, he was free to explore other strategies – such as how to get the best deal for his retirement. It was not easy, but a year later, he told me that it had been the best decision he'd ever made.

So the key issue is to try to avoid brooding on anger. Try to work out strategies for coping. If there are things that can be done, do them. If there are others who can help you, seek their help. But brooding on injustice, going over the same ground over and over again, does not help. Giving up an unwinnable fight is one strategy, but at other times you may need to learn how to become more assertive and stand your ground (*see* Chapter 14).

Anger to Avoid Pain

Caroline was angry with her parents because she thought they did not love her enough. As long as she felt angry, she avoided the great sadness and need to grieve that were underneath her anger. Anger gave her some feelings of power. Sadness and grief made her feel very vulnerable.

Anger can be used to prevent the recognition of being hurt, but it is often hurt and shame that need healing and this often involves sadness. Some people may imply that all you need to do is to get your own back on the person who has harmed you or to stand up to them. However, although this can be helpful it is not always so. Underneath, we still have a wish to be loved and approved of. I remember a patient who had done quite a lot of work with another therapist on learning to stand up to her abusive parent and express her anger. But, despite this, she was still depressed and mistrustful. What she had not done was grieve for her lost childhood or allow herself to feel and accept the feelings of vulnerability in grieving.

In working with anger in depression (and I stress 'anger in depression' because not all anger is like this), it is sometimes important to find someone who will help you move through the grieving process. In grief, we acknowledge our pain and vulnerability. And in the grieving *process* itself, anger is often the first or a very early response – but we have to work through this stage rather than get stuck in it.

Bypassed Anger: Ten Common Reasons for Avoiding Anger
Sometimes people try to avoid feelings of anger altogether. If you bypass anger, you might go straight to feeling hurt, but also feel a victim (powerless subordinate). You will also bypass becoming assertive (*see* Chapter 14). You may feel that you have no power to do anything about certain situations. You might think that you feel hurt because you are weak, and you may not be able to focus on the fact that it is at least partly the attitude of the other person that is the cause. It is important to recognize your hurts without, at the same time, becoming a powerless victim.

. Here are ten self-beliefs that may stop you from exploring your anger and learning how to use it in an assertive way. Following each one, I offer some alternative ideas.

1 Others are more powerful than me. I will never win in conflict with them.
Alternatives: It's not about winning and losing. Even if you don't

achieve the outcome you want, it is important to try to put your point of view. If you tell yourself that you have to win, otherwise it's pointless, you are defeating yourself before you start. If you attempt to put your point of view, at least you will have tried. Trying to be assertive means that you are less likely to be angry with yourself if you don't get the outcome you want.

2 I learned in childhood that anger is bad.

Alternatives: Because your parents could not cope with your anger does not mean that anger is bad. Anger is part of human nature, and it can be useful. Consider compassionate anger [*see above*]. If we never felt angry about things, would we be motivated to try to change anything? Anger is really important because it reveals where you are hurting and what you value. True, aggression and lashing out are not good, but anger turned to assertiveness has many uses. Although your parents taught you that anger is bad, they may not have taught you how to be assertive. They did not give you any positive way to deal with conflicts – so maybe the problem was that they did not know themselves. You'll need to learn this for yourself.

3 When I am angry, I am bad and unlovable.

Alternatives: Of course, you might prefer never to be angry but that's not possible. To say that you are unlovable is all-or-nothing thinking and self-labelling and discounts the positive aspects of your life. When you think of being unlovable, you may be thinking of being unlovable to *someone*. So who is the person you feel unlovable to? If it is your partner, you can think of it this way: Relationships are like boats. If your boat can only sail in a calm bay, it is not much of a boat. We need boats that will not capsize even if a storm blows up. If you see yourself as unlovable when you feel angry, you are also saying that your relationship can't cope with the odd storm – but, in fact, clearing the air and being honest and frank with your partner are likely to strengthen your relationship, not ruin it.

Of course, it is true that, at the moments of conflict, you are not sharing loving feelings. But love is like the climate; it remains no matter what we do. Anger and conflicts are like wind and rain – they come and go. Just as one thunderstorm does not change a climate, so your anger does not make you unlovable. You can learn to survive conflict.

4 When I am angry, I am being disloyal.
Alternatives: Sometimes, when you confide in people you trust about the anger you feel towards others close to you, you can have strong feelings of being 'disloyal'. However, confiding in others might help you to get your anger in perspective. If the person you are angry with has done things that have hurt you, keeping them hidden is really colluding in a secret rather than showing loyalty. You confide in others because you want to sort out your feelings. It is understandably difficult if you feel that you are 'breaking loyalties'. However, remember that people have done all kinds of bad things out of loyalty. If you showed compassion, you would try to change things.

5 I must not hurt others.
Alternatives: Deliberately hurting others is not, by most people's standards, a moral thing to do. But the anger we are talking about here is not like that. Rather you want to use your anger to draw attention to the fact that something is causing you pain or hurt and needs to change. You have no wish to harm others for the sake of it, but to help them see how they are hurting you and to stop them doing it. In this sense, your anger is defensive. Others are far less likely to be hurt if you explain your position and show respect for them rather than attacking them. But if they are hurt, they need to understand why and sort that out. You can't be held responsible for everyone's feelings – that's giving yourself too much power. In any case, you might, in the long run, be more hurtful to them and your relationship if you are not honest with them about your feelings.

6 I can't stand the feelings of anger.
Alternatives: Angry feelings can be frightening if you are not used to feeling them. You may block your angry feelings if you feel that you might lose control. However, you are far less likely to do this if you learn how to be assertive (*see* Chapter 14).

7 I might lose control and damage people.
Alternatives: It is your responsibility not to do that. But you need to

consider a number of things. First, are you seeing your anger as more damaging than it is? Are you secretly telling yourself that you are a very powerful person and that everyone around is so fragile that they could not possibly cope with your anger? If so, try to think of the reasons why you might wish to believe that. Then work out the evidence for this belief and the evidence against it. Lashing out at people – going into the red zone – is not a good idea, but this is no reason to avoid being assertive with others.

8 I might lose control and make a fool of myself.
Alternatives: It may be that you are prone to feeling shame if you express your feelings, so you can work on that. It may also be true that if you become very angry, you might say things that you do not mean or become tongue-tied. The main thing is to try to focus on the issue, the message you want to convey, rather than your anger.

If you have become angry, try to find out if you are having internal bullying thoughts and calling yourself names (e.g. 'I'm stupid, 'I'm a fool'). If you are, recognize this is all-or-nothing thinking and discounting the positive aspects of your life. Remind yourself that your anger is one element that you may wish to change, but it does not make you a fool or stupid.

9 I only feel I have a right to be angry if I am 100 percent sure that I am in the right.
Alternatives: There are few things in life where one can be 100 percent right. This is all-or-nothing thinking. Maybe no one is right or wrong, but everyone has a different point of view. Sharing these differences can be a source of growth.

10 I would be ungrateful or selfish to show anger.
Alternatives: 'Selfish' is, of course, a self-label and you are probably discounting all those times when you have given of yourself. Even if you feel grateful to someone, this does not mean that there cannot be disagreements between you. You can show gratitude when the situation warrants it, but positive things can be achieved in not hiding your discontent. Be cautious not to let your gratitude turn into a trap of obligation, for then you may feel more resentful.

Key Points
- Anger is part of life and can be aroused in situations when we perceive actual or potential damage to something we value.
- In depression, we can become too angry and 'blow up' or we can hide our anger.
- We may resort to rather underhanded ways to avoid open conflict, get our own way or get revenge.
- Anger is very often related to shame – our greatest rages often occur in situations where we feel shamed – whether we recognize it or not.
- At times it is important to consider whether we are overestimating the amount of damage that can be, or has been, done (e.g. to self-esteem).
- Anger itself is not all-or-nothing, and it is useful to learn how to control it rather than allowing it to control us or locking it away.
- Brooding on anger leads to an aroused (hyped-up) state, which is often very unpleasant and not helpful.
- There are a number of primary self-beliefs that make anger difficult to deal with because they do not allow it to be worked through and it stays hidden.

Exercises
- Write down your thoughts about the last time you became angry. Ask yourself questions like: 'What am I saying about this event?' 'What implications am I drawing?' 'What do I think this event (or the other person's attitude) says about me?' 'What am I saying about myself?' When you have written down some of your thoughts, explore whether you are engaging in any of the following: all-or-nothing thinking, overgeneralizing, discounting the positives, thinking in 'musts' or 'shoulds', and so forth.

  Let's work through the example of Emma becoming angry with Chris over him not helping with the housework. The following are her main thoughts and the possible coping responses she came up with:

continued on next page

I'm always left with the housework while he goes off with his friends.
Well, actually he does help sometimes. I am overgeneralizing here. And I am ignoring some of the other positive things he does to help. Still I do feel strongly that he should do more. I need to sit down with him to talk about it – when I don't feel so angry and upset.

This is really unfair. If he cared about me, he would help out.
Is doing housework the only sign of caring? Chris is behaving in a way that is traditional for males. His father was the same. I may not like it, but I may be exaggerating if I think this shows that he doesn't care about me. I need consistently to point out that this is a concern to me and that he can learn to change.

He just takes me for granted.
I might feel taken for granted, but is this true? What evidence is there for and against this idea of being taken for granted?

Maybe that's all I'm good for. If I was more lovable, he would be more attentive.
I recognized a problem about who does the housework. However, I'm going to feel much worse if I start to think Chris's lack of interest in housework is a lack of interest in me. It is this blaming myself and feeling unloved that is making me depressed. It could just as easily be a typical male attitude. I need to train him!

- If you tend to become too angry, try to spot the danger signs early. Think back to the last time you were angry. What was going through your mind? What were your early feelings? Was there any build-up to it? Could you spot the danger signs – feelings of getting wound up? If so, learn to say to yourself, 'I am entering my danger zone and need to back off – keep my distance.' If you find yourself getting too angry, move away

continued on next page

continued from previous page

from the other person. Blowing up at others is not helpful. However, if it is appropriate, try to come back to the issue that was behind your anger when you feel calmer. Don't avoid the issue but avoid the strong anger that might lead you to say things you later regret.

- Use the 'count to ten' approach. If you suddenly feel very angry, stop, then count to ten slowly, then take a deep breath. Learn to avoid acting when you have hit the red zone. You may also try leaving the room. The key idea is to distract yourself, and give yourself time to calm down sufficiently to stay in control.
- If any of the 'ten common reasons for avoiding anger' (*see* pp. 208–11) apply to you, make your own flash cards and try challenging these thoughts. Think of the advantages and disadvantages for changing them.
- If you are frightened of the feelings of anger, try expressing anger when you are alone. Get a rolled-up newspaper, kneel by the side of your bed and hit your bed with it. As you do, speak (or shout) your thoughts about your anger. Allow yourself to feel your anger. Remind yourself that no one can be hurt by this exercise – the point of it is to help you become less fearful of the feelings of anger. When your anger has subsided, you may wish to cry. Allow yourself to do this.

Then, and most importantly, before leaving the room lie on your bed and carry out a relaxation exercise. Think to yourself, 'This anger episode is over and I will let it go.' Imagine a stormy sea that becomes calmer. The idea is to recognize that you can become angry but will also calm down. Learning how to do this is important, because it helps you avoid brooding on your anger. At the end of the exercise, note that you were able to become angry and to calm down afterwards – so the feelings of anger themselves need not be frightening, even though, of course, they may not be pleasant. But you were able to control your anger by directing it at the bed. This exercise is not designed simply to release anger but to allow you to experience

continued on next page

it without fear. Go step by step, and learn that, even when you are very angry, you can still stay in control of your feelings.

Next, when you feel calmer, write down what you said when you were angry – what went through your mind? Explore to see if some of your thoughts were extreme and should be challenged. The next stage is to recognize where you are hurting and what your anger is about.

14

From Anger to Assertiveness
and Forgiveness

We now need to think about what we do when we feel angry – given that, in depression, anger is often related to hurt and vulnerability. The main issue, however, is not to express anger as such – at least not in a raw, over-the-top or impulsive way – but that we need to learn to pin-point what it is that is really upsetting us, and learn how to act *assertively* rather than aggressively.

Assertiveness

What is Assertiveness?
Before we can think about acting assertively, we need to clarify what we mean by assertiveness. Research has suggested that assertiveness is related to many types of behavior. Willem Arrindell and his colleagues in the Netherlands have studied assertive behavior and suggest there are at least four components to it:

1 *Display of negative feelings:* The ability to, for example, ask someone to change a behavior that annoys you, show your annoyance, stand up for your rights and refuse requests. This is what most people are thinking of when they talk about 'being assertive'.

2 *Expressing and coping with personal limitations:* The ability to admit to ignorance of something and making mistakes and to accept criticism. In addition, the ability to ask others for help without seeing this as a personal weakness.

3 *Initiating assertiveness:* The ability to express opinions and views that may differ from those of others, and to accept a difference of opinion between oneself and others.

4 *Positive assertion:* The ability to recognize the talents and achievements of others and to praise them, and the ability to accept praise oneself.

This chapter focuses primarily on the 'display of negative feelings.' In Chapter 12, which dealt with shame, we discussed how we can accept personal limitations without attacking ourselves. In Chapter 11, on approval, we explored how important it is both to accept and to give praise. In many ways, therefore, some of the types of behavior discussed earlier can be seen as helping you become more assertive and raise your self-esteem.

Non-Assertive, Aggressive and Assertive Behavior

When people have problems in acting assertively, they are either highly submissive, fearful and prone to back down when faced with conflicts, or they become overly dominant and aggressive. The table below outlines some differences between these forms of behavior, showing the contrasts in non-verbal behavior, feelings and thoughts. Although there are occasions when coming to terms with and expressing angry feelings is useful, I am not encouraging you to express extreme anger, but to become assertive and more in touch with your hurts and vulnerabilities. A table of non-assertive, aggressive and assertive behavior is shown on p. 218.

Interestingly, non-assertive and aggressive people can share similar beliefs. For example, both can think in terms of winners and losers. In a conflict situation, there are thoughts of 'I'm not going to let them win this one' or 'I can't win this one' or 'I always lose.' Aggressive people are determined not to be losers or be placed in a subordinate position. Depressed people can feel that they have already lost and are in a subordinate position. Sometimes this seems like a replay of how they experienced their childhoods. Parents were seen as powerful and dominant and they (as children) felt small and subordinate. Depressed people can, however, be aggressive to those they see as subordinate to themselves (e.g. children). The important thing is to remind yourself that while it might have been true that, as a child you were in the subordinate position, you don't have to be now. You can look after yourself and treat others as your equals. You are an adult

Non-assertive	Aggressive	Assertive
	Nonverbal Behavior	
Looks down or backs away	Stares and 'looks' angry, threatening	Meets eye contact but avoids 'the angry face'
Tries to signal 'no-threat'	Wants to signal threat – to be obeyed	Wants to signal 'listen to my point of view'
Allows other to choose for self	Chooses for (and imposes on) self and others	Tries to reach agreement
	Feelings	
Is fearful of the other	Is angry or enraged with the other	Tries to control both anger and fear
Hurt, defeated	Feels a victim and sense of injustice	Recognizes that one can't have everything one wants
	Thoughts	
My view is not important	My view is the most important	All views have a right to be heard
I don't deserve to have this need, want or desire	My wants and needs are more important than other people's	Each person's needs and wants are important
I will lose	I will (or must) win	It is preferable for no one to win or lose but to work out how to give space to each person
I am inadequate or bad	I am good and in the right	Right and wrong is all-or-nothing thinking and labelling. It is preferable to work out what the issues are rather than labelling or attacking the person or oneself
Just here to please others	Others should do as I want	We should try to please each other in a mutually sharing and caring way
Self-attacking	Other attacking	Avoids attacking

now. So you might use the motto: 'That was then. This is now.'

One way to feel more equal to others is to try to eliminate the 'all or nothing' from your thinking (powerful/powerless, strong/weak, winner/loser) by telling yourself that 'It is not me against them. Rather we each have our own needs and views.' To be assertive then is to not see things in terms of a battle, with winners and losers. This may mean that you have to be persistent but not necessarily aggressive. The angry-aggressive person wants to win by force and threat; the assertive person wants to achieve a particular end or outcome and is less interested in coercing others or frightening them into submission – and will often accept a compromise.

The second aspect of assertiveness is that it focuses on the issue, not the person. To use a sporting metaphor, it involves learning to 'play the ball, not the player.' In this case we speak of our wants or hurts without alarming others or employing negative styles of thinking. For example, these are typical responses of someone who is angry and aggressive towards someone else:

- You are a stupid person (all-or-nothing thinking and labelling).
- You are always so thoughtless (overgeneralizing and discounting the positives).
- I can never trust you (all-or-nothing thinking and discounting the positives).
- You are a selfish bastard (just about all the styles!).

All these statements attack the other person. When people feel attacked, they tend to go on to the defensive. They lose interest in your point of view and are more concerned with defending themselves or attacking back. The assertive response focuses less on threatening/attacking the other person but more on ourselves and the quality of our relationships with others. Thus, in acting assertively we would explain in what way a particular action or attitude is hurtful. For example:

- When you behave in that way, I feel hurt because I think that you don't care about me.
- If you say things like that, I feel you are discounting my point of view.
- I feel much happier when you behave like this towards me.

- I accept that you feel like that, and have a right to, but that is not my point of view.

Can you see the steps here?
1 Acknowledge your anger.
2 Recognize in what way you feel hurt (and, of course, try to discover if you might be exaggerating the harm/damage done).
3 Focus on what this hurt is about and your wish to have the other person understand your feelings and your point of view.
4 Don't insist that the other person absolutely *must* agree with you.

In assertiveness, we try to remain respectful of the other person. Winning, getting your own back or putting the other person down can have a negative outcome. In fact, even if you are successful (i.e. you win), the other person may still feel resentful and wait for a chance to get their own back on you! Winning can create resentful losers.

Avoiding Spreading Guilt
One word of warning. When you acknowledge your hurts assertively, this doesn't include making the other person feel guilty or ashamed. Sometimes people don't want to share with others what they want to change but just make the others feel bad. When they discuss the things they want to change, they do it in a rather whining, 'poor me' way. Or they may say, 'It's all your fault that I'm depressed.' They may think: 'Look what they've done to me – I'll make them feel guilty for that. Then they'll be sorry.' Now this is understandable but not helpful. Getting your own back by trying to make people feel guilty is not being assertive. You may at times wring concessions from others, but usually people feel resentful if they have to give in because they have been made to feel guilty.

Sometimes we might even do things to ourselves to try to make the other person feel guilty. After an argument with her mother, Hilary went home and took an overdose. Later she was able to recognize that she had been thinking: 'She'll be sorry when she sees what she made me do.' Now nobody can *make* us do anything – short of torturing us. It was Hilary's anger that was the problem. Her mother had been critical of her, but at the time, Hilary had not said anything, although she had felt anger seething inside her. Her overdose was a way of trying to get her own back. With some effort, Hilary was able to be assertive with her mother and could say things like: 'Look, Mother, I don't like the way you criticize me. I think I'm doing an okay job with my children. It would help if you focused on what I do well, not on what you think I do badly.' This took her mother aback, but after that, Hilary felt on a more equal basis with her mother.

Sometimes depression itself can be used to attack others. Hilary also came to realize that, at times, she did feel happy but refused to let others know it. She wanted to be seen as an unhappy, suffering person, and that this was other people's fault and they should feel sorry for her and guilty. It was also an attempt to evoke sympathy from others – although it rarely worked. She had the idea that, if she showed that she was happy, she would be letting others off the hook for the hard times she had had in the past.

Sometimes there is a message in our depression. It may be to force others to look after us or it may be to make them feel sorry for us. We find ourselves turning away from possible happiness and cling to misery. It can be helpful to think carefully about how you want others to respond to your depression. It can be a hard thing to do, and you might see that sometimes you use your depression to get your own way or get out of doing things. Try not to attack yourself about this, for you are not alone in doing it. Your decision is whether to go on doing it or whether you can find other ways to make your voice heard.

Avoiding Sulking

Another non-assertiveness problem is sulking, or 'passive aggression'. In sulking, we don't speak of our upsets but close down and give people the 'silent treatment'. We may walk around with an angry 'stay away from me' posture, or act as if we are really hurt, to induce guilt. Indeed, our anger is often written all over our faces even as we deny that we feel angry. We have to work out if our sulking is a way of getting revenge on others and trying to make them feel guilty. Are we sulking in order to punish others?

You may feel powerless to bring changes. This may be because you believe that direct conflict would get out of hand, or to show anger is to be unlovable or because you think you would not win.

However, sulking does have powerful effects on others. Think how you feel when someone does it to you. The problem with sulking is that it causes a bad atmosphere and makes it difficult to sort out problems. When you sulk, you give the impression that you don't care for others. Sulking is likely to make things worse. Another problem is that sulking often leads to brooding on your anger. The more you do this, the more you will want to punish others.

You will find that, if you can learn to be assertive and explain what it is that you are upset about, you will feel less like sulking. Because sulking can have powerful negative effects on others and relationships, I would strongly suggest this is a power that you could give up. You can recognize your tendencies to sulk, work out why you do it and try becoming more assertive. This is likely to take time, but once you decide that you have had enough of being a sulker, you are at least set on a path out. Here are some possible alternatives:

- I sulk because I feel hurt or want to punish others.
- This is not helping my relationships – even if it works at times.
- Maybe I'm saying that the other person should be as I want him or her to be. I can challenge this.
- I can learn to recognize that the other person's attitude is not what I want and try to act assertively.

Anger at Failed Assertiveness

If we hold some of the beliefs about ourselves outlined above, we will have problems in becoming assertive. One extremely common occurrence in some depressions, and even in life in general, is that we can become angry with ourselves for not being assertive. We have probably all had the experience of getting into a conflict with someone and not saying what we wanted to say. Then later we felt very cross for not standing up for ourselves. We felt that we had let the other person win or get away with something. Afterwards we thought of all kinds of things that we could have said but didn't think of at the time. Then we started to brood on this failure to be assertive and our internal bully really got going.

Roger was criticized in a meeting which he felt was mildly shaming. He actually dealt with the situation quite diplomatically but, in his view, did not defend himself against an unfair accusation. Later that night and for a number of days afterwards, he brooded on his failure to say what he had really wanted to say. These were his thoughts about himself:

- There you go again – letting people walk all over you.
- You never stand up for yourself.
- You've shown once again that you're made of mush.
- You've failed again.
- You're a really weak character.

Roger had a strong ideal of himself as a 'person to be reckoned with,' but of course, he rarely lived up to this. As in the case of Allen (discussed in Chapter 13) who had to take early retirement, when Roger was out of the situation he started to activate his own internal fight/flight system and brooded on what he wished he had said. At one point, he had fantasies of revenge, of physically hitting the person who had criticized him. As with Allen, Roger's thoughts led to some agitation.

The following are alternative coping thoughts that Roger could have considered:

- I am bullying myself again and getting angry with myself.
- I am exaggerating the degree of harm I sustained.
- I am discounting what I did say and looking at it in all-or-nothing terms.
- I was criticized – in my view, unfairly – but this is not the same as being 'walked all over'.
- Criticisms are not always fair.
- True, if I had thought about it, I might have been able to respond better, but that only shows that there is room for improvement.
- I am sensitive to criticism because I often see it as a major attack on me as a person. This means that I need to learn how to keep criticism in perspective.
- Other people later agreed that the criticism was unfair, so they don't see me as weak.
- In reality, I don't want to be seen as an aggressive person, and anyway I would rather sort out conflicts amicably and reasonably. I can at least give myself credit for that.

You will be aware by now that the most damaging aspects of Roger's internal attack were the thought of having failed and labelling himself as weak. These thoughts placed him in a highly subordinate position and were quite at odds with his ideal self. They activated a desire for revenge. Because of the way our brains work, it is quite easy to get into this way of thinking if we feel that someone has forced us into a subordinate position. So we have to work hard to stop this more primitive brain response from running away with us. Here are some alternative coping thoughts that interrupt this more automatic subordinate thinking style:

- By globally labelling myself as weak, I feel bad. This is all-or-nothing thinking and ignores the positive aspects of my life. It makes me feel much worse.
- It may be true that I need to learn how to be more assertive, but this is going to be hard to do if I take each failure to assert myself as evidence of weakness. There are many areas of my life where I have shown some courage, but in any case, conflicts are often complex and cannot be reduced to simple ideas of weak/strong.
- If I'm not careful, I will have to cope with two problems – the criticisms that come from outside and the criticisms and attacks I launch on myself.
- If a friend had been in a similar situation, I would not have attacked him or her in the same way that I attack myself – for I know that this would have made him or her feel much worse.
- If I feel under threat from the outside, it is preferable that I learn how to give myself some support rather than just running myself down and listening to my own internal bully.

Now these alternative thoughts are intended to halt the slide into the depressive spiral. We are obviously going to feel some disappointment if we think that we could have stood up to others better than we did, but we don't have to attack ourselves or allow our minds to rush into fantasies of revenge. Moreover, if we approach the problem rationally, we might identify a need to use assertiveness. So we could then plan what we wanted to say (but didn't) and calmly try it out. The problem for Roger was that he never tried assertiveness but only felt disappointed with himself and then became angry. He never gave himself the chance to improve his assertiveness.

We want to be heard and listened to without being seen as aggressive, overpowering or pushy. This may not be an easy thing to achieve. If we are sensitive to these difficulties, recognize that assertiveness is a skill that takes time to learn, and which sometimes we will get wrong, we can avoid getting trapped into labelling ourselves as weak by our internal bullies.

Anger and Assertiveness in Intimate Relationships

Anger associated with depression, in intimate relationships, can result not from single events or short-term problems but from longer-term difficulties. You may have felt that, for years, you have not been taken seriously. In some relationships, one person may feel constantly subordinated to the other, or may be storing up a lot of anger and brooding on events from 'way back'. These can be difficult things to sort out in a relationship. If this is the case for you, it is worth considering marital or relationship therapy. However, it can be very helpful to begin by learning how to be assertive and more open with your partner/family.

Intimate relationships are often riddled with conflicts of interest and, sometimes, power plays. These are all quite normal and are what make intimate relationships so challenging. Maybe it's preferable to accept conflicts as challenges and allow yourself to grow and evolve through conflicts rather than trying to avoid them. As with any learning in life, we often get better as we cope with more and more difficult things. It does not matter if you are learning a new language or how to drive a car or training to become a doctor, the more difficult the things are you learn to do, the better you become at doing them. It's a step-by-step process. It's the same with intimate relationships: we grow and develop by passing through difficult as well as good times. By facing your conflicts, you are improving your capacity for intimate relating, not reducing it.

Forgiveness

Reconciliation

Disagreements, arguments and conflicts are normal in nearly all relationships. It is just not possible to see eye to eye all the time, or never to be in a bad mood. Indeed, some marriages can have high levels of conflict, but still survive. How is this possible? Well, it is usually because the conflicts themselves are not feared. However, some depression-prone people do fear conflicts, especially if they think arguments might become heated. We have already explored some of the reasons for this in Chapter 13 (e.g. 'I am unlovable to get angry', 'I will be rejected if I get angry'). But there are other reasons for a fear of arguments. One is a belief that 'something will be damaged beyond repair.'

Some depressed people also have difficulty in reconciling after conflicts have taken place. Couples and families with high levels of conflict but with good reconciling behaviors, and who basically value each other, tend to suffer less depression. When we reconcile and make peace, our anger and arousal subsides. Chimpanzees, our nearest primate relatives, actually seem better at reconciling their differences than humans. Research shows that, after a conflict, they will often come together for a hug and embrace and they rarely stay distant for long.

So why is it difficult for some people to reconcile? In some cases, it is because as children they were never taught how to do it, and now as adults, they feel awkward about it. Perhaps neither they nor their partners know how to make the first move to make peace. Another reason is that one or both parties in the conflict will not reconcile until they are given the dominant position: they must win, get their own way and assert their authority. The one who reaches out to make peace is perceived as the one who has submitted.

For example, Angela said that, when she was a child, it was always her and not her mother who had to say she was sorry. If she didn't, there would be a very bad atmosphere between her and her mother, which she found intolerable. He mother would sulk, sometimes refusing to speak to Angela until she had apologized. And when the girl did, her mother would remind her of the conflict and how naughty Angela had been. At a time when Angela was reaching out for acceptance, her mother would make her feel bad, ashamed and guilty again. So Angela developed an expectation that, if she apologized, the other person would use this to make her feel bad about herself and would not accept her peace-making efforts without 'rubbing her nose in it.' She was therefore very frightened of conflicts because there was no way she could reconcile afterwards without always feeling in the wrong.

Jake thought that to say 'Sorry' always meant that he was admitting he was in the wrong. If he had been angry with his children, he would have strong desires to apologize and, yet to apologize was, in his mind, to be seen as weak.

So there are a number of things that can stop us from peace-making:

If I apologize and want to reconcile, it means:

- I was in the wrong.
- I am giving in.
- I have lost.
- I am weak. Strong people do not apologize.
- Others will think I have taken full responsibility for the conflict.
- I am in a subordinate position.

There are various alternatives to these ideas. For example:

- I can apologize for my actions if I think I have hurt someone, but this does not mean that the conflict itself was all my fault. Indeed, it is preferable to think in terms of 'differences of opinions or desires' rather than in terms of blame.
- Assertiveness is not about winners and losers but about being clear about the reason(s) for a conflict and attempting to resolve it.
- The ability to apologize and repair a relationship is a 'positive' on my part, not a weakness.
- I don't have to grovel when I apologize but rather to get together with the other person again because I care about the relationship.
- I can focus on the issue of coming together rather than on just relieving myself of guilt.

Reconciliation, like much else in assertiveness, is a skill that can be learned. It may be difficult at first, but if you set your mind to it, you are more likely to improve. Learning how to 'make up' after a conflict makes them less frightening. You learn that you can survive them and may often benefit from them. Making up is only a submissive position if you tell yourself it is.

Try to avoid sulking, which may be used to punish others. Reconciliation in intimate relationships may involve hugs and other physical contact, but of course, you can't force this on others. If others are not ready to reconcile, all you can do is to state your position – that you'd like to make up. Try to be honest and offer an apology if you need to, and wait for the other person to come round in their own time. If they don't, try to avoid getting angry with them because they don't wish to go at the same pace as you.

One other thing that men especially need to be cautious of is encouraging their partners to *prove* that they are now reconciled with them by agreeing to have sex. If you do this, it is possible that your efforts at reconciliation will not be seen as genuine, but only as a tactic to get your own way. If your partner does not want to have sex, you may read this as 'Well, he/she does not really care for me, otherwise he/she would.' This can lead to anger and resentment again. If you feel that there is not enough sex in your relationship, this is best sorted out at some other time, calmly, and with no threat of 'If you loved me, you would.'

Some typical thoughts that can make forgiveness difficult include:

- I must make them pay (feel guilty) for upsetting me.
- If I forgive them (or me) I am letting them (or me) off the hook.
- If I forgive them then I can't express my dissatisfactions.
- I will have to be nice.
- Forgiveness is a position of weakness.
- It has more benefits for them than me.

Resentment and Revenge

Forgiveness does not mean that what happened in the past does not matter. Rather, it is the effort made to give up the desire for revenge or punishment. Forgiveness can be a lengthy process that requires an acknowledgment of much hurt. Some people may try to forgive without acknowledging their own pain and anger, but when they do this, resentment usually remains. So forgiveness can be a painful process. However, learning how to forgive is about learning how to let go of hurts. A need for revenge can be damaging to ourselves and our relationships. We may hold on to anger rather than work through it. We may tell ourselves how justified we are to be angry regardless of how useful this is.

Judy felt much anger against her parents for their rather cold attitude, and blamed them for her unhappy life. In doing this, she was in effect saying to herself: 'I cannot be better than I am because my parents have made me what I am. Therefore, I am forever subordinate to them – for they held the power to make me happy. Therefore, I can't exert any power over my own happiness.'

Gradually Judy came to see that it was her anger (and desire for revenge) which locked her into a bad relationship with her parents. Forgiveness required a number of changes. First, she needed to recognize the hurt she felt, which to a degree was blocked by her anger. Second, she needed to see that she was telling herself that, because her parents were cold towards her, she was 'damaged' and destined to be unhappy – that is, she was giving up her own power to change. She realized that she felt a 'victim' to her childhood. Rather than coming to terms with this, she felt subordinated and controlled by it. While it is always preferable to have had early loving relationships, it is still possible to move forward and create the kind of life one wants. As Judy came to forgive her parents (but not condone them), she let go of her anger and felt released from the cage in which she had felt trapped.

If we strongly resent someone or something, we can also feel that we are 'the other's victim.' This is a subordinate position that may seriously interfere with our ability to feel in control of our own lives. We may also develop deep distrust of others, which makes it difficult to have meaningful relationships. Forgiveness – letting go of the desire for revenge – is one way out of this. When we forgive, we are saying, 'I let the past go and am no longer its victim.' One patient of mine said that, by giving himself the power to forgive, he was giving himself the power to live. Forgiveness is not a position of weakness. Some people find that 'letting go' feels like a great release.

To forgive *ourselves* means that we treat ourselves with compassion. We do not demand that we be perfect and not make big mistakes from time to time. There are many spiritual traditions that recognize the great importance of forgiveness. Buddhists have a meditation that they call 'loving kindness', designed to help individuals treat themselves with more compassion and learn the art of forgiveness.

Key Points
- It is the message or meanings in anger that need to be considered rather than the anger itself.
- In learning how to be assertive, we focus on the hurt and the issue(s) behind conflict rather than attacking either ourselves or the other person.
- Non-assertive behaviors include aggression, inducing guilt, sulking and fearfully backing down.
- Anger at our own lack of assertiveness is a common experience. This self-directed anger can be more damaging to us than the lack of assertiveness.
- Because anger and assertiveness nearly always arise in situations of conflict, it is important that, after the conflict has passed, there is reconciliation and forgiveness. These may not take place if there are specific beliefs that stop them – for example, 'to apologize is to admit I was in the wrong or that I am letting people off the hook.'
- Forgiveness is actually an assertive action because we give ourselves the power to forgive and thus release ourselves from feelings of having been a victim for which we must seek revenge.

Exercises
- Focus on examples of assertive behaviour. These include:
  – Avoid attacking the other person for that will just put him/her on the defensive.
  – Work out what you want to say, focusing on a specific issue.
  – Be prepared to 'trade' and compromise. Avoid seeing either as signs of weakness.

  Here's an example involving Emma and Chris, who we met in Chapter 13. Emma was angry about Chris's lack of helping

continued on next page

---

around the house. However, she waited until they were relaxed together and then said:

> *You know, Chris, I wish we could spend more time together. However, I'm so busy with the house and it would be really helpful if you could lend a hand. I feel really left out when you go off to see your friends and I'm stuck here doing the ironing. It's not that I want to stop you going out but that I want to have more time, too. Look, I've worked out that, if you do more of the shopping and vacuuming I would have more time for myself. I'd really feel a lot better and not feel so taken for granted.*

Of course, this may not do the trick straight away but it's a start. Sometimes it helps to rehearse what you want to say – that is, rehearse your assertiveness skills. Remember, it is a step-by-step process and does not have to go perfectly first time. By preparing what you want to say, rather than waiting until you get angry and rushing in with attacks, you are more in control and will often achieve more.

- If you are prone to getting angry with yourself for not being as assertive as you would like to be, review the example of Roger on pp. 222–3. Work out if you are attacking yourself. Then rehearse the types of assertive things you would like to say. Say them out loud. Get used to speaking them and hearing yourself say them. Try to avoid brooding on your anger and on all the really nasty things you could say. You know that you probably won't say them so there is no point in rehearsing them. Try out only those things that you think you should say.
- An important aspect of acting assertively is 'slowing your thoughts down' to give you space to think. If you get into a conflict situation, don't feel that you have to respond immediately. One way to do this is to ask the other person to tell you more about what concerns him or her, rather than trying to defend yourself immediately.

You then might say to the other person, 'I can see how you could think of it that way, but this is how I see it.' Try to be factual

continued on next page

continued from previous page

rather than accusing. Try to stick to the issue at hand rather than trade personal attacks.

- Spend time thinking about forgiving others and letting go of the past. Write down the advantages and disadvantages of doing this. If you could let go of the past (and any desire for revenge you might feel), how would this help you? What stops you? What are your thoughts here? Try to use your rational/compassionate mind to challenge any negative beliefs you might have.

  If you feel that some of the hurts from the past are very serious, and it is impossible for you to embark on this journey alone, think about seeking help. The moment you say, 'I no longer want to remain a victim of my past,' you are taking the first step up and out.

- Try the Buddhist 'loving kindness' meditation. First, sit or lie down somewhere comfortable. Go through a relaxation exercise of the type given in Chapter 4. It does not have to be elaborate; just enough to get your breathing to subside to a calm rhythm. Now, think of yourself as a feeling, conscious being who needs loving kindness. Imagine yourself lying there and think that this person (i.e. you) needs loving kindness. Imagine the feeling of loving kindness directed at you. This may seem odd at first, but with practice, it may come. If there are things that you feel bad about, allow yourself to feel forgiveness for them. Admit to them and let them go. Sometimes people like to imagine themselves in a white or golden healing light. If you feel tearful, allow yourself to cry. Whatever works for you, use it. The idea is to develop the inner art of forgiveness. Forgiving yourself does not mean an end to trying to improve. It just means that improving and changing will be easier for you if you don't hang on to things from the past that cannot be changed.

  When you feel that you are succeeding at this, think of others close to you and of loving kindness directed at them. Gradually expand your feelings to as many other people as you would like. If others have hurt, you imagine forgiveness for them. This does not mean condoning their negative attitudes or backing down but rather letting go of destructive vengeance.

15

Dealing with Frustration, Disappointment and Lost Ideals

This chapter considers one of the most common reasons for anger – frustration. This usually involves the experience of being blocked or thwarted in the pursuit of something important. Both humans and other animals often react to frustration in specific ways, anger and irritation being the most common. Disappointment, also common to depression, is similar to frustration and usually involves some hope or expectation that does not turn out as desired.

Our emotional reactions to frustration and disappointment depend on the importance we place on things. Clearly, finding that we can't have things that we don't particularly want or value does not cause much upset, but if it is something we have set our hearts on, that's a different matter.

We can feel frustrated and disappointed about many things, but the most common are:

- When *things* don't work right or as we think they should.
- When *others* do not behave, or feel about us, as we want them to – e.g. don't show us enough affection, break promises.
- When we *ourselves* lack an ability to do or achieve something.
- When we *feel* certain things (e.g. feel depressed and lose energy, don't feel as positively about someone as we would wish, feel disappointed in ourselves because we lose the ability to feel affection or lose sexual feelings).

'Shoulds' and 'Oughts'

Disappointment is a major area where our 'shoulds' and 'oughts' come to the fore. We can believe that things, ourselves or other people 'should be like this and should not be like that.' The problem here is that, life being what it is, it will not respect our 'shoulds' and 'oughts'. Some people feel that we should not have to die, and instead of coming to terms with it, they rage about the fact that life 'shouldn't be like this.' Sometimes our 'shoulds' stop us from doing the emotional work we need to do in order to come to terms with things as they are and work out the best solutions for dealing with them.

We can develop a strong sense of 'should' when it comes to our own attitudes – e.g. 'I *should* work harder,' 'I *should not* make mistakes,' 'I *should not* be angry,' 'I *should* love my parents.' However, we can feel very disappointed when we don't turn out as the 'should' says we should. And 'shoulds' often involve anger and attempts to force ourselves to be different. When we strongly apply the 'shoulds' to ourselves, we inevitably end up bullying and attacking ourselves. It is as though we struggle to avoid accepting our limitations, setbacks or true feelings. The American psychotherapist Karen Horney called the shoulds 'a tyranny'.

When we apply 'shoulds' to other people, we often feel angry with them when they disappoint us. Instead of seeing them as they really are, we simply say 'they *should* be like this' or 'they *shouldn't* be like that.' Strong 'shoulds' often reduce our tolerance for frustration, and as we shall see shortly, 'shoulds' can lead to serious problems with disappointment. Indeed, Buddhism has recognized for thousands of years that much human misery stems from our frustrations and the way we think that we should have things or be a certain kind of person or that others should be a certain way. We can also become too attached to certain ideals and find giving them up painful.

Frustration Tolerance

Our ability to tolerate frustration can change for many reasons. You have probably noticed that, some days, you can cope with minor problems without too much effort, but on others, almost anything that blocks you can really irritate you. If we are driving somewhere in a hurry, we might see others on the road as 'getting in our way' and become angry. In extreme cases, we may even try to show them who is boss on the road. A situation such as this – called 'road rage' – becomes a primitive fight for dominance. As our feelings and attitudes become more urgent, we start to demand that things 'should be' different from the way they are.

Fatigue, tiredness and being under pressure are also typical everyday things that reduce our frustration tolerance. And depression itself can lower frustration tolerance.

The degree of frustration that a person feels can relate to a fear of shame. For example, Gerry lost his car keys on the day he had an important meeting. He became angry with himself and his family because the keys could not be found. In the back of his mind, he was thinking, 'If I don't get to the meeting on time, I will walk in late. Everybody will think I'm a person who can't keep to time and they will think I'm unreliable or careless.' At times, we may blame ourselves with thoughts like 'If only I were more careful, I wouldn't lose things.' Probably everyone could tell stories of how, when things are lost (e.g. the string or scissors are not in the drawer as expected), they became angry and irritated: 'Why are things never where they should be?'

Depression is most commonly associated with blocks to major life goals. It is often helpful therefore, to explore in what way you feel blocked in your goals and/or feel socially thwarted, frustrated and disappointed. This frustration and disappointment will relate to your expectations, hopes, aspirations and ideals.

Lost Ideals

Perhaps one of the most difficult things in life is coming to terms with disappointment. In Arthur Miller's play *Death of a Salesman*, the main character cannot come to terms with the way his life has turned out and that he did not make it big. The American dream has eluded him and his sense of disappointment over this broken ideal destroys him.

We can be set up for disappointment because our ideals, hopes and expectations are unrealistic. Instead of coming to accept the world, other people and ourselves as they or we are, we try to enforce our standards and ideals on them and ourselves. Sometimes it is our values and ideals that lead us deep into frustration.

At times, life can bring us down with a heavy bump. In Greek mythology, Icarus flew too high, melted his wings and fell back to earth. Like Icarus, our ideals can be overvalued and unrealistic. This can be a painful thing to admit to.

A serious thwarting of our life goals and ideals can trigger depression, especially if we see this as having a lot of social implications (e.g. loss of status, loss of a loving relationship) as well as implications for how our lives will be in the future. So to think about depression often means that we have to think about:

- What our ideals are.
- In what way we feel thwarted in reaching them.
- How we deal with the frustration and anger that comes when they are not met.
- What conclusions we can draw about ourselves, others and the future.
- Whether we are caught up in a strong sense of 'should'.

You can show this more clearly by writing out two columns of the *ideal* and the *actual* and then think about what I call the 'disappointment gap'. The disappointment gap leads to four possible outcomes: attack and blame the self; attack and blame others; give up; accept reality without seriously attacking either self or others.

Because attacking is a common response to frustration, we can see that we have found a root source of our internal bully – none other than our frustration. The more frustrated we are with ourselves, the more we may tend to bully ourselves. The internal bully does not really exist at all! It is, in effect, our 'attack self' response to frustration.

Let's work through some examples and see how this works.

Brian had set his sights on an important promotion. For over a year, he had worked hard to put himself in a good position, and his bosses had indicated that the promotion was within his grasp. He began to anticipate and plan how the new position would make his work easier and more interesting and how the extra money would allow him to move house. Unfortunately, two months before the promotion was due, Brian's company was taken over and all promotions were put on hold. Then, to make matters worse, the new company brought in some of their own personnel, and Brian found that the position he was going for had been filled by a younger man. He became angry and then depressed. All the plans, hopes and goals associated with the promotion seemed thwarted. He told himself that things never worked out for him and there was no point in trying to improve himself. His intense disappointment and anger in part fuelled his depression. He ruminated on the injustice of what had happened but had little power to change the situation – in effect, in his mind he kept fighting an unwinnable battle and thus saw himself as constantly frustrated and defeated. So his ideal–actual self looked like this:

Ideal	Actual
Get promotion	Didn't get promotion
Advance in career	Stuck in career
Move house	Stuck in same house

— *Disappointment Gap* —

- *Attack self:* I should have seen this coming. I should feel confident enough to try to get another job, but I'm not. If I were more assertive, I'd make them give me my promotion. I'm weak for not coping with this.
- *Attack others.* They're just using me. They're unfair, and they should be fair and realize that this promotion was promised to me by the old company. They have snatched an opportunity away at the last moment.
- *Give up:* I can't get out of this. Nothing will change. My future is ruined.

It is, of course, understandable why Brian felt bad about this lost promotion, but his anger and self/other-attacking made a bad situation worse. For him to come to terms with what happened – the fourth possible outcome – he had to recognize his sadness about it (rather than block it out with anger) and the depth of his 'shoulds' and stop attacking himself. He soon realized that he could not have 'seen it coming' and that it was not a matter of him not having been assertive enough. He gradually began to work out ways that he could get around this setback, waited a while and sought employment elsewhere. Coming to accept the situation and then working out how he could deal with it were important steps in his recovery.

'It's All Been Spoiled'

Depressed people often have the feeling that things have been spoiled. Susanne had carefully planned her wedding, but her dress did not turn out right and it rained all day. This was disappointing, but her mood continued to be low on her honeymoon. She had thoughts like 'It did not go right. It was all spoiled by the weather and my dress. Nothing ever works out right for me. Why couldn't I have had one day in my life when things go right?' She was so disappointed and angry about the weather and her dress that she failed to consider all the good things of the day, and how to put her disappointment behind her and get on and enjoy the honeymoon. She dwelt on how things had been spoiled for her. Later, when she considered possible positives in her life, she was able to give up her all-or-nothing thinking and to recognize that she was seeing the weather and the dress as almost personal attacks. She realized how her anger was interfering with her pleasure. She also acknowledged that many kinds of frustrations and disappointments in life are often activated by thoughts of 'everything has been spoiled.' She had to work hard to come to terms with her wedding 'as it was', but doing this helped to lift her mood.

The sense of things having been damaged and spoiled can be associated with the idea that things are irreparable and cannot be put right. In these situations, it is useful to work out how best to improve things rather than dwell on a sense of them being 'completely' spoiled. Of course, we might need time to grieve and come to terms with disappointments. I am not suggesting that one can simply rationalize disappointments away. The feelings can be strong indeed.

When we are depressed, we can sometimes feel that we are spoiling things for others or are a disappointment to them, or that they would be better off without us. Some children feel that they are a disappointment to their parents and live with feelings of guilt. They may think that they should have been different or better offspring. This can arise because they tend to focus on only the negatives and underestimate the positives. And it can be because they are actually disappointed in their parents – they did not praise them enough or give them enough attention. In a few cases, people can feel that they are spoiling things for others so much that they are a burden to them. To these individuals, suicide may seem like a good idea.

If you think that something has gravely spoiled things for you or that you are spoiling things for others, it can help if you talk about these feelings openly – don't make assumptions. It is the depression that is the problem, not you as a person. So, once again, check out if you are thinking in all-or-nothing terms, overgeneralizing or discounting the positives in your life. Has *everything* been spoiled? Are there some things that remain good or even just okay? Are you seeing more damage in a situation than there is? Are you seeing yourself more negatively than other people do? Are you attacking yourself? Are you making overly negative predictions about the future? What possibilities for the future are you cutting yourself off from?

Loss of a Positive Relationship

When we fantasize about our ideal partners, we usually see them as beautiful or handsome, kind and always understanding. And when it comes to sex, we may think that they should be like a battery that never goes flat. When we think about our ideal lover, we don't think about their problems with indigestion, the times when they will be irritable and stressed or take us for granted or that they could fancy other people.

As an adolescent, Hannah had various fantasies about what a loving relationship would be like. It would, she thought, involve closeness, almost telepathic communication between her and her lover and few if any conflicts. She believed that 'love would conquer all'. This type of idealizing is not that uncommon, but when Hannah's relationship started to run into problems, she was not equipped to cope with them because her ideals were so easily frustrated.

The early courting months with Warren seemed fine and they got on well. Sex was good and Hannah was sure that theirs was going to be a good marriage and she had many hopes and ideals for it. However, after six months of marriage, they had a major setback. The negotiations for a house they wanted to buy fell through. Then, while they were trying to find another, the housing market took off and they found that they had to pay a lot more for one of similar size. Warren felt cheated by life, his mood changed and he became withdrawn and probably mildly depressed. Hannah, who was also upset about the house problems, was more concerned about the change in her relationship with Warren. The gap between her ideal and the actual relationship started to widen. This was how the discrepancy in her ideal–actual relationship looked:

Ideal	*Actual*
Have fun together	Can't go out, short of money
Have few conflicts	Increasing conflicts
Always feel understood	Don't feel understood
Feel close to each other	Feel increasing distance

— *Disappointment Gap* —

- *Attack self:* Maybe I'm doing something wrong. If Warren cared for me, he would talk to me more. Maybe he doesn't love me any more. I get irritated with him so maybe it's my fault. He's lost interest in sex, therefore I am not sexually exciting any more. I should be able to cope better. Maybe I made the wrong choice of partner.
- *Attack other:* This is a different side to him. He should cope better and recognize my needs. He's being selfish and moody.
- *Give up:* There's no point in talking about what's wrong. We can't change the housing market. I'm stuck.

Warren had had similar ideals and expectations about their relationship. The problem was that, when these ideals were not met, he and Hannah both tended to blame either themselves or the other – and this made the situation much worse. To move out of this position, they first had to give up attacking themselves and each other and unite to tackle their common problems. Second, they had to recognize that the ideals they had held were rather unrealistic – and that was painful to do.

Gradually Hannah began to recognize that their problems were not about love but the hard realities of living. There was nothing wrong with her as a person if Warren felt down, nor was there anything necessarily wrong with the relationship. They had to learn to deal with their problems in a different way by encouraging each other to talk about their feelings. Hannah had often avoided this for fear that Warren would blame her or say that she was, in some way, part of the reason why he was feeling down. She also had to give up attacking him when he did not give her the attention that she wanted.

She slowly moved away from thinking that all problems in their relationship were to do with a lack of love. Warren had to acknowledge that his anger at the house problem was damaging their relationship and that he needed to work through his sense of injustice and belief that 'This is unfair and it shouldn't have happened.' He also had to recognize the effect his moods were having on Hannah. They eventually learned to build on the positives in their relationship rather than fighting over the frustrations.

The Ideal 'Other'

We often have fantasies of an ideal 'other'. This may be an ideal friend, sexual partner, child or parent. But reality being what it is, these ideals are rarely met. If our ideals are too far from reality, we are going to be mightily disappointed.

Anna felt that her mother never really loved her, and so she created in her mind a picture of her ideal mother – loving, warm and kind. In many ways, this image was very helpful to her. In therapy, she was encouraged to dispute her negative self-attacking thoughts by thinking about what her ideal mother would say. Unfortunately, Anna also wanted her real mother to be more like her ideal mother – and this her real mother could not be. Anna thought: 'Why can't she be like my ideal mother? She should treat me better. Maybe if I tried harder, she would be nicer.' But, sadly, her real mother never was the way Anna wanted her to be.

It can be useful to create images of the kind of person we would like to relate to if this helps us challenge negative self-attacking thoughts. However, the moment we say, 'Others should be like this,' and confuse fantasy and ideal with reality, we are likely to run into problems. We will, at the least, feel terribly disappointed.

We may also feel a continuous sense of disappointment with other people, even when they try, to their best ability, to be reasonable and kind. If our ideals are too high, we will always find fault. Rather than take and show pleasure in what they do, we tend to focus on what they don't do. And if we are honest, we can get a little selfish about it. We focus only on how far the 'other' meets our standards of what they should be like. We may feel resentment when they don't come up to scratch.

Disappointment and Frustration with What we Feel

So far we have discussed how we can be disappointed in things and people that block our goals and affect our relationships. Another key area of disappointment centres around personal feelings. Some depressed people go to bed hoping that they will feel better in the morning, and it is a great disappointment when they don't. If they can say, 'Yes, I am disappointed about this, but it takes time to get out of depression. I will go a step at a time today and see how far I can get,' they may be spared some pain. Unfortunately, depressed people often feel (understandably) angry and deflated when they wake up and don't feel full of energy. But they also make matters worse by attacking themselves, predicting that the day will go very badly and telling themselves they 'should' be better. There are many other feelings that can be a source of disappointment. Let's look at some examples.

Don's problem shows clearly how difficulties can arise when our hopes and ideals are disappointed by our own feelings. Don had suffered from anxiety attacks for many years and, as a result, felt that he had missed out on life. He developed a strong fantasy that, if someone could cure his anxiety, he would be able to be like other people and especially more like his brother who was successful in the art world. When I saw him, I found that his attacks were focused on a fear of being unable to breathe and of dying. However, by looking at the evidence that he was not going to die when he had an anxiety attack, and learning how to relax to gain more control over his attacks, he made progress. In fact, he did so well that he went on a trip to Europe. But when he came back, he went to bed, got depressed, felt suicidal and very angry.

We talked about the problem as one of unrealistic ideals. Don had the fantasy that, if his anxiety was cured, he would do a lot of things and make up for many lost years. In his fantasy, he would be like others, able to travel, be successful and, in his words, 'rejoin the human race at last.' He believed that normal people never suffered anxiety. Also he had hoped that there would be some magic method that would take the anxiety away, and that once it was gone, it would be gone for good. He explained that, on his European trip, he had suffered more anxiety than he'd expected.

We wrote out two columns that captured this situation, headed 'Ideal me' (i.e. without anxiety) and 'Actual me' (i.e. how I am now).

Ideal me	*Actual me*
Like others	Not like others/different
Able to enjoy life	Life is miserable
Confident/successful	A failure
Explorative	Frightened

Our conversation then went something like this:

PAUL. It seems that you did quite a lot on your trip, but you feel disappointed with it. What happened when you got back?

DON. I started to look back on it and thought, 'Why does it have to be so hard for me, always fighting this anxiety?' I should have enjoyed the trip more after all the effort I put into it. I should have done more. It's been a struggle. So I just went to bed and brooded on how bad it all was and what's the point.

PAUL. It sounds as if your experience did not match your ideal.

DON. Oh yeah, it was far from that.

PAUL. Okay, what went through your mind when you found that the trip wasn't matching your ideal?

DON. I started to think I should be enjoying this more. If I were really better, I'd enjoy it more. If I felt better, I'd do more. I'll never get on top of this. It's all too late and too much effort.

PAUL. That sounds like it was very disappointing to you.

DON. Oh yes, very, terrible, but more so when I got back.

PAUL. What did you say about you?

DON. I'm a failure. I just felt totally useless. After all the work we've done, nothing has changed.

PAUL. Let's go back to the two columns for a moment and see if I've understood this. For many years, you've had the fantasy of how things would be if you were better. But getting there is a struggle and this is disappointing for you. When you get disappointed, you start to attack yourself, saying that you're a failure and it's too late. That makes the 'actual' you seem unchanged. Is that right?

DON. Yes, absolutely.

PAUL. Can we see how the disappointment of not reaching the ideal starts up this internal attack on yourself, and the more of a failure you feel, the more anxious and depressed you get?

DON. Hmm, yes.

PAUL. Okay, it was a disappointment to have anxiety again. Were you anxious all the time?

DON. No, not all the time.

PAUL. I see. Well, let's start from the other end so to speak. If you had to pick out a highlight of the trip, what would it be?

DON [thinks for a moment]. There were actually a few, I suppose. We went to this amazing castle set up on the hill . . .

As Don started to focus on the positive aspects of his trip, his mood changed. He became less focused on the negatives and more balanced in his evaluation of the trip. Now I am not saying that you should simply 'look on the bright side' but to focus on the possibility that there may be some positives on which you can build. It is easy to become focused on disappointment. By the end of the session, Don was able to feel proud of the fact that he had been to Europe, whereas a year earlier, that would have been unthinkable. He was not magically cured of his anxiety but well on the way towards that goal.

Don was able to work with the links between his ideal, his disappointment and the attacks he made on himself. Because he was also prone to discount, or filter out, the positive things in his life if what he experienced did not match his ideal, we explored the successes of the trip. He saw his frustration and anger as 'destroying and ripping up' the good things that happened to him. This was all-or-nothing thinking fuelled by various 'shoulds'. For Don, the 'shoulds' were deep wishes, hopes and aspirations.

He began to lose his depression when he began to accept that his ideal might not be possible, and that he may have to grieve for some of the lost years. However, the more he focused on what he could do, rather than on how much he was missing out or how unfair it was to have anxiety attacks, the less depressed and self-attacking he became.

Disappointed with Oneself

We can feel that we have let ourselves down because we have not come up to our own standards or ideals. Here again, rather than accept our limitations and fallibilities – that maybe we have done our best but it did not work out as desired – we can go in for a lot of self-attacking. It is as if we feel we can't trust or rely on ourselves to come up with the goods. We start attacking ourselves like a master attacking a slave who hasn't done well enough. This frustration with oneself can be a major problem.

Lisa wanted to be confident like her friends. She wanted always to be in a good state of mind and never feel intense anger or anxiety or be depressed. She had two clear views of herself – her ideal and her actual self – and these would go hammer and tongs at each other.

Ideal self	*Actual self*
Relaxed and confident	Fearful and anxious
Hard-working	Lazy
Caring of others	Angry with others

— *Disappointment Gap* —

- *Attack self*: Oh God, I've let myself down again. Why do I have to be so anxious all the time? Why don't I just get on and do things? I am a useless, pathetic person.
- *Attack others*: Why do others always seem so confident? I hate them. They don't understand how difficult it is for me.

- *Withdraw*: I had better not try too much because it will not work out. I'm bound to fail and let myself down. I just can't rely on myself.

Both Lisa's ideal self and actual self were unrealistic. Her ideal self could not be met all the time. Her actual self (which she identified as her depressed self) was prone to discount the positives, think in all-or-nothing terms and overgeneralize.

It may be true that we can't rely on ourselves always to be anxiety free or make the best of things or be a mistake-free zone. The main thing is how we deal with our mistakes and disappointments. Attacking ourselves when we feel the anger of frustration is not helpful and, in the extreme, can make us very depressed. Learning to accept ourselves as fallible human beings, riddled with doubts, feelings, passions, confusions and paradoxes can be an important step towards self-acceptance.

Fiona had wanted a baby for about three years. She would fantasize about how her life would be changed with a child, and she engaged in a lot of idealized thinking of smiling babies and happy families. However, the birth was a painful and difficult one, and her son was a sickly child who cried a lot and was difficult to soothe. She found it difficult to bond with him and, within a short time, became exhausted and felt on a short fuse. At times, she just wanted to get rid of him. She took such feelings not as a natural (and indeed not that uncommon) experience of women after childbirth, but as evidence that she was a bad mother. When her son could not be soothed by her efforts, she thought that he was saying to her: 'You're not good enough.' She thought that, if she had been a better mother, she would not have had a sickly child, and she would have been loving and caring from the beginning, regardless of her fatigue. She felt intensely ashamed of her feelings, and could not tell her family doctor or even her husband of the depths of her exhaustion or feelings of wanting to run away. She felt her feelings made her a bad person. The reality of life with her small son brought a whole set of ideals crashing down around her head.

We can explore Fiona's ideal of her motherhood and her depression.

Ideal self	*Actual self*
Happy and relaxed	Tense and fraught; many sleepless nights
Feel loving towards my child	Want to run away, feel aggressive
Be able to soothe him	He is difficult to soothe

— *Disappointment Gap* —

- *Attack self:* I thought that I was a caring person but I feel so awful when he starts crying. I just want to leave him, to shut the door on him so I can't hear him. I can't cope, therefore, I'm a weak, inadequate and bad person. If people knew what was going through my mind, they would hate me, lock me up or take my son away. Maybe I don't deserve to be a mother. I hate myself for feeling this way.
- *Attack others:* Why does my son have to cry so much? He doesn't like me. If he'd only sleep like a normal child, it would be better. It's not fair. Why do others seem so happy with their babies? I hate them. It's not fair.
- *Give up:* There's nothing I can do. I should just passively accept this state of affairs or get away. No one could understand me.

Depression and exhaustion after childbirth are not uncommon. If this happens to you, try your best not to be ashamed of it – you are far from alone. Speak to your doctor and tell him or her exactly how you feel – that you want to run away, feel aggressive or whatever. You may need expert help, counselling or drugs to help lift your mood. Or you may need to talk to other mothers who have had similar feelings. The moment you stop attacking yourself and recognize that you may need help, you are taking the first steps towards recovery. Becoming depressed after childbirth is intensely sad and disappointing, and you can experience many odd feelings, but try not to be ashamed about this. Try, to the best of your ability, to get your rational/compassionate mind to speak to you.

Inner bully says	*Rational/compassionate mind says*
You are not coping and are failing as a mother.	Many complex changes have taken place in my body.

You are useless/bad.

It is natural to feel tired and exhausted.

Sometimes the changes that happen in childbirth produce some strange and odd feelings.

If I'm not coping too well, maybe I need extra help. I will talk to my doctor and seek his/her advice and help.

I'm not going to listen to the bullying part of myself, which will simply run me down. I can take my feelings seriously and try to find out what I can do about them.

If I don't bully myself, I'm less likely to feel ashamed about my feelings. They may be a great disappointment to me, but these feelings can and do happen to some women. There is nothing bad about me if I have these strange feelings – but I do need to try to obtain some help.

When we have these feelings of intense disappointment, there is often some bright spark who tells us to pull ourselves together, or who seems able to cope with everything. It may be someone in our lives who is being very critical of us, or who likes to tell us how well he or she coped with things and who can make us feel that, compared to him or her, we are failing. Try not to be too influenced by these people. What we feel is what we feel, and rather than attacking ourselves, it is preferable to look at the ways we can cope and sort out our problems in the ways that best suit ourselves.

Key Points
- We can be disappointed with things – e.g. blocks to major life goals, relationships and personal feelings.
- The anger and frustration of disappointment often set in motion

continued on next page

---

a train of thoughts that are either self-attacking and/or 'other' attacking.

- If we can learn to identify these thoughts early, we can take steps to challenge them and work through them.
- As the anger grows in us, there is a tendency to use many of the thinking styles we have met in earlier chapters (e.g. all-or-nothing thinking, overgeneralizing, disqualifying the positives, dwelling on the negatives).
- Although disappointments are always upsetting, we can perhaps learn to limit their effects on us and try to prevent them from driving us into depression.
- In reality, there is no internal bully as such – it is created by our own reactions to disappointment and frustration. It's the 'attack self' response.

Exercises
- Think of the last time you felt disappointed and angry about something. Then write down your 'Ideal' thoughts and your 'Actual' thoughts in two columns.
  Now find out if you do any of the following:

Attack self: Write down any self-attacking thoughts that have been produced by this disappointment.
Attack others: Write down any 'other-attacking' thoughts that have been produced by this disappointment.

- Now that you have worked out how you tend to react to disappointments, first *acknowledge your anger*. Ask yourself:
  Am I going in for all-or-nothing thinking?
  Am I discounting the positives? What remains good or okay?
  Am I saying that *everything* has been spoiled (i.e. over-generalizing).
  What would I say to a friend who had this disappointment?
  What would I like someone who cares for me to say to me?
  What evidence is there that shows I can cope with this? (Don't

continued on next page

continued from previous page

focus on the evidence against – which would be easy.)

- Look out for 'It–Me' problems. Distinguish clearly between your actions and your 'self'. For example, ask yourself: If I fail an exam, does this make me – a person, my whole being, my totality – a failure? I might *feel* like a failure but this does not make it true. Are you saying, 'I only accept *me* if I do *it* well'?
- *'Shoulds' and 'Musts':* Explore the pressure of the 'shoulds' and 'musts' in your life and how they can produce more emotional pain.
- *Shame:* Are you disappointed because somehow you feel ashamed at not meeting your ideals? (If so, look at the shame exercises in Chapter 12).
- And finally, the most painful bit, in a friendly voice ask yourself, 'Are my ideals realistic?'

16

Perfectionism and Competitiveness, or How the Secret of Success is the Ability to Fail

Depressed people are often surprised when I suggest that 'the secret of success is the ability to fail.' So much in our society concentrates on succeeding and achieving things that we have actually become incompetent at failing. Yet, if you think about it, success, like love, looks after itself. Most of our problems don't come from succeeding or doing well but from failing and not doing well. The way we cope with disappointment and setbacks can do much to throw us into depression, especially if we spiral into self-attacking and self-dislike. Learning how to fail without self-attacking can be a useful means of exerting more control over moods.

One reason why failure becomes a serious problem is because, perhaps without realizing it, we have become perfectionist and competitive people to whom the idea of failure is a terror. I should also say that, while I will sometimes refer to people who are perfectionists, this is only for simplicity's sake, since it is more accurate to refer to perfectionist styles. Indeed, we can become more perfectionist in our thinking as we become depressed.

Before exploring perfectionism, it is useful to remember that failure is part of life. It is inevitable. Think of learning any new skill: learning to play the piano, tennis and so on, or a baby learning to walk. The chances are that, in the beginning, the failures will greatly outweigh the successes. If, for example, a baby gave up trying to walk the first time it fell over, it would never get going. But there are times later in life when we expect ourselves to get everything right from the beginning. This, of course, is not humanly possible.

If we can cope with failure and not be terrorized by it, we are much more likely to succeed and be more relaxed in the process. Perfectionism and competitiveness, along with unrealistic ideals, are reasons why failing can be so hard. If you hold highly perfectionist attitudes, you are going to run into many failures simply because it's tough being perfect.

Perfectionism

In some ways, perfectionism relates to having high ideals and believing that we must reach them or else we are worthless and bad in some way. However, perfectionism is a little more complex than this. Research by the Canadian psychologists Paul Hewitt, Gordon Flett and their colleagues has found that there are three forms of perfectionism:

- *Self-orientated perfectionism:* Here the focus is on high standards and the need to be perfect. When people fall short of these standards, they can become highly self-critical and experience a lot of frustrative anger.
- *Other-orientated perfectionism:* Here people demand high standards of others. They can become angry with others if the latter are not up to the mark. The other-orientated perfectionist may look for how far people fall short of a standard rather than how good they are.
- *Socially prescribed perfectionism:* Here people believe that it is others who expect high standards of them and that they will be rejected or shamed if they don't come up to those expected standards.

At present, it remains unclear how far perfectionism drives certain depressions. One reason for perfectionism is the fear of failure. This is related to the competitive side of our personalities. It may be the fear of failure that is the real problem in perfectionism – especially if a person is prone to intense self-criticism. It is also possible that perfectionism leads to frequent instances of disappointment and 'defeat', and that this sense of defeat results in depression.

Competitiveness

Are you happy being average? If someone said that you are an average lover, wife, husband, doctor, driver or cook, how would you feel? There are probably some areas of your life where you would be content to be average, and if you are very poor at doing something (e.g. playing a game), being average might actually be good. However, would you be content to be average in all areas? If you cook a meal for people, would you be happy for them to say, 'Thanks for the average meal?' If you make love to someone, would you be happy to know that he or she felt your love-making was average? Well, perhaps, but often we want to feel special, at least some of the time and to some people (e.g. our parents or lovers). Most people might feel a little upset if they thought that their parents loved them no more than any other person. I think most people would recognize that this desire to feel special, at least some of the time, is normal. Indeed, telling someone that they are average is occasionally seen as a put-down: 'What! Only *average*?'

You can tell where your competitiveness lies by asking yourself two questions. First, in which areas of your life would you not settle for being average? And second, in what areas of your life are you concerned by what others have, are doing or are achieving? Your answers will tell you your areas of competitiveness. This competitive drive – to be socially successful, and seen as special – can play a role in depression.

Some forms of perfectionism are related to competitiveness. Competitive perfectionists tend to see life as a competition. There are two forms of competitive perfectionist styles. The first I will call 'keep up' competitiveness: these people strive to be as good as others, are highly focused on what others are doing or thinking, and are likely to say things like 'Other people can do this so, so should I.' They are running in a race to 'keep up', and their main fear is of not being as good as others and being seen as inadequate or inferior. Much of their thinking is dominated by social comparison, with negative thoughts and feelings being triggered when they see others doing better than themselves.

For example, Veronica discovered that her friend had decorated her bedroom and made new curtains. Veronica thought: 'My friend does things so easily. I ought to be able to achieve similar things. I don't cope as well as she does and am therefore inferior to her and inadequate.' Veronica was continually trying to reach standards set by others, and seeing what others could do became a driving force to achieve the same. Many people are like this to some extent, but perfectionists demand that they should *always* be at the same standard as others, or else they attack themselves. They drive themselves to reach high standards because they think others are already at this level. They may deny that they do this, but it is relatively easy to find in them a desire to avoid being seen as inferior. When they engage in this style of activity, they tend to take their standards from those around them and find it difficult to set their own.

The second style is 'get ahead' competitiveness – to be seen as special, unique and/or superior. Some people who are perfectionist about their diets or weight are like this. Ursula had an eating disorder and saw control over her body and its appearance as making her superior to others, and giving her an advantage over them. Edgar was a keen tennis player and the best at his club until another man joined who was better than he was. Edgar became preoccupied with his own playing and his need to be better, and became intensely self-critical if his performance was less skilled than the new member's. The motto of those who subscribe to the 'get ahead' competitive style is: 'There is only one place to be and that is at number one.' Of course, some people try to get ahead by cheating or 'wheeling and dealing', but although they may be highly competitive, they are not perfectionists. They will settle for whatever gives them an advantage. What marks the competitive perfectionist is the focus on and drive to meet standards.

Competitive perfectionists do not always admit that their actions are designed to make them superior or special, but they certainly behave as if this is the case. They do not like to come second and can feel upset if others (and especially those who they regard as inferior) do better. Like the 'keep up' competitive person, their standards can be taken from those around them and are not set by themselves, and they are very sensitive to what others think about them.

Many of us have these aspects in our psychology to some degree. Indeed, from an evolutionary point of view, those individuals who were not competitive would not leave many genes behind them. As we have seen, most human beings want to keep up, have some means of impressing others, feel accepted and, at times, special. However, in the perfectionist, these traits are marked. To fail to reach those standards is, for them, to risk inferiority or a loss of admiration and approval. This results in anger, frustration and self-attacking.

It turned out that it was not just in playing tennis that Edgar was competitively perfectionist. A couple of years earlier, the man next door had put in a new kitchen. Before he went to see this, Edgar had had no thoughts of changing his own, but you can guess what happened. As soon as he saw the new kitchen, he had to have a new kitchen himself *and* it had to be better than the other man's. While he was putting it in, he became easily frustrated if it would not fit correctly. When I asked him to focus on the thoughts going through his mind, they were : 'I bet he didn't have this much trouble putting in his kitchen. I've got to make mine better than his; if not, I will feel that he has got one up on me and I will feel inadequate.'

Some people demand high standards of themselves even if these standards cannot be reached. Frank was an artist who thought that his work should be recognized by others as exceptional. He was intensely self-critical but also full of resentment at how others seemed to lack appreciation of his work. And if he heard of other painters (whom he regarded as less able than himself) winning prizes or gaining recognition, he would feel enraged and depressed. He always perceived people as trying to ignore him, put him down and prevent him from gaining the admiration he needed. At no time, before therapy, did he consider that his paintings were good but no more than that. They *had* to be great and others *had* to be full of admiration for them!

Perfectionist behavior can be activated in social situations that are seen as competitive. Many socially anxious people feel they have to be *really* interesting; to be boring or average is seen as a terrible thing to be. So they continually monitor their behavior for its 'interest' level, which increases their anxiety and makes easy conversation very difficult. Just imagine for a moment that you go to a party and every time you try to say something, you tell yourself, 'The others will find this boring. It's not interesting. I won't be able to hold their attention. They would rather speak to someone else.' Eventually, you would get really anxious, which, of course, is what happens to the socially anxious person. Their ideals of being good conversationalists are extreme and they think that they will be rejected if they are not good at this.

Despite what many people think, perfectionism and constantly striving to keep up, win and succeed are not that helpful, at least not if you want to live a reasonably happy life. One thing research has shown us is that perfectionists don't have a good time. They are prone to get depressed, anxious, irritable and suffer from various other conditions such as anorexia and drink problems. And the reason for this is that failures and setbacks ignite much anger and self-attacking. These people take failures very badly.

Doing Your Best

Now before we go any further, let's be clear about one thing. Most of us accept that trying to do our best is a good idea. If something is worth doing, it's worth putting some effort into it. The problem is: how much effort? Even if you work twenty hours a day, you might, in principle, say that you could have worked twenty-one hours a day. If perfectionists fail, they inevitably say they could have done more. The problem is clear – the goal posts keep moving.

It's similar for 'other-orientated' perfectionists. Even if you put a lot of effort into something, the other-orientated perfectionist will still say that you could have done more. Sara studied hard for her exams and got reasonable grades but not all top marks. Her parents indicated to her that she could have tried harder even though she had studied many hours a day. Sara was not able to see the unreasonableness of this but accepted their view and felt guilty and ashamed. It was as if her parents did not notice how much work she had done, but only focused on the comparatively few times when she took breaks from studying. Later in life, Sara may well have problems in judging what is reasonable effort and what is not.

So another problem with perfectionists is that they only judge themselves and others by the results and not their efforts. No effort is good enough if it does not produce the desired results.

Doing It All

Tina was often confronted by a feeling of being overwhelmed at home. There was the house to clean and the children to take to school, and never enough time. Her main belief was: 'I must do it all.' I used to feel exhausted just talking to her! Behind this belief were the following ideas: 'If I don't do everything, I will be letting others down. They expect it of me. Other women can do these things *and* go out to work. Therefore, I am inadequate, if I don't keep up.'

After some work together, Tina and I worked out some alternative thoughts:

- I am imposing these standards on myself.
- I can prioritize and recognize that I don't need to do it all.
- Frankly, some of this housework is boring and I'm lonely at home. That's why I don't feel like doing these things – it's not because I'm inadequate.
- I need to put time aside to do things I enjoy, such as visit friends – even if this means that I don't get everything done.
- I can go step by step and break down the chores rather than focus on all of them.

It also turned out that Tina could not let her husband help because she saw the home as 'her territory'. Moreover, although he was keen to help, when Tina allowed him to he was often less thorough than she was. Her perfectionist attitude meant that she was often dissatisfied with other people's efforts to help her. And she felt guilty and inadequate for needing her husband's help.

Letting others down and feeling guilty can be a driving force behind some perfectionist styles. So can a need to be 'in control'. Tina had the fear that, if she were not in control, 'everything will fall apart and disasters will happen.' This gave her some feeling of importance (i.e. she was needed) but not in a helpful way. The idea that 'others can't cope without me' is not uncommon in some perfectionist styles.

The Loss of Pleasure

Perfectionists can also cut themselves off from many positive pleasures. They are less likely to enjoy things for 'the thing in itself' but only focus on the results. For example, when painting pictures non-perfectionists may enjoy getting out in the fresh air to paint or simply putting paint on canvas. They may try out new things and have fun messing about with new ideas. Perfectionists, however, can enjoy few of these things, for in the back of their minds is always the question: 'Is it good enough?' Frank the artist told me how he would fly into rages and rip up his work if he could not make the image that he had in his mind appear on the canvas. Even in sex perfectionists may be more focused on how they perform than on getting lost in the pleasure of it. They have to 'do it right.' A patient of mine who used to go hiking complained that he could have been walking anywhere; what seemed to matter more was how many miles he covered. He would set himself tests – 'Can I walk twenty miles today?' Even if it had been a bright and beautiful day and the countryside had been in full bloom, he would hardly notice this, because he was so intent in doing his set number of miles – often as quickly as possible.

At one level, we may see this as 'gaining pleasure from achievement.' However, in depression there is often a sense of not achieving enough and certainly a loss in the ability to enjoy the simple pleasures of life.

The disappointment and dissatisfaction with performances that perfectionists feel can result in a number of difficult emotions: guilt, anger, frustration, shame, envy and anxiety. These negative emotions can make life a misery.

Perfectionism and the Internal Bully

One problem with perfectionism and competitiveness is that frustrative anger tends to get directed at the self by the actions of the internal bully. A competitive person can even 'adopt' the bully and believe that, unless they bully themselves, they will never do what is necessary to succeed. Consider Barry. He was well aware that there was a strong bullying and self-critical part to himself. He hated failure. Yet, although he knew that this was partly a source of his depression, and the reason why he had trouble with close relationships (he'd get moody if he had setbacks, or his lover did not come up to his standards), he was very reluctant to tackle the bully. When I invited him to 'let the bully speak', the bully 'said':

Barry is basically a lazy person. He needs me to kick him into action. Without me, he would never make anything of his life. He'd end up miserable and down and out. No one would respect him and he would constantly fail. He is basically a weak, useless person.

When Barry focused on these thoughts, he was at first surprised by their strength but they also seemed true to him – he agreed with his bully in a passive accepting way. On reflection, he realized that the bully was the voice of his father, so initially he felt unable to challenge it. But in time he learned to fight back. He came up with the following:

Actually, I'm not half as lazy as you think I am. To be frank, it is you, bully, when you hit me so hard, who makes me depressed. This depression causes most of my problems. You like to kick me when I'm down. If you are really as keen on success as you say you are, the best way to treat me is with kindness and support when things are tough. If I feel confident, I'm likely to do far more than if I'm full of fear, anger and disappointment.

It took a while but Barry finally began to bring his bully under control. The first step was for him to see how, for years, he'd accepted the messages of his inner bully and had never tried to fight back but only submitted to and placated it. But as I say to all my patients: Never try to placate bullies – they feed off that and only grow stronger.

If we don't control our inner bullies (which originate partly from frustration), they knock us down when we fail. Then it is difficult to recover from a setback and keep going. Moreover, they won't allow us to take time out to enjoy the simple pleasures of life. Their message is: 'Do, do, do, and when you've done, do more.'

Barry had also come to believe that he had no real motivation of his own, that there were few things that he was interested in or could aspire to – all his successes had been obtained because of the bully. This was very sad because, in fact, Barry was a very caring and passionate man. He would achieve more if he allowed himself to be motivated by his own inner desires rather than being bullied into action. Indeed, we can get so used to doing things because we are bullied into them that we lose the sense of our own joy of life, of excitement and the desire to succeed. Think about it this way. Suppose you have sex because you think you ought to, that this is what you are supposed to do. How can you then discover your own sexuality and its pleasures? How can you come to explore your sexuality and be motivated to satisfy your own desires? You can't. The most control you can exercise is to say 'No' to it!

When people decide that they don't want to do something, this decision can be seen as an act of rebellion against being bullied – not laziness. Many people find this out after leaving school. For example, I hated English and my teachers thought I was lazy – I had to force myself to do it. Later, without the pressure to pass exams I got to really enjoy writing and studying – but only after I did not have to do it.

So, if you only do what is expected of you by others, or because of your internal bully, you will tend to lose interest in doing that thing. You will, at one level, feel resentful at having to do it. Yet free yourself from this pressure (challenge that internal bully) and you may find a new source of energy that motivates you.

Hope for Success and the Fear of Failure

At times our competitive side can be carried away by fantasies of success. Ideals are set so high that they are impossible to achieve, so we live with a constant background sense of disappointment. Sometimes this reveals itself in the idea: 'I want to be a somebody rather than a nobody.' Anything that seems to block the path towards achieving these ideals is met with anger and frustration. Now, ideals are fine as far as they go, but if we fall into the trap of saying, 'I must reach my ideal, otherwise all else is worthless,' we are heading for trouble. We often fail to explore and enjoy the pleasures of living 'now' and focus only on where we want to go and how far from our ideal we are.

The other side to this is that 'hope for success' can hide a deep 'fear of failure'. What research has shown is that those people who have a high fear of failure tend to be:

- more attentive to the cues that signal possible failure rather than to cues that signal possible success.
- prone to self-criticism.
- prone to feelings of worthlessness.
- lacking in energy and concentration.
- likely to have difficulty in making decisions.

The constant fear of 'getting it wrong' takes a terrible toll.

Now there is one other important aspect to a 'fear of failure': sometimes it is not related to hope for success. I have found that people who suffer from a fear of failure rarely enjoy successes. Instead, they only feel a sense of relief from not having failed. For example, when Harry passed his exams, his main feeling was one of relief at not having failed, and he found it difficult to enjoy his classmates' celebrations. When he got married, his main feeling was: 'Oh, thank God, I got through that.' And when he obtained his first promotion, he thought: 'What a relief! I've made it through my first big test.' Harry rarely thought: 'Wouldn't it be wonderful if I succeed?' but rather 'Wouldn't it have been terrible if I failed?' Life was a constant struggle of dodging problems.

Proving Oneself and Self-centredness

Some forms of perfectionism and competitiveness are very self-centred. Indulging in these types of behavior can actually block our ability to relate openly with others. Suppose you came to see me for therapy. Which would you prefer: that I am concerned to do all I can to help you because I am interested in you, or that I try to ensure that I do the best I can because I don't want to fail or be seen to fail – I am more concerned with my reputation than with you? Or suppose your lover has sex with you. Which would you prefer: that he or she wishes to share the experience with you, or that he or she makes love to prove that he or she is good at it?

Sadly, some perfectionists are so self-centred that they turn nearly all activities into reflections of themselves. If they fail, thoughts such as 'What does this mean about me?' dominate their thinking. Because they have not got control over their inner bully, they cannot afford to fail. It is not so much concern with others but how they feel about themselves. Of course, it is not quite as 'all or nothing' as I am making out – it is a matter of degree – but I hope that you see the issue here. The more you control your inner bully (and your frustration if you do poorly), the less self-focused you will be and the more you may be able to develop more satisfying relationships.

Perfectionism, Pride and the Desire to Impress Others

Sometimes we develop perfectionist and competitive standards as a way of dealing with shame. We have the motto: 'If we are perfect, we are beyond reproach, beyond shame or criticism.' Moreover, because we believe that our perfectionist standards are worthy of approval, we may only feel good if we reach them.

Kay, a dancer, was known to be a perfectionist. She was moody and rarely satisfied with her performance. At times she would push herself to the point where she would ignore small injuries, which would then become major problems. At these times, she would become depressed and angry with her body for letting her down. True, she did reach high standards but never seemed to enjoy her successes or, if she did, they were short-lived enjoyments. She had the motto: 'You are only as good as your last performance.' In therapy, we explored the origins of these standards and found that they came from her relationship with her father. She had always wanted to do something that her father would be proud of, and she was desperate to win his approval. Her father never showed strong feelings, either positive or negative, but Kay believed that, if she became famous or did something special, in some way he would have to take note of her and admire (and love) her, and so would other people. Gradually, as she moved into adulthood, she became less aware of how her father's approval was a driving force in her perfectionism.

Kay demonstrated a very common element in perfectionism – that it sometimes originates in the desire to do things to make someone proud of us, to see us as special and worthy of affection and attention. We are concerned to impress others. It may be that we think that they demand high standards or it may be that we think that achieving high standards is the way to their hearts.

Ask yourself: Why do I want to reach the standards that I've set myself? You have to be really honest in your answers. Here are some that others have given:

- I want to impress others.
- I want to be a somebody rather than a nobody.
- I want others to see how good I am.
- I don't want others to see the bad side of me or my flaws.
- I want to avoid being criticized and thought of as worthless.
- Life is pointless if you don't succeed.
- I must not let others down.
- There has to be something I am good at.

It does not matter too much what your wants, wishes and hopes are provided that you can cope with them not coming to fruition. If you say, 'I'd like to impress others,' that may be fine. But if you say, 'I *must* impress others, otherwise they will see me as inadequate and I will feel useless,' you have a problem. And the reason why is that failure and setbacks will generate such anger with yourself and others that this can drive you into depression.

Personal Pride and Perfectionism

Some people with eating disorders, who become very thin, are often highly perfectionist and competitive. However, they have a pride in themselves because they exert control over their eating and weight. Often the problem starts when they get on the scales, see that they have lost weight and feel a thrill or buzz of pride from the achievement. To put on weight produces a feeling of deflation and shame. They can become obsessed with every calorie and type of food they eat. This is an example of shame turning to pride. They may feel ashamed of their bodies or believe that there is not much about them to be proud of – but then they hit on the idea of weight loss, and the pride of losing weight drives them on.

When shame turns into pride, it takes a real struggle to change this. Helping these people to put on weight may be seen as taking away the only thing (losing weight) they feel good at. This kind of problem is a very different one from, say, panic attacks. Nobody wants panic attacks, so therapist and patient can line up together against the common problem. But anorexic people want to be thin; they want to maintain their perfectionist standards.

It is the same with all forms of perfectionism and competitiveness, be it cleaning the house, playing a sport well, working long hours and so on. *The person does not want to give up these things.* However, it is the reactions to failure and setbacks that have to be changed. If the sports person becomes depressed because he or she is not playing well and loses confidence in him/herself that is hardly helpful.

Pride and Confidence

Pride is actually quite different from confidence. In fact, we may call pride 'false confidence'. The reason for this is that pride depends on your performance – on what you think others will value. That is not confidence, although if you can reach your standards, you might feel confident. But this can be a fragile confidence. What happens the moment you fail? Your confidence disappears like the morning dew.

Real confidence comes from a belief in yourself as a person. That is, whether, succeeding or failing, you are able to cope without generating intense disappointment and anger that turns to self-attack or thoughts of hopelessness. You are neither carried away by success nor seriously deflated and depressed by failure and setbacks. You may have a strong desire to do well or look good and put much effort into these things, but your inner self is able to accept you as you are. This is the source of confidence – self-acceptance. You learn to be accepting of yourself for good or ill. Anything else means that you are only a fair weather friend to yourself. But real friendship and acceptance is standing by someone when the chips are down.

Envy and Competitiveness

Some styles of competitiveness can also generate envy of others and an inability to accept that others may, in some situations, be better and more capable than oneself. Alex, who was training to be a therapist, was an able student, but he took my suggestions on improving his skills very badly. I wondered if I was putting my suggestions across too critically. But every suggestion I made seemed to put him on the defensive and he would argue against it. After a time, I admitted to feeling rather irritated by him. He could take nothing from me and seemed to devalue whatever I said. I commented to him that he seemed to want to be a 'great' therapist without having to go through the difficult learning process.

After some difficult conversations, he reflected that his early life had been full of perfectionist and competitive demands from his parents. He had never been allowed to fail. So in his mind, if I showed him how he could improve, he viewed this as him 'not being good enough.' He had an easily activated sense of shame, and as a result, he was unable to acknowledge that others had things of value to offer him. In groups, he was envious, competitive and prone to run down others. If he had seen that others knew more than he did, he would then have had to acknowledge that he could improve, and to Alex that meant that he had to acknowledge that he was not perfect. A recognition of a need for something, like advice and training, was (to him) an acknowledgment of his limitations and thus not being (in his mind) good enough.

Shame-prone individuals who become competitive can be a problem to themselves and others because they go so easily on to the defensive. They feel bad if others criticize them or are more able than they are. Another person's gain is their loss. Competitive envy causes many problems in depression because it stops people acknowledging their need for others and their own vulnerabilities. They also begrudge the attributes, success, rank, status and attention accorded to other people. They may fail to offer assistance to those who succeed and try to undermine their efforts.

Envy can also come from a feeling of powerlessness and anger at being in that position. The American psychotherapist Althea Horner gives this example in her book *The Wish for Power and the Fear of Using It*:

A woman who characteristically clung to a powerless position in order to force her mother to take care of her, as well as to protect the mother against the hate of her own envy of the older woman's power, said of an associate, 'I hate her, and there's nothing that can be done about it. I spoil her by thinking her seams are crooked or that she only seems nice because she is so shallow. I am powerless with her. I do want to smash her, to get rid of her, to tell her what I think of her. And I hate you [the therapist] for being so strong. I feel impotent. I can't change you. I kiss ass and walk away hating you. It's a passive ragefulness.'

Although she used to think of herself as competitive, she came to understand the critical difference between competitiveness and envy. This difference resides in the degree of hostility and the wish to spoil or destroy that go with envy. One can value the competitive rival and have no wish to harm that person. In competitiveness, unlike envy, the only wish is to win.

If these are experiences you can identify with, you can try to change them. First, you can see that you are not alone in feeling this way. Second, by recognizing them, you are closer to understanding and challenging these thoughts. Try not to attack yourself if you realize that you have envious feelings, thoughts and attitudes. In fact, this is a step forward. When we are depressed, we can often feel envious of those who are not. As one patient said to me, 'Sometimes I would just like to wipe the smiles off their faces and let them feel what I am feeling. Then they would not be so smug about it.' When you feel angry with others it can sometimes be that this anger comes from envy.

Challenging Competitiveness and Perfectionism

To challenge competitiveness and perfectionism requires us to first recognize them in ourselves. However, it is often the case that we don't always see these styles in ourselves.

One way of exploring your competitive and perfectionist styles is to write down the advantages and disadvantages of failing and to explore your fears (the disadvantages) of failing. Here's an example.

Pauline felt that she had constantly to keep up with the housework but denied that she was a perfectionist. The very idea seemed a joke to her – 'That,' she said 'is the last thing I am.' But look at the advantages and disadvantages of keeping her house up to scratch that she wrote down. Her first thoughts were: 'There is so much to do and I must do it all.' If she did do it, then:

Advantages of keeping house tidy
- I'll feel I've achieved something.
- If I feel I have achieved something, I'll feel better about myself.
- I'll prove to myself that I am not lazy.
- I'll prove that I am as good as other people.
- The family expect it of me.
- They'll like, love and respect me more.

Disadvantages of not keeping house tidy
- I'll feel lazy.
- I'll have let my family down.
- I'll have shown once again that I cannot cope.
- My family will be disappointed in me and be angry – even if they don't admit it.
- I'll feel that I have failed.
- I'll feel useless.

You can see that showing through these advantages and disadvantages are perfectionist styles of thinking. There is the expectation that others (the family) will be disapproving of her; there is the feeling of being lazy and worthless for not succeeding; and there is a social com-parison (others can do these things so I should also be able to).

It might be interesting for you to reflect on Pauline's thoughts and think how you might help her. What would you say? Would you agree with her? If your answer is 'Yes', then look at the implications. What this means is that, if you went to Pauline's house and found her sitting depressed in her kitchen, not able to get on and do things, you would say to her: 'Look, Pauline, you are being very lazy. Other people can keep their houses clean, so why not you? Your family expects it of you and you are letting them down. They are going to be rightly angry with you. You are not as good as other people and are worthless.'

The chances are that you would not treat someone who was

depressed like this. You would probably not even think like this when dealing with someone else. (If your internal bully was in control of your thoughts, it's possible that you might think it but you would not say it.) Why? You don't need to be a psychologist to know that it would push her further into depression.

So let's imagine that, when you visit Pauline, you come as a helper and healer. What would you say? First, you would be sensitive to her feelings.

Look, Pauline, you are feeling depressed right now, so all this must seem like a mountain to climb. Let's try to plan a couple of things that you might be able to do, and go from there. If you can do one thing, you are one step further on.

Next, you might start to tackle her self-attacking thoughts.

You know that, when you feel well, you can do the housework okay. This problem has nothing to do with being lazy. If you were simply lazy, you'd put your feet up, read the newspaper and enjoy not doing anything. Maybe you're bored with housework and this makes it even more difficult. Maybe you feel very lonely here on your own, struggling to do the housework when the family have all gone to school or work. If that's true, we can think about it and try to see what we can do to change the situation. But first, you need to see that this is not about laziness.

Next, you might deal with her habit of comparing herself to others.

Sure, other people can do housework when they are not depressed, but most people struggle when they are. By comparing yourself with others, you will feel worse. Let's focus on what you can do rather than what others can do, and move on from there.

Next, you might discuss her family's expectations.

Could you ask them for more help? Ah, I see that you think that this will make you dependent on them or feel inferior to them. Well, right now the important thing is to get the help you need and to express your feelings. Sometimes we need to learn how to let others help us for a while. You think that your family will be critical of you for needing help? Do you have any evidence for that? Even so, maybe they are expecting too much. But the thing is, even if they are critical, this doesn't mean that you have to accept what they say as being true about you. Maybe they don't understand how bad depression feels. That's lucky for them, but then they are not in a good position to judge, are they? Of course, if you are angry with them and attack them for not helping, this will put them on the defensive, but if you are open and reasonable, they might understand. Have you tried that? Have you tried being thankful for help or have you always accepted it grudgingly?

Now you have an idea of how you might help Pauline. First, you would recognize the depression, then focus on doing small things, going step by step. Then you would try to help Pauline stop attacking herself and engaging in all-or-nothing thinking ('I have to do it all'). Then you might assist her to address the problem of asking her family for help because you recognize that their help could be useful to her. You might also focus on her thinking: does she discount the positives in her life or does she overgeneralize? The last thing you would want to do is to be negative towards her, for this would not work.

Now that you have seen how this kind of approach might help Pauline, you can use the same principles to deal with your own problems.

I have discussed Pauline's situation because it may not, on the surface, appear to involve competitiveness or perfectionism. But both of these styles were definitely in play, for two reasons. First, because if Pauline had believed that everyone had the same sorts of problems, she would have been less negative about herself. Second, because her thinking focused on trying to do everything rather than going a step at a time. Thus, it is preferable to learn to cope with being able to do less than one ideally would like. Another reason for using this example is because the problems it brings to light are relatively common in depression. Now in fact, it would not matter if we were perfectionist about our work or about achieving certain outcomes, such as a painting; the principles are the same. People often want to do more than they can, and it is when they fail to achieve their goals that problems begin.

And to get out of these problems means coming to accept our

limitations: that we are less than perfect; that we can survive failures and setbacks without attacking ourselves or becoming overly despondent. We may not be able to 'do it all,' but that doesn't mean we can't go some way towards doing some things.

It is not doing your best that is at issue. It is how we cope with failure and disappointment that may cause trouble. This is why the key to success is the ability to fail. When we fail, we have to learn to treat ourselves kindly. Anyone can feel good about themselves if they succeed. We have to find ways of minimizing our bad feelings if we don't do something well. We also have to learn to prioritize and decide what has value to us and what does not. Is it better to spend all your time making the house spotless, or is it preferable to be more relaxed about housework and focus on relationships with your family? Are achievements more important to you than relationships?

Key Points

- We can direct competitiveness and perfectionism towards ourselves or others or because we think others expect these styles of thinking of us.
- Some of our perfectionism is competitive – used because we want to avoid being seen as inferior or because we want to be seen as superior and special.
- It is sometimes a 'pressure to succeed' that reveals our perfectionist and competitive styles.
- We can become very self-centred if we drift into perfectionism. This is often because we have let our internal bully have too much control.
- The main problem with these styles of thinking is that they can lead to anger, frustration, guilt and anxiety about failing.
- These feelings can result from, and increase, the amount of attacking that we do to ourselves and others. This can spin us into a spiral of feeling more depressed.
- There is nothing wrong with high standards themselves, but it is how we cope with ourselves and others when, life being life, they cannot be met.

Exercises

- Your competitive and perfectionist styles will show up most clearly when you fail at something. So think about a time when you failed to achieve something. Now ask yourself the following questions:
  - What standard was I trying to achieve?
  - Why would it have been good if I had achieved that? What did I hope to get out of it?
  - Was I trying to avoid being seen as inferior or did I want to be seen as superior?
  - Are these my own standards or ones I think others expect of me?
  - Was I trying to impress others?
  - Am I a person motivated to succeed – seeking the pleasures of success – or am I someone who is primarily motivated to avoid failure? If the latter, I can start to learn to enjoy the pleasures of success by praising myself for small successes. If you think your successes are in some way 'fakes', review Chapter 10.

- Failing involves disappointment. So think back on the last chapter and explore what you do when you fail.
  - Attack myself (write down what you say about yourself).
  - Attack others (write down what you say about others).
  - Give up (write down why you give up).

  Remember: writing things down helps to make your thoughts clearer, rather than having them zoom about in your head.

- Consider carefully the things you have written above and examine them for the typical depressive styles of thinking outlined in earlier chapters – for example, all-or-nothing thinking, discounting the positive aspects of your life, being overly focused on the negatives.
- Decide that coming to terms with failures and setbacks and learning how to fail are the real achievements here. Once you can fail, you are free to succeed. But if failure is a terror to you,

continued on next page

continued from previous page

the path to success becomes a dangerous and frightening place to be. So now, using your compassionate/rational mind to support you in your hour of need, answer the following questions:
– What would you say to someone else?
– What would you like someone who cares for you to say?
– How can you challenge your negative thoughts about yourself?
– What are some of the alternatives to your negative thoughts and feelings?
– If you can't 'do it all,' is there some smaller part that might be achieved?
– Can you go step by step, focusing on what you have done rather than what you haven't?

Also consider:
– Are there enjoyable things in your life or is it full of chores? Could you do one thing for yourself today?
– How might you gain help from others?

- Try enjoying success. Allow yourself to say, 'That was good and I am going to enjoy my success.' Try praising yourself more, even for small successes. The more you experience this enjoyment of success, the more motivated you will be to try harder at achieving things. If you do something only out of fear, this can become very exhausting. It is useful to try to motivate yourself through rewards rather than through fear of punishment. You are using a different part of your brain when you are motivated to succeed rather than to avoid failure.
- Recognize that confidence comes from within. Try to avoid confusing it with false pride, which can be taken away from you the moment you fail. Pride may give us a buzz, but we can't depend on it.

17

Summing Up

Depression is probably one of the darkest winters of the soul. Researchers throughout the world are trying to work out why we have this capacity to feel as terrible as we do – and many have come up with their own explanations. In this book, I have given one view. This is that depression is a potential state of mind that evolved in our brains many millions of years ago. Our brains also evolved with a need to form social relationships. We are therefore, highly motivated to be wanted, valued and have status in our relationships. When we obtain the signals that these things are coming our way, we tend to feel happy. But if we feel that we are not wanted or valued or if we lose status, our mood goes down, and it can slide into depression if we think that chances of our obtaining these 'social things' are low. So depression speaks to our need to live as social beings, in communities of familiar and trustworthy individuals. It is thus more likely in situations of social isolation and fragmentation. It is marked by inner feelings of being distant and cut off from others.

This does not contradict the idea that depression also relates to states of defeat and feeling blocked and inferior, for it is usually the social implications of a defeat that matter most to us. A defeat that does not lower your status or leave you feeling inferior or cause you to downgrade your self-esteem and social standing will have less impact on your mood than a defeat that does. This is when your thinking begins to play a part. The more a defeat or setback activates thoughts of inferiority and worthlessness, the more the depression will increase. Conversely, the more you are not inhibited by shame or are not grossly disappointed by unrealistic ideals, and you develop the ability to control your anger and stop putting yourself down, the greater are your chances of reaching out to others and getting out of the depression.

This linking of thoughts with internal evolved potential states of mind is only one approach to depression. There are others. Geneticists might see depression as related to some genetic disposition. They might point to the evidence of increased susceptibility in identical twins: if one twin suffers depression, the risks of the other one also suffering from it are higher than for the population in general. Those who study families might see depression as related to early family life experiences. Indeed, many of the most negative views that we develop of ourselves and others can often be traced to what happened to us in early life. Those who study the social environment might see depression as one consequence of the fact that our social environments no longer nurture us with long-term, committed relationships and because of our increasingly competitive and over-idealized expectations of how life should be. They may point to the differences in rates of depression in different countries and communities. Thus, there can be biological, psychological and sociological aspects to depression, each addressing different dimensions of our humanness. One, some or all these factors might apply to you.

I think that we do those who suffer from depression a great disservice if those of us who work in these fields become competitive about our theories. Depression is too complex and varied for there to be only one cause or one answer. In treating depression, one cannot be a 'one-club golfer.' One approach does not rule out another.

Nevertheless, I believe that, in many cases, people can become trapped in depression by the way they think, and also by the difficulties of facing up to things that have to be changed. This may well be the case for you. If you attempt some of the things suggested in this book, you'd be no worse off for trying – what have you got to lose? Try things out. See what works for you. Get your own evidence for what is helpful.

So I hope this book has given you some insight, into the psychology of depression. It has been a long journey and no doubt you may want to visit various parts of it again. In closing, there are a few points that I would like to mention again.

- Depression is a very varied problem. It ranges from the mild to the severe. Some depressions are associated with much anxiety, others with much anger. Some come on slowly, others quite quickly.
- There is a psychological component to every depression, and indeed this book has focused on this, but this does not mean that psychological change is all you need to get out of it. Some people benefit from medication and others require a change in social circumstances.
- If you have a number of problems in your everyday life, it is possible that changing the way you think and behave can help you approach these in a different and more productive way.
- Self-help books can be very useful, but do not necessarily eliminate the need for professional help. It may be that reading this book has encouraged you to consider whether you might benefit from therapy or other forms of help. If so, contact your family doctor, who can refer you to a properly trained person. No self-help book can cover the richness of the experience of depression or all that goes on in therapy.
- Shame can be one of the main reasons why you may be reluctant to seek help, but try to remember that depression is one of the most common problems that mental health professionals work with. You are far from alone. A similar case can be made for talking with friends.
- Although you may need extra help, there are also many things that you can do to help yourself or at least avoid making your depression worse by the way you think.
- Getting out of depression often takes time, effort and patience.

The ten key steps that can help to control depression
1 Seek help if you need it – don't suffer in silence.
2 Go step by step.
3 Break problems down into smaller ones rather than trying to do everything in one go.
4 Introduce more positive activities into your life.

continued on next page

---

continued from previous page

5 Become more attentive and aware of your thinking and the ideas that go through your mind when you are depressed.

6 Try to identify your typical thinking styles (e.g. all-or-nothing thinking, discounting the positive aspects of your life). Note especially what you think about yourself, and how you label and treat yourself. Look out for your internal bully. Remember that this can drive you further into, rather than out of, depression.

7 Try writing down your thoughts to aid clarity and to focus your attention.

8 Try to identify the key themes in your depression (e.g. your need for approval, shame, unhappy relationships, unrealistic ideals, perfectionism). This will allow you to spot more easily your personal themes when they arise – and to challenge them.

9 Learn to challenge your thinking with the use of your rational/ compassionate mind. The more you treat yourself with compassion and give up thinking of yourself in terms of inferior, bad, worthless, and so on, the easier it will be for your brain to recover.

10 Try challenging negative thoughts and developing new ways of behaving. However, also expect setbacks and disappointments from time to time.

Finally, remember:

• Your depression may be a state of mind you are in, but your depression is not you.
• Your anxiety may be a state of mind you are in, but your anxiety is not you.
• Your anger may be a state of mind you are in, but your anger is not you.

These states of mind are to do with how your brain was designed over millions of years. They are part of human nature. Whatever

continued on next page

judgments of 'you' that your emotions come up with, they are about as reliable as the weather. The more compassionate you are with yourself, the less you will be a 'fairweather friend' to yourself. If you can stay a true friend to yourself, even though depressed, you are taking a big step forward. You're on the way up.

Appendix 1

Monitoring and Challenging Your Thoughts

These forms and how to use them
are explained in chapters 5 and 6

Thought Monitoring and Challenging Form
Worked example 1

A	B	C	D
Triggering events, thoughts, feelings or images	Beliefs and key thoughts	Feelings/ Behaviors	Alternatives and challenges to negative thoughts
Too much work to do.	I can't get it all done. I will never succeed.	Depressed.	I can focus on what I can do rather than on everything at once.
	I'm incompetent and a failure.	Do nothing.	I am bullying myself with all-or-nothing thinking and labelling myself rather than supporting my efforts. I am assuming the worst before it happens. If I was helping a friend, I would help them go step by step. I can break these problems down into smaller ones. And I am depressed right now which means that I'm probably exhausted, so I can't expect myself to be as energetic as I used to be. If I can give myself praise for small things, I will start to boost myself up again. I call myself a failure because I am discounting my positives and feel frustrated, but these feelings do not make me a failure.

Key questions to help you identify your thoughts

What actually happened?	What went through your mind? What are you thinking about yourself? What are you thinking about others? What are you saying about your future? Look in the Quick Guides section, p. 284.	What are your main feelings and behaviors?	What would you say to a friend? What alternatives might there be? What might a more balanced view be? Look in the Quick Guides section (p. 284) and try generating alternatives.

Thought Monitoring and Challenging Form
Worked example 2

A	B	C	D
Triggering events, thoughts, feelings or images	Beliefs and key thoughts	Feelings/ Behaviors	Alternatives and challenges to negative thoughts
Argument with partner.	I am going to end up rejected. It's all my fault. I must be very unlovable.	Depressed.	Hold on. There are problems in the relationship but I can't take all the blame. There are things that we are both unhappy with and need to sort out. If I take the blame then we can't work together. I am self-blaming and getting more depressed which actually stops me from trying to make the relationship work. It is upsetting to have arguments, but if I avoid all-or-nothing thinking about my lovability I am more likely to see them through. Anyhow, I have friends who like me, and we have had good times together in the past, so I can't be as bad as I am painting myself.

Key questions to help you identify your thoughts

What actually happened?	What went through your mind? What are you thinking about yourself? What are you thinking about others? What are you saying about your future? Look in the Quick Guides section, p. 284.	What are your main feelings and behaviors?	What would you say to a friend? What alternatives might there be? What might a more balanced view be? Look in the Quick Guides section (p. 284) and try generating alternatives.

Thought Monitoring and Challenging Form
Worked example 3

A	B	C	D
Triggering events, thoughts, feelings or images	Beliefs and key thoughts	Feelings/ Behaviors	Alternatives and challenges to negative thoughts
I want to run away from my family.	I should want to stay with my family. I can't cope with all their needs. I must be a very uncaring person.	Depressed. Guilt.	The desire to escape is often strong in depression. It may mean I feel exhausted. I probably need to create some space. First I can break the problems down and think what it is *specifically* that I would like to run away from. Although difficult I can try to explain these things to them and see if it is possible to get extra help if I need it. I can try to create more space for myself without feeling guilty (which makes me feel worse) – then I won't feel so smothered. I can focus on those things I can cope with rather than on those things that seem overwhelming. Most importantly, I can recognize that there is nothing wrong or bad about me because I need space. I cannot be an inexhaustible supply of care to everyone. The more I break the problem down, rather than just feeling bad about it, the greater the chances are that I can start to work out some solutions.

Key questions to help you identify your thoughts

What actually happened?	What went through your mind? What are you thinking about yourself? What are you thinking about others? What are you saying about your future? Look in the Quick Guides section, p. 284.	What are your main feelings and behaviors?	What would you say to a friend? What alternatives might there be? What might a more balanced view be? Look at the Quick Guides section (p. 284) and try generating alternatives.

Thought Monitoring and Challenging Form

This form has been left blank for you to fill in (you will find more blank forms at the end of the book)

A	B	C	D
Triggering events, thoughts, feelings or images	Beliefs and key thoughts	Feelings/Behaviors	Alternatives and challenges to negative thoughts

Key questions to help you identify your thoughts

What actually happened?	What went through your mind? What are you thinking about yourself? What are you thinking about others? What are you saying about your future? Look in the Quick Guides section, p. 284.	What are your main feelings and behaviors?	What would you say to a friend? What alternatives might there be? What might a more balanced view be? Look in the Quick Guides section (p. 284) and try generating alternatives.

Appendix 2

Quick Guides

To identify your negative thinking style, pay attention to your feelings. Then ask yourself:

- What is/was going through my mind?
- What am I thinking about me?
- What kind of judgments am I making about myself?
- What judgments or assumptions am I making about other people?
- What am I thinking about my future?

The way you think about things can affect the way you feel. Below is a summary of some typical ways of thinking that can worsen depression. If you can learn to spot these styles of thinking in yourself, then this is a good first step to disputing and changing them. We all use these styles of thinking from time to time; no one is 100 percent logical or compassionate all the time. But in depression they get taken to extremes.

Jumping to conclusions This involves the tendency to make decisions rapidly, especially when under stress. For example, you might jump to the conclusion that someone does not like you because they ignore you. You may predict the future, e.g. that nothing you do will work out. Jumping to conclusions means that you don't *look at the evidence*. Instead, you go for immediate gut reactions and assume these to be true.

Emotional reasoning This involves an over-reliance on feeling to guide judgments e.g. 'I feel this is dangerous, therefore it is.' You assume that negative feelings reflect the way things actually are: 'I feel it so it must be true.' Feelings are often poor guides to reality.

The 'power' of feelings comes from our more primitive brains having more control over us than is often good for us. Remember to test out feelings: look for alternatives and explore the evidence for and the evidence against.

I must These thoughts involve feelings of being compelled to do something. 'I must be in a relationship to be happy; I must achieve things to be a worthwhile person; I must never be criticized; I must never fail.' Try to turn musts into preferences, e.g. 'I would like to do this, but if I can't then it does not mean that I am a no-good person or that I can't be happy.'

Discounting and disbelieving the positives This involves the tendency to ignore or dismiss positive attributes, events or achievements. You either take them for granted or think that 'anyone could do that'. When you disqualify the positives it is difficult to get started on the way up. Focus on what you can do rather than on what you can't.

Discounting and disbelieving others This involves thinking that other people's (good) opinions of you don't count. You think that either they don't really know you or that you have kept things hidden and deceived them. At other times you may think that others only say positive things to be nice but they don't, in their hearts, really mean it. This often involves a loss of trust.

Amplifying the negatives When you are depressed it is all too easy to dwell on negatives and difficulties. They take on more importance and you are very attentive to possible rejection, put-downs or failures. You can easily lose perspective by amplifying negatives and dwelling on them. Try to regain perspective by generating alternatives and avoiding emotional reasoning.

All-or-nothing thinking This is also called 'black-and-white', or 'polarized' thinking. You see things in 'either/or' categories. If your performance falls short of what you wanted, you see it or even yourself as a total failure. You may think, 'either X loves me or s/he doesn't. Either I succeed or I fail.' However, life is full of indeterminate areas. Love is not either/or; there are degrees of love. Success is not either/or. There are degrees of success. Hence, it is more useful to think of the degree of success rather than the degree of failure.

Overgeneralizing   You take a single negative event and see it as a never-ending pattern of defeat. Here, one swallow does make a summer. You may think that things can never change, or that one failure means that everything you have done was a failure or faked.

A Quick Guide to Recognizing Your Self-Attacking Thoughts and Styles

Self-criticism   This is when part of you becomes like an observer and judge. You are constantly passing negative judgments on yourself, as if a critical parent were sitting on your shoulder. You are more focused on what you do wrong or badly rather than on what you do well.

Personalization and self-blaming   This involves the automatic tendency to assume that you are in the wrong or are responsible for negative events. You may not look at the evidence or consider alternatives, or reflect that most things are caused by a number of different factors.

Self-labelling   This involves 'all or nothing' in your thinking about yourself as a person. If your behavior fails, you think you are a failure, unlovable or inadequate, etc. In depression this type of thinking involves blaming and name calling (e.g. useless, inadequate, weak, a nuisance, a fake, worthless, bad, etc).

It-me   This involves the tendency to judge yourself rather than your behavior. You think that only your behavior matters; if that is not good then you are no good. But behavior and self are quite different. A self is a conscious, feeling being, with hopes, desires and wishes. A behavior is just a behavior, that may or may not be disappointing.

Self-attacking   This involves a degree of anger and hostility directed at yourself. It is more than being critical – after all, not all criticism involves hostility. But in self-attacking one is hostile with oneself.

Self-hatred   This is an extreme form of self-attacking. It is more than just anger with the self and often involves judgments and feelings of being bad, evil or disgusting. Unlike self-criticism, which aims to improve through punishment, self-hatred can be about wanting to destroy and get rid of.

Social comparison　Although social comparison is probably inevitable, try to be more aware of when you do it. Check out how your mood changes and ask yourself if the social comparison is valid. Does it help you? Are you engaging in envious thoughts? Do such thoughts help you?

A Quick Guide to Challenging Negative Thoughts and Styles

Once you have identified your depressing thoughts, consider:

- What would I say to a friend or someone I care about who was in the same situation?
- What would I like someone who cared about me to say to me to support and encourage me?
- Have I given enough weight to the fact that when I am depressed my 'brain-state' tends to look on the black side?
- How would I see this if I was not depressed?
- What might be a rational-compassionate way of thinking about this?
- Have I tried to look at alternative ways of seeing this? What might these be?
- Have I got enough evidence to support my view? What is the evidence that does not support my (negative) view?
- Am I letting my internal bully get away with too much?
- What are the advantages and disadvantages of thinking in this way?
- Did I put enough effort into trying to change or did I assume, from the start, that it would turn out badly? What have I got to lose by giving it a go?

A Quick Guide to Making Your Own Flash Cards

Throughout this book I have offered ways to challenge some of your thoughts. Here are some thoughts for flash cards to deal with common depressing ideas and thoughts.

I am Weak to be Depressed

- Depression is a state of mind. Just as I can have other states of mind (e.g. happy, relaxed, angry, anxious), I can be depressed.
- Depression is unpleasant, but sadly many millions suffer from it because to the brain this is just one of its patterns for feeling.
- Depression can affect anyone – even people who are often regarded as strong (e.g. Winston Churchill).
- Depression is a horrible state to be in, but it is not evidence of weakness.
- Depression is most often about becoming exhausted, trying too hard, feeling defeated, losing hope. By understanding it more, I can try to bring my rational-compassionate mind to help tackle it.
- There may be very real problems in my life that have exhausted me and made me vulnerable to being depressed.

If I Need an Anti-Depressant Drug it Means I am Weak

- Depression is not about weakness, but can be about being exhausted.
- I need to get the evidence of whether an anti-depressant would help me. If it can help me sleep better and boost my mood and confidence, then that might help me to get on top of my depression.
- Millions of people take anti-depressant drugs.
- Whether I choose to take an anti-depressant drug or not is my own decision. I don't need to prove that I can cope without one as some kind of test of my strength.

If I Need some Therapy I might have to Reveal my Anger or Shame

- It is understandable to be anxious about revealing personal things to someone else, like a therapist.
- Properly qualified therapists are well aware that it is the things we are ashamed of that cause us problems.
- I have no evidence that a therapist will look down on me if I tell him/her the things that I am ashamed about. Indeed, just as a surgeon expects to deal with blood and guts, so therapists expect to deal with the less pleasant sides of life.

- The more I am prepared to face up to what I feel ashamed about, the more I may get to know myself and learn how to let these things go or see them in a different way.
- A therapist can't force me to talk, so I can go at my own pace and decide whether the therapy is helpful.

I Can't do What I Used to do, Therefore I am a Failure

- I am depressed right now, so it's natural not to have my normal drive.
- Even though I can't do what I used to, I can still do some things.
- I can praise myself for what I do do, rather than attacking myself for what I don't do.
- There is no way I am going to bully myself out of depression.
- I can go step by step.
- By praising my steps, no matter how small they may be, I am moving forward.

I am Worthless

- To sum up a person (e.g. myself) in simple terms of good-bad, worthwhile-worthless is all-or-nothing thinking.
- Just because I feel stupid and worthless this does not mean that I am.
- If I over-identify with feelings of worthlessness then I am more likely to get depressed.
- The idea of worth can be applied to objects like cars or soap powder, but not to persons.
- If I say 'worthless' is just one of a number of possible feelings that I, as a human being, can have about myself, then I can keep a perspective on these negative feelings.

I am so Filled with Anger I must be Bad

- Anger is, like other feelings, something we are all capable of.
- High levels of anger usually point to high levels of hurt or vulnerability.
- My anger tells me that there is something I want to change and push against.
- True, flying into rages is not helpful, but I can learn to be more honest with my own needs and put them assertively.
- I can learn to understand my anger rather than just labelling myself as bad and trying to push my anger away.

I am not as Competent as other People, therefore I am a Failure

- It is natural to want to compete in the world and feel that we are up there with others.
- All human beings are unique and need to go at their own pace. Just because some people seem more able than me does not make me a failure. I dare to be average.
- I can focus on what I can do and what is important to me, in my own unique life, rather than on what others are doing.

Nothing Ever Seems as Good as I Want it to Be, Therefore there is no Point in Trying

- Disappointment is part of life and I can learn to cope with it if I keep it in perspective.
- I can learn to focus on what I do get out of doing things rather than how far short they fall of my expectations.
- I can check out whether I attack myself when I am disappointed and learn how to be kinder with myself.
- This type of thinking is rather all or nothing. Therefore I can learn to focus on what I enjoy rather than on what I don't.

I Will Never get Better

- After reading this book, I realize that there are many ways to tackle depression and these work for many people (e.g. drugs, psychotherapy, family therapy, etc.).
- I don't have to suffer in silence.
- If I need extra help, I can talk to my family doctor and see what is available.
- I haven't always been depressed, so depression is a state of mind that I am in right now, but this does not mean that I'll always be depressed.
- I may have been trying to deal with my depression but, as this book points out, maybe I have been enduring it, trying to soldier on, rather than really tackling it.

Appendix 3

Antidepressants

If you are depressed, it is important to consider taking an antidepressant medication. The evidence from research suggests that in severe depressions drugs work better than therapy alone. If you suffer from severe depression you may need to see a psychiatrist. Although depressed people often don't like taking drugs they can be extremely beneficial, even in less severe depressions. This is especially so if you're exhausted, can't sleep, feel bereft of hope and/or intensely anxious. Three common reasons that people do not wish to take drugs are:

- Beliefs such as 'I should be able to conquer this alone', 'It is shameful to take drugs', or 'I am weak for needing drugs' (see flash card on page 288).
- Problems with side-effects.
- Fears of becoming addicted and not able to cope without drugs.

Antidepressants are not addictive, but some people rightly worry that at times drugs can be used to deal with depressions arising from social and personal problems. The other side of this coin, however, is that if you feel less depressed then you will be better able to face up to your personal and social problems. If a drug helps you, this does not mean there aren't important personal and social issues to deal with. Nor does it mean that you could not benefit from therapy. As I stressed in the first chapter, the treatment of depression should be biopsychosocial; meaning that it often requires us to treat body, mind and social issues together.

Only medically qualified professionals can advise and prescribe drugs. They should explore with you the ones that will best suit you, the doses that you may require, and check that you are not suffering from any physical disorder that may be contributing to your depression.

How do Drugs Work?

For many years research has concentrated on three chemicals in the brain that seem to be involved with mood. These are dopamine, noradrenaline (called norepinephrine in the USA) and serotonin. Collectively these are known as monoamines. Antidepressant drugs work by either increasing the levels of these chemicals and/ or by changing how efficiently they work (on receptors) in the brain.

There are three basic classes of antidepressant. These are monoamine oxidase inhibitors (MAOIs for short), tricyclics and selective serotonin re-uptake inhibitors (known as SSRIs). A fourth medication, lithium, is often used for people who have various swings in mood between depression and mania, as it helps to stabilize mood.

Most drugs have both a chemical name and a trade name. A trade name is given by the drug company which produces it. As trade names can vary from country to country, I will give only the chemical name.

MAOIs include isocarboxazid, phenelyzine and tranylcypromine. These may be useful when anxiety (social and generalized) dominates the clinical picture. Patients taking these drugs must be extremely careful to avoid certain foods as these can cause very serious reactions. The list of foods to avoid includes things like cheese, red wine, yeast extracts and pickled herrings; your family doctor will provide you with information on what to avoid. You will also need to avoid certain medications such as decongestants and cough medicines.

Tricyclics work in a different way to the MAOIs. The most common tricyclics are amitriptyline, clomipramine, dothiepine, imipramine and lofepramine. There are no dietary restrictions with these drugs although alcohol should be avoided with all antidepressants.

The SSRIs are a new group of drugs that came to be used during the 1980s. Generally, they have fewer side-effects than the tricyclics, are safer and are increasingly becoming the drugs of first choice for depression. The most common ones are fluoxetine, fluvoxamine, paroxetine and sertraline. These drugs are believed to be more specific in their action and primarily affect serotonin systems. They can be especially useful when obsessional problems are present. As I write this guide, I should point out that new antidepressants are appearing all the time. This is a new generation of drugs called SSNRIs, meaning that they work on both serotonin and noradrenaline systems in the brain.

Generally, antidepressants take three weeks or more to work on lifting mood although they may help with specific symptoms such as sleep before this. The reason for this 'delayed action' has been the focus of much research. You should not use antidepressants as you might use a tranquillizer because they have to build up in the body, and thus they need to be taken regularly. It is also important that they are taken at doses that are therapeutic. Too low a dose may not be helpful. Psychiatrists generally suggest that one should stay on a medication for six months or so after improvement.

All antidepressants have side-effects. Sometimes these will fade over the first few weeks. Tricyclics can give a dry mouth and affect sexual functions and weight. Different antidepressants have slightly different side-effects and your family doctor or psychiatrist will advise you on these. Sometimes, changing the time of day a drug is taken can be helpful.

There is also evidence that some patients do better on certain drugs than others. So if you find, after a reasonable trial, that a drug does not work for you, discuss this with your doctor. Don't give up if a particular drug does not suit you. Even within a class of drugs, e.g. the SSRIs, I have seen patients do better on one than another – although the research evidence for this is still being gathered. Very occasionally, some drugs increase irritability and if this is so for you, you should explore whether a switch to another medication would be helpful. It is extremely important that you and your doctor try to find a medication that you feel suits you, because choosing one that causes you too many side-effects increases the risk of non-compliance, and thus loss of therapeutic effect. Around 60 percent of patients respond to antidepressants first time, although the figure climbs to nearer 80 percent if the treating professional tries different drugs to suit the person. Looking at this another way, 40 percent of people may not respond well to the first drug used, but 20 percent may have a disappointing response to antidepressants generally.

Once prescribed a drug, you should stay in regular contact with your family doctor so that he/she can monitor your progress. If things are not working out, or if you are having problems taking your medication, try to avoid thoughts like, 'Well, my doctor has done what he/she can. If this medication does not work, none will. He/she will get fed up with me. I just have to bear it.' Depression is a condition where we can easily give up if something doesn't work out quickly. However, treating depression is not always easy, and you and your doctor may need to work together to find what might best suit you and the help you might need.

If you want to know more about drugs and how they work, you can consult Spike Milligan and Anthony Clare's book *Depression and How to Survive It* (Arrow, 1994). An excellent, quick overview which goes into more details than I can offer here is given in David Burns' *Feeling Good: The New Mood Therapy* (Morrow, 1980). Dr Burns also explores eight common beliefs that stop people from using antidepressant medication and how to challenge these beliefs. In addition, some of the self-help organizations that I have listed in Useful Addresses can be helpful to consult.

Finally, let me stress again that depression has many different causes and takes many different forms. The most important thing is for you to avoid feeling ashamed about being depressed. So, 'own' your depression and explore what you can do to change it or turn it off. Don't suffer in silence. There are many different types of antidepressants, and there are many different types of therapists and therapies. At the end of the day it has to be your decision on how you will treat yourself. Professionals can only advise you. Although there are no recipes for a pain-free life, and for some people life is full of hardships and difficulties, there are many things that can be done to ease the pain of depression.

Useful Books and Addresses

Useful Books

A.T. Beck, *Love is Never Enough* (New York, Harper and Row, 1988)
Useful book pointing out that it is often our beliefs about how relationships 'should' be and how others 'should' act that cause problems in relationships. Offers a practical guide for dealing with relationship problems.

David Burns, *Feeling Good* (New York, Morrow, 1980)
Old classic and still very popular. David Burns has also written a workbook (1986) and one on intimate relationships.

Dennis Greenberg and Christine Padesky, *Mind over Mood: A cognitive treatment manual for clients* (New York, Guilford Press, 1995)
Very practical step-by-step approach. Lots on recording thoughts and behavior.

Paul Gilbert, *Depression: The evolution of powerlessness* (Hove, Lawrence Erlbaum, and New York, Guilford Press, 1992)
This offers a more technical approach to understanding depression. If you are interested in the evolutionary aspects in general you might wish to consult *Human Nature and Suffering* by me and the same publishers. Two excellent and fascinating books that explore the evolutionary approach are: Robert Wright, *The Moral Animal: Why we are the way we are* (Abacus, 1996); and Randolph Nesse and George Williams, *Evolution and Healing. The new science of Darwinian medicine* (Phoenix, 1996).

Hal Stone and Sidra Stone, *Embracing Your Inner Critic: Turning self-criticism into a creative asset* (New York, HarperCollins, 1993) Explores in detail some origins and consequences of self-criticism. Not specific to depression.

Alan Stewart, *Tired All the Time* (London, Optima, 1993) Explores common causes of tiredness, including things like allergy and diet.

Spike Milligan and Anthony Clare, *Depression and How to Survive It* (London, Arrow, 1994) Mostly a psychiatrist's medical view of depression. Good on the role of genes and drugs (which types and how they work) and other physical treatments, less good on the psychology and self-help.

You might also wish to contact this publisher, Robinson, for details of other self-help books – e.g. on anxiety and on eating problems – in the same series as this one.

Useful Addresses

If you want to know more about self-help organizations here are some useful addresses.

MIND, The National Association for Mental Health
Granta House
15–19 Broadway
Stratford
London E15 4BQ

Tel.: 0181 519 2122

A very helpful organization than can offer advice on services for a wide range of psychological difficulties. It also has a wide range of literature.

Association of Post-Natal Depression
25 Jerdan Place
Fulham
London sw6
Tel.: 0171 386 0868

Manic-Depression Fellowship
8–10 High Street
Kingston-Upon-Thames
London KT1 1EY
Tel.: 0181 974 6550 and 0181 546 0323

Depressive Alliance
PO Box 1022
London SE1 7GR
Tel.: 0171 721 7672 (Recorded information)

Institute for Neuro-Physiological Psychology
Warwick House
4 Stanley Place
Chester CH1 2LU
Tel.: 01224 311414

Seasonal Affective Disorder (SAD) Association
PO Box 989
London SW7 2PZ
(No telephone number available)

United States

American Mental Health Foundation
2 East 86th Street
New York
NY 1008
(Written enquiries only)

Association for the Advancement of Behavior Therapy
305 7th Avenue
New York
NY 10001
Tel.: 212 647 1890

The Behavior Therapy Center of New York
115 East 87th Street
New York
NY 10028
Tel.: 212 410 6500

Behavior Therapy Institute
San Francisco
Tel.: 415 989 2140

Behavioral Psychotherapy Center
23 Old Mamroneck Road
White Plains
NY 10605
Tel.: 914 761 4080

Institute for Behavior Therapy
137 East 36th Street
New York
NY 10016
Tel.: 212 686 8778

Institutes for Neuro-Physiological Psychology:
Dr Larry J. Beuret, MD
4811 Emerson, Suite 209
Palatine
IL 60067
Tel.: 847 303 1800
and

Mrs Victoria Hutton
6535 North Shore Way
Newmarket
Maryland 21774
Tel.: 301 607 6752

Australia and New Zealand

Institutes for Neuro-Physiological Research:
Dr Mary Lou Sheil
80 Alexandra Street
Hunters Hill 2110
Sydney, Australia
Tel.: 298 796 596
and
Heather Jones
501 North Willowport Road
Hastins
New Zealand
(No telephone number available)

INDEX

Index

Extra Monitoring Sheets

Thought Monitoring and Challenging Form

This form has been left blank for you to fill in

A	B	C	D
Triggering events, thoughts, feelings or images	Beliefs and key thoughts	Feelings/ Behaviors	Alternatives and challenges to negative thoughts

Key questions to help you identify your thoughts

What actually happened?	What went through your mind? What are you thinking about yourself? What are you thinking about others? What are you saying about your future? Look in the Quick Guides section, p. 284.	What are your main feelings and behaviors?	What would you say to a friend? What alternatives might there be? What might a more balanced view be? Look in the Quick Guides section (p. 284) and try generating alternatives.

Thought Monitoring and Challenging Form

This form has been left blank for you to fill in

A	B	C	D
Triggering events, thoughts, feelings or images	Beliefs and key thoughts	Feelings/ Behaviors	Alternatives and challenges to negative thoughts

Key questions to help you identify your thoughts

| What actually happened? | What went through your mind? What are you thinking about yourself? What are you thinking about others? What are you saying about your future? Look in the Quick Guides section, p. 284. | What are your main feelings and behaviors? | What would you say to a friend? What alternatives might there be? What might a more balanced view be? Look in the Quick Guides section (p. 284) and try generating alternatives. |

Thought Monitoring and Challenging Form

This form has been left blank for you to fill in

A	B	C	D
Triggering events, thoughts, feelings or images	Beliefs and key thoughts	Feelings/ Behaviors	Alternatives and challenges to negative thoughts

Key questions to help you identify your thoughts

What actually happened?	What went through your mind? What are you thinking about yourself? What are you thinking about others? What are you saying about your future? Look in the Quick Guides section, p. 284.	What are your main feelings and behaviors?	What would you say to a friend? What alternatives might there be? What might a more balanced view be? Look in the Quick Guides section (p. 284) and try generating alternatives.

Thought Monitoring and Challenging Form

This form has been left blank for you to fill in

A	B	C	D
Triggering events, thoughts, feelings or images	Beliefs and key thoughts	Feelings/ Behaviors	Alternatives and challenges to negative thoughts

Key questions to help you identify your thoughts

| What actually happened? | What went through your mind? What are you thinking about yourself? What are you thinking about others? What are you saying about your future? Look in the Quick Guides section, p. 284. | What are your main feelings and behaviors? | What would you say to a friend? What alternatives might there be? What might a more balanced view be? Look in the Quick Guides section (p. 284) and try generating alternatives. |

Thought Monitoring and Challenging Form

This form has been left blank for you to fill in

A	B	C	D
Triggering events, thoughts, feelings or images	Beliefs and key thoughts	Feelings/ Behaviors	Alternatives and challenges to negative thoughts

Key questions to help you identify your thoughts

What actually happened?	What went through your mind? What are you thinking about yourself? What are you thinking about others? What are you saying about your future? Look in the Quick Guides section, p. 284.	What are your main feelings and behaviors?	What would you say to a friend? What alternatives might there be? What might a more balanced view be? Look in the Quick Guides section (p. 284) and try generating alternatives.

Thought Monitoring and Challenging Form

This form has been left blank for you to fill in

A	B	C	D
Triggering events, thoughts, feelings or images	Beliefs and key thoughts	Feelings/ Behaviors	Alternatives and challenges to negative thoughts

Key questions to help you identify your thoughts

What actually happened?	What went through your mind? What are you thinking about yourself? What are you thinking about others? What are you saying about your future? Look in the Quick Guides section, p. 284.	What are your main feelings and behaviors?	What would you say to a friend? What alternatives might there be? What might a more balanced view be? Look in the Quick Guides section (p. 284) and try generating alternatives.

Overcoming Depression Feedback Form

We hope that you found *Overcoming Depression* helpful. We always appreciate readers' opinions and would be grateful if you could take a few minutes to complete this form for us.

1. How did you discover this book?

   Came across it by chance   —
   Recommended by a friend   —
   Recommended by a therapist or doctor   —
   Read an article in a magazine or paper   —
   Saw a TV feature   —
   Saw an advertisement   —

2. How much of the book did you read?

   All of it   —
   More than half of it   —
   Less than half of it   —

3. Which chapters were most helpful? ....
   ....

4. Which chapters were least helpful? ....
   ....

5. Overall, how useful to you was *Overcoming Depression*?

   <u>Not at all</u>   <u>Slightly useful</u>   <u>Somewhat useful</u>   <u>Very useful</u>   <u>Extremely useful</u>

6. What did you like best about the book? ....
   ....
   ....
   ....

7. What did you like least about the book? ....
   ....
   ....
   ....

8. Have you used other self-help books for managing depression?   Yes/No

   If 'yes', how did *Overcoming Depression* compare?

   <u>Much worse</u>   <u>Worse</u>   <u>About the same</u>   <u>Better</u>   <u>Much better</u>

9. Would you recommend this book to a friend?   Yes/No

Thank you for your help. Please send this to: Robinson Publishing Ltd, 7 Kensington Church Court, London W8 4SP.